Language Teacher Research in the Middle East

*Edited by Christine Coombe
and Lisa Barlow*

Language Teacher Research Series

Thomas S. C. Farrell, Series Editor

Teachers of English to Speakers of Other Languages, Inc.

Typeset in Sabon and Adelon
by Capitol Communication Systems, Inc., Crofton, Maryland USA
Printed by United Graphics, Inc., Mattoon, Illinois USA
Indexed by Pueblo Indexing and Publishing Services, Pueblo West, Colorado USA

Teachers of English to Speakers of Other Languages, Inc.
700 South Washington Street, Suite 200
Alexandria, Virginia 22314 USA
Tel. 703-836-0774 • Fax 703-836-6447 • E-mail info@tesol.org • http://www.tesol.org/

Publishing Manager: Carol Edwards
Copy Editor: Terrey Hatcher Quindlen
Additional Reader: Carol Edwards
Cover Design: Tomiko Chapman

ISBN 9781931185417
Library of Congress Control Number: 2007924034

Table of Contents

Acknowledgments

We would like to thank Series Editor Tom Farrell for taking his vision of the field and dedication to teacher research and turning it into this wonderful and much needed book series. Maintaining schedules and meeting deadlines is never pleasant, but Terrey Quindlen managed to make the task eminently manageable and minimally stressful. Her expertise, eye for detail, and good cheer were much appreciated. Our thanks are also extended to our esteemed colleagues, the authors of the articles in this collection. Their willingness to share their research and reflections is of tremendous value. Finally, we would like to thank our families for their support and encouragement. A written acknowledgment could never sufficiently convey our gratitude to them.

Christine Coombe and Lisa Barlow, Editors

Series Editor's Preface

The Language Teacher Research Series highlights the role language teachers at all levels play as generators of knowledge concerning all aspects of language teaching around the world. This idea may seem alien to many language teachers. Often, they either think that they have nothing to say about their teaching or that what they have to say is of little significance. Teachers generally are accustomed to receiving knowledge from so-called *real* researchers.

In my opinion, language teachers have plenty to say that is valuable for colleagues around the world. One of the main reasons for the Language Teacher Research Series is to celebrate what is being achieved in English language classrooms each day, so educators can encourage and develop communities of like-minded language teaching professionals who are willing to share these important experiences.

In this manner, the TESOL community can extend its understanding of English language teaching in local, regional, and international settings. The series attempts to cover as many of these contexts as possible, with volumes covering Asia, Europe, the Americas, the Middle East, Australia and New Zealand, and Africa. Each account of research presented in the Language Teacher Research Series is unique in the profession. These studies document how individual language teachers at all levels of practice systematically reflect on their *own* practice (rather than on other teachers' practices).

When practicing language teachers share these experiences with teachers in other contexts, they can compare and contrast what is happening in different classrooms around the world. The ultimate aim of this series is to encourage an inquiry stance toward language teaching. Teachers can play a crucial role in taking responsibility for their own professional development as generators and receivers of knowledge about what it means to teach English language learning.

How This Series Can Be Used

The Language Teacher Research Series is suitable for preservice and in-service teacher education programs. The examples of teacher research written by practitioners at all levels of teaching and all levels of experience offer a window into the different worlds of English language teachers. In this series I have attempted to impose some order by providing authors with a template of headings for presenting their research. This format is designed so that language teachers with varied expertise and educational qualifications can pick up a book from any region and make comparisons about issues, background literature, procedures taken, results, and reflections without having to work too hard to find them. The details in each chapter will help readers compare and evaluate the examples of teacher research and even replicate some research, if so desired.

This Volume

This fourth volume in the Language Teacher Research series, *Language Teacher Research in the Middle East*, documents different forms of practitioner inquiry that involve systematic, intentional, and self-critical studies of language teaching in different Middle Eastern settings. Again, it will be interesting to compare and contrast these Middle Eastern research stories with studies from the other volumes appearing in the series.

Thomas S. C. Farrell, Brock University, Canada

CHAPTER 1

Language Teacher Research in the Middle East

Christine Coombe and Lisa Barlow

Teachers in the Middle East, as in other parts of the world, are expected to engage in professional development (PD) activities and to build on and develop their skills as educators. What constitutes good PD for teachers? In the past decade, educators have developed a vision of good PD that focuses on issues teachers deem important in their daily work, that respects and builds on their knowledge and skills, and that nurtures and supports teachers' intellectual leadership capacity (Corcoran, 1995; Little, 1993). An increasingly common activity that potentially addresses all three of these criteria is teacher research. Teacher research is a form of inquiry that involves teachers in developing their own research questions and investigating their own classroom practices. Teacher research can be broadly defined as "systematic and intentional inquiry carried out by teachers" (Cochran-Smith & Lytle, 1990, p. 3). It is a process of actively engaging teachers in the reflective investigation and critical evaluation of their own practice (Stenhouse, 1975).

In the field of foreign and second language education, teachers have traditionally been seen as subjects or consumers of research done by others. Teacher research involves teachers directly in the selection of immediate, compelling, and meaningful topics as they explore their own practice. It is the teachers themselves who carry out the research on their own work to improve what they do. Therefore, in teacher research, teachers participate actively in directing their own work and, ultimately, their own professional development.

Advocates of teacher research cite its many advantages and describe it as a valuable form of professional development. Zeichner (1999) espoused teacher research because it allows teachers to become better at what they do. In addition, it helps teachers become more flexible and open to new ideas. A third advantage is that it narrows the gap between teachers' aspirations and realization. Zeichner went on to state that teacher inquiry heightens the quality of student learning and stimulates positive changes in the culture and productivity of schools. Teacher research also raises the status of the teaching profession in society. A final advantage Zeichner noted is that teacher research produces knowledge about teaching and learning that is useful to teachers, policy makers, academic researchers, and teacher educators.

Practitioner inquiry provides abundant opportunities for teaching faculty to collaborate with peers, make critical instructional decisions, and implement these strategies in their own classrooms. The literature clearly shows that teachers who have carried out research often report significant changes to their understanding of teaching (Richards & Farrell, 2005). Studies also have found that teachers who engaged in research have experienced professional and personal growth and a decrease in feelings of frustration and isolation (Goswami & Stillman, 1987; Maloy & Jones, 1987; Noffke, 1997; Oja & Pine, 1987). Research by Boudah and Knight (1996) reported positive effects from participation in teacher research in terms of improved teacher attitudes toward research, increased feelings of self-efficacy related to low-achieving students, and increases in positive interactions with students. Finally, teacher research processes may also help to create a positive school culture—one that supports teacher reflection and experimentation (Francis, Hirsch, & Rowland, 1994).

The goal of this volume is to improve teaching and learning in the English language classroom, and the studies were conducted during the process of regular classroom teaching. Most were small-scale in nature and were intended to solve problems rather than simply do research for research's sake. They were carried out by teachers either individually or collaboratively. The classroom research studies began from a specific issue or classroom problem arising from the profession. The teacher researcher then set out a systematic process for formulating an inquiry, collecting information or data, critically reflecting on it, and taking corrective action if warranted.

The teacher researchers followed different research methodologies. Several of the chapters focus on controversial aspects of education in the Middle East and Arabian Gulf. What all of the studies have in common is that the research questions they attempted to answer originated in the classroom.

Margaret Agbalizu's chapter, "How Does Language Anxiety Affect Performance in the English Language Classroom?" discusses the effect of foreign language anxiety on the speaking and writing performances of female high school students. The study divided students into two academic groups, or streams:

science, typically high achievers, and arts, usually poor performers. Agbalizu's results show that speaking and writing activities were identified as provoking anxiety because the two language skills are product oriented and often exam based. The anxiety caused by these two factors can restrict students' speaking abilities and reduce the volume and quality of their writing.

In the chapter "L2 Learners and Student Evaluations of Teaching: Issues of Language Comprehension," Ahmad Al-Issa and Hana Sulieman outline the steps they took to measure students' understanding of what they read on their university's Teaching Evaluation Form. The results of their study show that only 17% of the total sample of second language (L2) learners was able to comprehend all seven questions of the survey. In their reflections, the authors suggest ways of making the evaluation form more understandable for English as a foreign language (EFL) students.

Next, Maher Bahloul's chapter, "Spelling Errors of Arab Learners: Evidence for Intergraphemic Mapping," analyzes the spelling errors of 88 male adult Saudi EFL learners to gain an understanding of how these students construe and misconstrue the graphemic structure of their second language. He argues that the students' first language, Arabic, accounts for almost one third of the learners' spelling errors.

In "What Makes a Good Teacher? Investigating the Native-Nonnative Speaker Issue in the Arabian Gulf," Christine Coombe and Mashael Al-Hamly report on a study they conducted to investigate EFL students' attitudes toward native-English-speaking teachers (NESTs) and nonnative-English-speaking teachers (NNESTs) in tertiary institutions in Kuwait and the United Arab Emirates. Their study concludes that their students had a definite preference for NESTs, with 47.7% favoring NESTs, 17% favoring NNESTs, and 35.3% stating no preference. In their reflection, Coombe and Al-Hamly express the need to try to effect change and make students aware of the special attributes that all teachers bring to the classroom.

In the chapter titled "Multicultural, Coeducational Group Work Experiences: Creative Collaboration or Problematic Partnership?" Cindy Gunn outlines the process she went through to determine how she could continue to incorporate group work with male and female students productively into her classes and at the same time better meet the sociocultural needs and concerns of her students. Gunn concludes that the results of her research were not decisive, but she does suggest that fellow teachers should be cognizant of student concerns regarding mixed-gender collaborative activities.

In "To Mediate or Not to Mediate: Surviving in an Exam-Based EFL Context," Naziha Ali Jafri reports on the results of an investigation into the awareness and practice of facilitated EFL learning at a Pakistani community school in the United Arab Emirates. Jafri surmises that although teachers perceived the importance of mediation in L2 learning, they found that time constraints, large class size, and an exam-driven curriculum did not allow for facilitated learning. Her conclusions also show that students felt teachers were ignoring their need to communicate in English in authentic occupational contexts.

Paul MacLeod's chapter, "The Effectiveness of Learning Contracts With Arab Learners of English," outlines the author's research into the use of learning contracts with students who were frustrated in their repeated attempts to score 500 on the Test of English as a Foreign Language (TOEFL), which is a university-required benchmark. MacLeod's aim in integrating learning contracts into the course was to keep students optimistically focused on their goal of reaching a TOEFL 500. He found that his students rose to the challenge of taking more responsibility for their learning and were motivated to learn more.

In the next chapter, "Six Hats for Discussion and Writing," David Palfreyman and Fran Turner attempt to integrate de Bono's Six Thinking Hats model into their classroom to help develop students' thinking, discussion, and writing skills. Although both authors found the use of the model enriched their own teaching and raised their awareness of students' thinking skills and essay writing, they also questioned the practicality of the use of the model because of the existing curriculum and the time constraints they teach under each semester.

Next, Ali H. Raddaoui's chapter, "Teacher and Student Perceptions of Best Practices in Teaching," profiles what constitutes a good teacher and what constitutes a bad teacher in the eyes of students and teachers of English. Raddaoui finds that although students and teachers agreed on many aspects of what makes a good teacher—such as preplanned, organized lessons with a measure of improvisation—they disagreed on several points. Students' responses were sometimes surprising and contrary to what one would expect from students who will be entering a world of continual change.

Ali Shehadeh's chapter, "The Effect of Group and Individual Peer Feedback on Student Writing in an EFL Gulf Context," investigates the impact that feedback from a group of students had on students' writing as compared to the more commonly used technique of individual student feedback. Shehadeh's findings suggest that group feedback can provide students with a valuable tool to improve accuracy. In addition, he also proposes four practical advantages of group feedback for the writing classroom.

In the chapter, "Negotiating With Multiple Repeaters," Salah Troudi seeks ways to assist multiple repeaters in their English language achievement. To this end, he argues that an understanding of their educational and linguistic needs is crucial. The author also attempts to critically challenge common stereotypes used to label multiple repeaters. Troudi surmises that the students' confidence and interest in learning English increased when he involved them in negotiating preferred teaching styles and learning activities. He was also pleased to report that a surprisingly high number, 70%, of his multiple-repeater class passed his course during this teacher research project.

In the closing chapter, "Moodling in the Middle East," Jason M. Ward reports on research undertaken to determine how effective Moodle, the open-source course management system (CMS), is with his first-year writing class. According to students queried, 90% enjoyed using Moodle and thought it was useful for the course; a further 77% thought that they read or wrote more as a result of this CMS. Ward concludes that Moodle did enhance the learning environment by providing the students and faculty with more communicative, student-centered, and motivating activities in a much bigger world than the classroom.

The contributions to this volume support the view that teaching is a profession and that teachers, like all professionals, need to be constantly reflecting on what they are doing so as to improve their practice (Misson, 2006). To be an effective English language teaching professional, teachers must constantly upgrade their knowledge and understanding of language and language learning. But this is not enough; they should also develop as professionals. One way teachers can do this is by engaging in teacher research to develop a deeper understanding of what goes on in their classrooms. Teachers need to have the capacity for discovering and analyzing their students' needs and how as teachers they might best meet those needs. This means that every teacher must be a researcher.

Christine Coombe is coeditor of Language Teacher Research in the Middle East. *She is a faculty member at Dubai Men's College and an assessment leader for the Higher Colleges of Technology in Dubai, United Arab Emirates. Her research interests are teacher education, language assessment, and teacher evaluation. Her most recent publication is* A Practical Guide to Assessing English Language Learners *(2007, University of Michigan Press).*
Lisa Barlow is coeditor of Language Teacher Research in the Middle East. *She is a lecturer in EFL at United Arab Emirates University, Al Ain. Her research interests are testing and assessment in EFL and special needs. She is currently working on her EdD at Exeter University in England.*

CHAPTER 2

How Does Language Anxiety Affect Performance in the English Language Classroom? (*United Arab Emirates*)

Margaret Agbalizu

Issue

Experiences in teaching English as a foreign language (EFL) have shown that students are generally reluctant to speak in the target language. Similarly, students appear disinclined to engage in writing activities. Earlier investigations into these two areas have shown that students were afraid of committing errors (Price, 1991). This fear in classroom writing and speaking is an educational problem that cannot be ignored. Researchers refer to this tendency as *language anxiety* (Horwitz & Young, 1991). Gardner and MacIntyre described language anxiety as "a stable personality trait referring to the propensity for an individual to react in a nervous manner when speaking . . . in the second language" (as cited in Mitchell & Myles, 2004, p. 26). Although Horwitz, Horwitz, and Cope (1986) dismissed the possibility that anxiety might facilitate language learning, they argued that difficulties inherent in the language learning process are capable of challenging any learner's self-concept. In other research, Oxford (1999) found that low-level anxiety facilitated positive effects on the learner's foreign language performance. However, Scovel (1978) found that heightened anxiety might cause poor performance. Therefore, students' foreign language anxiety needs to be examined further in context for causes and possible remedies.

CONTEXT

Within the state-run schools in the United Arab Emirates (UAE), English is studied as a subject and taught using a combination of first and second languages (L1 and L2). Hence, English is viewed largely as a foreign language, and children in these schools seldom use English outside the classroom. In such situations, classroom foreign language learning can be affected by anxious feelings, especially if the learner has not achieved adequate proficiency in the target language.

Although research (Gardner & MacIntyre, 1993; Horwitz et al., 1986; Horwitz & Young, 1991; Price, 1991) has consistently revealed that anxiety can impede foreign language production, anxiety and the EFL learning situation in the UAE has not yet been examined. This study investigates Emirati female students' reluctance and fear when speaking and writing English in the public school classroom. Various researchers have studied the effects of foreign language anxiety on the language learning of EFL students in the United States and elsewhere, but almost no studies have examined the concurrent effects of the two anxiety constructs, foreign language writing anxiety and foreign language classroom anxiety, on foreign language learning. I have found no anxiety studies devoted to the EFL situation in the UAE and within the Middle East except the *Haifa Study* (Argaman & Abu-Rabia, 2000).

The public school system in the UAE tends to have two coursework streams that students follow: science and art. Students who join the science stream tend to be high achievers academically, and those in the arts stream tend to perform poorly on academics overall. The purpose of this study is to explore how foreign language anxiety affected the speaking and writing performances of the students in the two ability groups, and identify the group most affected by foreign language anxiety.

PARTICIPANTS

Participants in my study were 20 of my female 11th and 12th graders in a girls' secondary school in the Al Ain Educational Zone. Students were volunteers ages 17 and 18. To determine whether there were any significant relationships between the students' foreign language anxiety and their performance in a foreign language, their scores were grouped according to the streaming system (i.e., grade 11 and 12 science and grade 11 and 12 arts).

Background Literature

Reviews (Scovel, 1978) of the early research on the relationship between foreign language anxiety and performance found a considerable amount of ambiguity arising from the conflicting results (MacIntyre & Gardner, 1989). Young (1986) reported a negative correlation between foreign language class anxiety and scores on an oral proficiency measure called the Oral Proficiency Interview. Aida (1994) investigated the role of anxiety in university Japanese students. She found foreign language anxiety to be negatively correlated with final course grades. Relevant to the present study, Aida's investigations revealed that factors associated with the students' experience of anxiety in learning Japanese were mainly communication anxiety, fear of negative evaluation, and fear of failing the Japanese class.

Some inconsistent results with respect to the effects of L2 anxiety were obtained in Phillips (1992) and Ganschow et al. (1994). Of relevance in Phillips's study is one student of the highest ability who broke down during the oral exam. Nevertheless, she was able to recover enough composure afterwards and received a grade of 90 on the test. This suggests that anxiety may initially challenge a learner's self-concept but anxiety's effect may be adverse only when there is an existing low ability. Similarly, investigations conducted for the present study showed that the higher achievers who belonged to the science group had not been adversely affected by their experience of foreign language anxiety.

Sparks and Ganschow (1991) did not appreciate any relationship between anxiety and performance; instead, they advanced the Linguistic Coding Deficit Hypothesis (LCDH) theory. They argued that "the ability to use and understand language, rather than affective variables, is the important causal factor in foreign language learning within the classroom context" (Sparks & Ganschow, 1995, p. 236). MacIntyre (1999) and Horwitz (2001) strongly argued that anxiety is a multifaceted variable that can be both a cause and a consequence of poor language learning. As Horwitz (2000) put it, "the potential of anxiety to interfere with learning and performance is one of the most acceptable phenomena in psychology and education" (p. 256).

In a qualitative study, Price (1991) interviewed 10 anxious students. The students indicated that the most anxiety-provoking activity was speaking the foreign language in front of their peers. The problematic aspect of communicating in the foreign language within the classroom was also mentioned by participants in my study.

In terms of writing, Daly, Vangelisti, and Witte (1988) and Daly and Witte (1982) found that teachers' writing apprehension tended to determine students' general performance in writing-related tasks and the quality of student's written products. Research on foreign language writing anxiety (Cheng, Horwitz, & Schallert, 1999) found a significant negative correlation between L2 classroom anxiety and speaking in English. Relevant to the present study is that Cheng et al. also found that self-perceived inadequacy played a crucial role in the students' experience of foreign language writing anxiety. Argaman and Abu-Rabia (2000) found "highly significant but moderate negative correlation between language anxiety and the two measures of foreign language achievement, reading comprehension and writing achievement" (p. 156).

Procedures

To investigate the effect of foreign language anxiety on performance, I used two sets of English language learning questionnaires, follow-up interviews, and the students' term marks. Before beginning my study, I obtained permission from the headmistress of the school. I explained the purpose of the study to the students via a PowerPoint presentation. All instruments were piloted in both the translated and English versions. Data collection took place in three stages. First, the two questionnaires were used to collect data from 20 secondary school students enrolled in the science and arts sections. Teachers, my colleagues, allowed class time for study participation, and the participants completed questionnaires in class. The use of the questionnaires provided an opportunity to gather quantitative data, which was used to construct questions for the follow-up interviews. Next, I conducted semistructured interviews. Then, focus group interviews were organized with a mixed group of 12 participants. The interviews took place in an informal environment. I obtained the subjects' term marks and used them to assess students' performances. The term marks, together with the students' responses to the questionnaires, were coded and analysed. As a measure of appreciation, I gave thank-you cards and chocolates to students who participated in the study.

QUESTIONNAIRES

I adapted the Foreign Language Classroom Anxiety Scale (FLCAS) developed by Horwitz et al. (1986) and Daly and Miller's (1975) Writing Apprehension Scale (WAS). I modified the WAS to reflect foreign language learning and to suit EFL learning situations in the UAE, thereby creating the Foreign Language Writing Anxiety Scale (FLWAS). Based on comments collected in a pilot study, I further modified the FLWAS for the current study. I chose the FLCAS and the WAS because they have been used extensively and proven to be reliable and valid instruments. The questionnaires in this study had 20 questions each. The modifications were necessary for contextualizing the instruments in our own special Arabic-speaking situation.

SINGLE INTERVIEWS

From among the students who indicated a willingness to be interviewed, I chose 10. The group consisted of four students with high levels of foreign language anxiety, four with low levels of foreign language anxiety, and two presenting no anxiety at all. I included those two to see whether students not suffering from foreign language anxiety could offer any insights into the problem. The loosely structured interviews encouraged participants to pursue unanticipated topics or ideas. The interviews, organized around a question guide, lasted about 50 minutes. They were partly audiotaped, transcribed, and analysed. The guide contained the following questions:

1. Where do you speak more English?

2. What makes you anxious in your English class?

3. What do you think about your English curriculum?

4. Are there any kinds of exercises that cause you to panic?

FOCUS GROUP INTERVIEWS

I conducted an audiotaped focus group interview with 12 students, raising two research questions: (1) What are the sources of foreign language anxiety in your English class? (2) What do you suggest to reduce anxiety in your English class? Each interview lasted about 1 hour. Afterward, I transcribed and analysed the data.

To examine the relationship between the subjects' anxiety and performance in English language learning, I obtained the two term marks the subjects scored for their English speaking and writing examinations in the first term of the 2005–2006 academic year to serve as criterion variables in this study. They were speaking term marks (STM) and writing term marks (WTM).

I chose these combined data-gathering techniques so I could triangulate the data and thereby achieve a valid understanding and description of students' anxiety about classroom foreign language performance.

Results

Students' responses to the FLWAS and FLCAS were coded, scored, and then entered into a spreadsheet using Microsoft Excel. I completed statistical analyses using SPSS 13.0 for Windows. Because the FLWAS and FLCAS used a scale of five possible answers to each of the questions, ranging from 1 (strongly agree) to 5 (strongly disagree), the students' responses were scored in such a way that answers indicating the highest degree of anxiety received five points, and the answers indicting the least anxiety received one point. Negatively worded questions were reverse scored. In addition, Pearson's correlation was used to compute relevant statistical procedures.

In terms of qualitative data analysis, the process I used to analyze the interviews was based in part on the recommendations of Seidman (1991) and Weiss (1994). First, I transcribed the interviews in their entirety. Next, several readings of the transcripts identified four main categories or themes. Then, I employed *local integration,* as described by Weiss, to organize the ideas in the transcripts under those major categories. The aim was for the different categories, though diverse, to adhere or hang together. Within the categories, I identified connections among the various contributions of the participants and summarized the findings.

DESCRIPTIVE ANALYSIS

Looking at the arts group (see Table 1), the average scores on FLWAS (66.9) and FLCAS (69.3) were high. The similar scores on the two anxiety scales seemed to indicate that the arts group members experienced foreign language writing anxiety and foreign language class anxiety. On the achievement scores, 58.1 on the WTM and 64.8 on the STM were within average ranges. When I compared scores on the FLWAS (66.9) with the WTM (58.1) and scores on the FLCAS (69.3) with the STM (64.8), it appeared that, irrespective of the higher anxiety score on the FLCAS, the arts group performed better in speaking than in writing. However, according to t tests, a significant negative correlation ($-.65$ sig. = .042) was indicated between the group's writing anxiety (FLWAS) and speaking performance (STM). The expectation was that writing anxiety (FLWAS) would correlate negatively with writing performance (WTM), and that classroom anxiety (FLCAS) would correlate negatively with speaking performance (STM). The arts students' overall lower scores on the achievement measures were commensurate with their high anxiety scores. Based on the anxiety and performance scores, therefore, the group appeared to exhibit the negative effects of high levels of foreign language anxiety.

The science group's writing scores (see Table 2) were an average of 58.9 on the FLWAS, indicating moderate anxiety, and 81 on the WTM, which represented very good performance. On the FLCAS, the group scored an average of 49.4, which indicated less anxiety, and showed better performance on the STM, with an average of 86. The result of the correlations was .799 sig. = .006. This means there was a significant positive relationship between writing and speaking achievements. It suggests that as performance in writing increases, so does performance in speaking. The science group appeared unharmed by members'

Table 1. Arts Group's Average, Lowest, and Highest Scores

Item	N	Average	Lowest	Highest	Standard Deviation
FLWAS	10	66.9	58	79	7.288
FLCAS	10	69.3	49	91	13.933
WTM	10	58.1	28	84	24.231
STM	10	64.8	40	88	16.463

Table 2. Science Group's Average, Lowest, and Highest Scores

Item	N	Average	Lowest	Highest	Standard Deviation
FLWAS	10	58.9	49	67	6.024
FLCAS	10	49.4	28	75	14.96
WTM	10	81	58	98	13.63
STM	10	86	64	98	11.9

low to moderate levels of anxiety, because their performance on the achievement measures was high.

Based on *t* tests, the difference between the two groups' scores on the anxiety scale seemed not to be significant statistically, but the difference in the groups' scores on the achievement measures appeared significant statistically. Although both groups experienced some level of foreign language anxiety, only the arts group appeared to experience heightened anxiety, and its performance seemed to suffer as a result. Two ways that foreign language anxiety can affect performance have been considered here. On the one hand, the arts group appeared to suffer the debilitating type of foreign language anxiety that can lead to low performance or failure in a foreign language. On the other hand, the science group appeared to experience the facilitating kind of anxiety that can spur learners to higher achievements.

CORRELATION ANALYSIS

Using the data from the two groups combined, I applied statistical procedures. Between FLWAS and FLCAS the result was Pearson correlation coefficient $r = +.566$, which was highly significant at the .01 level (2-tailed). This meant that there was a positive correlation between the two sets of data and that a relationship existed between the students' experiences of foreign language writing anxiety and foreign language class anxiety. In other words, students who experienced foreign language writing anxiety also tended to experience foreign language class anxiety. Overall, the results showed that the population investigated tended to experience foreign language anxiety.

Between FLWAS and STM, the result yielded correlation coefficient $r = -.470$, which was significant at the .05 level (2-tailed). This result suggested that there was a negative relationship between the level of foreign language writing anxiety and students' performance in speaking. As students' anxiety about writing rose, speaking performance decreased or vice versa. This result seemed to have been influenced by the arts group's scores. Then, between WTM and STM, the result was a correlation coefficient $r = .600$, which was highly significant at the .01 level (2-tailed). This showed a relationship between the students' WTM and their STM, and implied that students whose performance was good at WTM would achieve a similar performance level at STM. This result appeared to have been influenced by the science group's scores.

To sum up, correlation analysis showed that all the students experienced foreign language anxiety. The higher language performances were contributed by the science group. These results seemed to confirm the hypothesis that science students tend to be higher achievers in academics overall, and arts students tend to perform relatively poorly. This result is consistent with the outcome of the descriptive analysis.

SOURCES OF ANXIETY

My qualitative investigations identified classroom-related sources of foreign language anxiety that encompassed personal and interpersonal anxieties, and I outline those here along with related student comments.

The Language Teacher and Peers

Fear of negative evaluation refers to a kind of "apprehension about others' evaluations, avoidance of evaluative situations, and the expectation that others would evaluate oneself negatively" (Horwitz et al., 1986, p. 128). In my study, speaking activities tended to be the main sources of anxiety. Students worried about their teachers' evaluative measures, especially because they appeared to perceive themselves inadequate and to view their teachers as fault-finders. A participant declared, "I don't speak English with the teacher because she is professional and she will catch my mistakes." The students feared being ridiculed by teachers. One participant remarked, "I am anxious when I tell teacher I don't understand; teacher say, 'You don't understand?! You must listen in the class. I just explained it to you' . . . and then, she said, 'silly'. . . . They make us ashamed and we not return to the teacher." Students broached the extensive use of L1 in the foreign language classroom. "If the teacher is good, the class will be good. Sometimes the teacher is boring, using Arabic all the time—we are not allowed to discuss anything, just right/wrong answers—she is teaching us to complete the exercises and homework." On the other hand, students feared being laughed at by peers: "I agree that the teacher makes us anxious, and I afraid from my girls in the class because they sometimes laugh—they laugh and we feel shy." Another participant offered: "Girls make me nervous. When I want to speak, girls giggle and make sounds." "Sometimes I feel calm, at other times I don't because some girls' attitude in the class—discouraging."

This nervousness can be called communication apprehension, which was defined originally by McCroskey (1977) as "an individual's level of fear or anxiety associated with either real or anticipated communication" (p. 78) with another person. An interviewee reported, "If she [the teacher] is near, I fear that she will ask me questions." Another reasoned, "Girls are uncomfortable about English class because it is difficult to understand, difficult to speak, and they don't know how to express ideas." One participant explained, "I can't speak English and can't understand what the teacher says. This makes me anxious. I am uncomfortable because I can't speak English."

The inability to understand the teacher and be understood by her and others is a main source of anxiety and embarrassment. "Speaking in the class makes me anxious—because it is a big problem," concluded an interviewee. Consequently, some students practice *failure-avoidance* behaviour, a term coined by Kleinmann (1977). Although students said they feared being harshly corrected and ridiculed by teachers, students said they felt relaxed speaking English with nonjudgmental friends and family members. One participant reported, "I talk English with my sister. She tells me what I say wrong, and I know what she says wrong. But the teacher?! 'O! You are wrong! You are this and that!'" Another participant disclosed, "I speak English sometimes with friends." Students seemed to cherish the mutual understanding they shared with other interlocutors and tried to avoid the sense of failure they felt when bullied and constantly evaluated by their teachers during classroom activities.

Instructional Materials

Students remarked that they found the course book irrelevant to their academic and social needs. "The book is so . . . stupid, it's like for kids not for big," declared one participant, adding, "we need real life; make us ready for real life." Another participant explained, "And in the class, we must use our imagination. The curriculum does not allow us to use our imagination. All that we know about English is the one class in school, not something we use in life." This dichotomy between the purpose of the course book and the students' sense of reality causes the students to doubt whether their present education can equip them for meaningful communication outside the school and for the demands of further education. A participant asserted, "Our language is many generation back. What we study in class is not the same in real life. When we get out of school, to real life, we will not be able" to converse easily.

Another aspect of the course book is the number of exercises. Students expressed dissatisfaction with the book because "it has too many exercises." Students complained that they "feel nervous, when we have functions or vocabulary," that "the worst thing is paragraph writing," and that "the book is big." There was a sense of inability to assess the book; an interviewee said, "I think the book is easy," yet went on to say, "but I can't read, even if it changes, I still can't read it." Another comment closer to the point was, "If it is changed, I don't think I will feel less anxious." This summarizes the whole aspect of the book and the exercises by demonstrating that the immediate cause of anxiety may not be the course book per se.

To sum up, in addition to the teacher's pedagogical practices and failed classroom techniques, inability to speak and understand English in the classroom made the students anxious. These problems led to silence instead of participation in the language classroom. This was aggravated by a curriculum steeped in exercises that demanded writing beyond the student's immediate command. The inability to speak and be understood, added to the inaccessibility of the course book, suggests that the students experienced anxiety about speaking as well as writing.

ANXIETY REDUCTION

The students interviewed suggested several strategies for reducing their anxiety.

Pair work and group work. Five interviewees suggested that students preferred pair work and group work to accommodate the wide range of abilities in their classes, which can often create anxiety. One participant observed, "Of course, some people learn languages more easily than others because maybe they started early, but for me it wasn't easy to learn."

Need for teacher support. Participants seemed to imply that students preferred a teacher who understood a student's weaknesses in the foreign language rather than an abusive one who embarrassed learners. One participant suggested, "And maybe in the class there is a girl who doesn't understand English well—the teacher refers to her as stupid—maybe we can encourage this girl." Students said they would prefer a teacher who treated them with friendship or with motherliness, who was capable of relating the course book to their lives and to reality. Another participant offered this comment, "The teacher should be our friend-mother, make the lesson touch our life. Teacher must encourage us even if we make a mistake. If the teacher encourages us, we will make good answer."

A session devoted to oral practice. Students expressed the desire to have a class dedicated solely to speaking to improve their language. One participant commented that if "only for two minutes, girls read the lesson, you can't learn speaking. English needs how to communicate and speak—even, no reading—teacher uses the recorder and we answer the questions." Another comment noted that because students "can't speak English in a good way, we like to speak English in the playground. . . . When I write in the structures, I get 90% or 95%, but we can't speak."

Students recommended shorter lesson periods. "We need to get out of the tension of studying, to refresh, because the lesson is 60 minutes. Too long, boring—brain is tired—so we need games to revive, maybe something visual, like movies. In the half of the lesson, we are sleeping, so we don't understand the entire lesson." Above all, students hoped that "if the curriculum changes, we will feel comfortable and less anxious. We want the style of the book to change. We love to see another kind—of the way of presenting the information. You must make students see movies in the school, during the class to learn—answer questions—have fun and learn at the same time—bring—read."

In sum, to alleviate their anxiety, students suggested a totally new English language curriculum that emphasizes speaking and offers activities in which group dynamics soothe their feelings. Students said that if their teachers were more understanding of their language needs, offered more friendship and assistance, and reduced the criticism, students would feel less anxious and would be encouraged to perform better in the language classroom.

QUANTITATIVE FINDINGS

Looking at the data from this study, correlation results supported that students overall experienced anxiety. Specifically, the study's results seem to indicate a negative relationship between foreign language anxiety and the performance of students in the arts group. Results from the questionnaires showed that the arts students scored higher than the science students in anxiety, indicating the high anxiety that the arts students experienced in their language learning and implying that the science students were less anxious. In addition, the arts students' writing anxiety (FLWAS) appeared to correlate negatively with their speaking performance (STM). As Tables 1 and 2 show, the arts students scored consistently high on the anxiety scales, and the science students scored consistently lower. The reverse is the case on the achievement measures: The science students scored higher marks, and the arts students scored lower marks. These results seem to suggest that the students in the arts section tend to experience higher levels of anxiety and perform poorly on achievement measures. For the arts students, their anxiety apparently acts as an affective filter that limits them from attaining their potential in the foreign language.

In this study, foreign language writing anxiety correlated negatively with speaking achievement, rather than with writing achievement. This seems unusual. I expected that FLCAS would correlate positively or negatively with writing or speaking achievements, because FLCAS is directly associated with foreign language speaking and writing achievements. However, I expected the FLWAS—based on Daly and Miller's (1975) WAS—to be directly associated with only foreign language writing achievement (Cheng et al., 1999). An explanation could be that, as Young (1991) maintained, students with self-perceived inadequacy will easily experience foreign language anxiety.

Previous studies (Aida, 1994; Argaman & Abu Rabia, 2000; Cheng et al., 1999; Horwitz et al., 1986; MacIntyre & Gardner, 1989; Phillips, 1992) also found a negative relationship between foreign language anxiety and achievement. Therefore, a range of research supports the view that foreign language anxiety can have adverse effects on foreign language performance.

QUALITATIVE FINDINGS

Looking at why students experienced anxiety, their comments shed some light on that tendency. Speaking and writing activities are identified as anxiety provoking in relation to the teacher's classroom strategies, because the two language skills are product oriented. The finished product must be presented on the spot, and this aspect causes anxiety. In addition, the two skills are exam based. Students asserted that "in the class, we are talking to get the right answer." If they do not get it right, they said, then the teacher "gets angry and embarrasses us" and "we feel shy." These concerns affected language proficiency by restricting the students' oral communicative abilities, and students' concerns acted to reduce the volume and quality of their finished written products.

Difficulty in language learning appears to be the result of an accumulated weakness owing to an absence of an early start, to an improper start, or to a learning plateau. In this study, difficulty with speaking might have been related to the strong negative correlation between foreign language writing anxiety and speaking performance noted for the arts group. Consequently, students expressed aversion toward classroom activities that had writing contexts, for example, functions, compositions, letter writing, and structures. All these aspects of writing skill are associated with grammar, and grammar is linked with rules that students find difficult to master.

Reflection

In view of the factors indicated by the students as anxiety provoking and the adverse effects of foreign language anxiety on the students' foreign language performance in my study, I aim to share the research outcome within the Ministry of Education. Following earlier discussions with immediate colleagues, we have adapted the existing curriculum. Further, initiatives are under way to bring the findings to the attention of education authorities.

My recommendations include a seminar advising the general body of language teachers on classroom foreign language anxiety and techniques to alleviate students' feelings of anxiety. During the process of this study, I have been informed of two major points: (1) In my EFL context, a language laboratory will help students hear authentic dialogues, visualize the contexts, and experiment with language. This exposure will reassure their self-concepts and reduce anxiety. (2) This study may imply that, in a system that uses no strict streaming of students, highly proficient students certainly will have positive effects on the least proficient ones. In conducting my research, I have noted that the qualitative strategies established powerful portrayals of the students' experiences and enhanced the benefits of more than one approach in investigating the effects of anxiety on performance. I also find that the small number of subjects may render any kind of generalization difficult. In order to generalize the results in the future, this study needs to be replicated with male students and a larger number of subjects. Then, the limitations of statistical analysis could be addressed. Specifically, future studies could explore and attempt to verify the correlation between writing anxiety score and speaking achievement score that I found in this study.

Margaret Agbalizu teaches at Umm Al Emarat
Secondary School for Girls in Al Ain, United Arab Emirates.

CHAPTER 3

L2 Learners and Student Evaluations of Teaching: Issues of Language Comprehension (*United Arab Emirates*)

Ahmad Al-Issa and Hana Sulieman

Issue

In a 2005 survey released by the Institute of International Education, the number of international students enrolled in American higher education institutions in the United States was 565,039, and this number is increasing rapidly. In addition, the number of American institutions outside the United States is on the rise, particularly in countries of the Arabian Gulf such as the United Arab Emirates (UAE), Kuwait, Qatar, and Bahrain. For example, since 1997, the UAE alone has hosted four new American-style universities, and several 2- and 3-year colleges have adopted an American-style curriculum.

Because many of these universities pride themselves on their American-Western education models, they also have implemented student evaluations of teaching (SET) to assess the effectiveness of their course offerings and their teachers. Often, American institutions in this region adopt from their U.S. sister universities the whole process of conducting SET, including the rating scales. Usually, these colleges and universities adopt the U.S. system without tweaking the instruments to fit the educational context (i.e., the linguistic and cultural backgrounds of the students).

As in most American universities, at the end of each semester the students at the American University of Sharjah (AUS) in the UAE rate the effectiveness of their teachers by filling out the university's teaching evaluation form (see

Appendix A). Although students attending this university are nonnative speakers of English (NNSs), English is the language of instruction as well as the language used on the evaluation form at AUS. We therefore were concerned about whether our students were having problems comprehending the English language used on the evaluation form. The quality of students' feedback (i.e., its validity and reliability) depends largely on whether or not students have understood the questions to which they have responded. If students, due to their limited English language proficiency, do not understand the intended meaning of a question on the rating form, then the validity of the instrument and the accuracy of the information provided by the students are questionable. Furthermore, because important personnel decisions (e.g., promotion, contract renewal, or merit increases) are usually made in light of the data obtained from SET, the use of invalid information to make these decisions would certainly be unfair to the evaluated faculty. The use of such data also would be misleading for any informative evaluation undertaken by teachers to improve their teaching or modify existing teaching practices.

AUS is considered one of the leading institutions of higher education in the Arabian Gulf and the Middle East. It was founded in 1997 by His Highness Sheikh Dr. Sultan Bin Mohamed Al Qassimi, ruler of Sharjah and the president of the university. AUS is a nonprofit, independent, and coeducational university which was accredited in 2004 by the Commission of Higher Education of the Middle States Association of Colleges and Schools, and further licensed by the Department of Education of the State of Delaware in the United States and by the Ministry of Higher Education in the UAE.

AUS attracts students not only from the Gulf region, but from around the Middle East, Africa, and the Indian subcontinent. It has a student body of about 5,000 students of mixed cultural and linguistic backgrounds representing more than 60 different nationalities and a faculty and staff representing more than 65 countries. The majority of the students are from Arab and Islamic countries, and English is their second, third, or even fourth language. However, the faculty body, which consists of more than 250 members, is mostly Western (from Canada, the United Kingdom, the United States, and European countries) and Arab-Americans who were either born and raised in North America or obtained their degrees from North America or Europe. The university, then, is an island of ideas, languages, cultures, and differing viewpoints in the arid lands of the UAE, a country in the Arabian Gulf that actually has more expatriates residing in it than locals. Students tend to choose AUS as an alternative to traveling to countries such as Canada, the United Kingdom, or the United States because of the opportunity to receive U.S.-style methods of instruction and diversity in the classroom while remaining close to home.

Because the language of instruction at AUS is English, students must obtain a score of 510 or higher on the Test of English as a Foreign Language (TOEFL) in order to matriculate. If students score less than 510 on the TOEFL, they are required to join the intensive English program to bring their TOEFL scores up. Each student, however, has had at least an average of 8 years of English language instruction before joining the intensive English program or the university.

Despite scoring a minimum of 510 on the TOEFL and their often impressive English speaking skills, some of our students join our university programs with noticeable difficulties in the areas of reading and writing. Thus, our classrooms, especially entry-level ones, usually consist of students of mixed levels of English proficiency. Students with lower proficiency levels usually have more problems coping with their course requirements. For example, in their writing assignments in response to various types of readings (e.g., personal responses to an assigned reading, summaries, or reflective papers), students show various levels of understanding the materials. Some students, we noticed, have problems comprehending what they are reading because of their limited English vocabulary. In addition to the weaknesses we noted in our regular classroom work, we also found that our students had great difficulty with any readings not directly related to the class. For example, we often do classroom research utilizing surveys and questionnaires. We also assist our colleagues' research by distributing different types of surveys. These topics may run the gamut from linguistics to sociology and psychology. However, what stand out are the constant questions our students ask us about word meanings. This factor has motivated us to pursue this research about SET.

The fact that some of our students have a problem comprehending English texts made us curious to find out how such a problem impacts English-related tasks that our students have to perform outside their course requirements. One of these tasks is the completion of the AUS teaching evaluation form at the end of each academic semester. If students were having problems even with teacher-aided tasks in the classroom, we wondered, then how well would they perform a task on their own that required comprehending each item or question without the help of the teacher? Knowing how important the outcome of the student evaluations is, not only for summative purposes but also for formative ones, we decided to investigate this issue. In other words, we decided to examine whether or not our students were capable of comprehending the questions on the actual teaching evaluation form used by AUS. We also wanted to know which demographic variables would influence students' levels of comprehension.

We were motivated to examine this issue because of our convictions that language teachers have the responsibility to examine how their students' language skills affect their performance on tasks designed to benefit the institution as a whole and help individual teachers improve their practices. To our knowledge, with the exception of Pennington and Young (1989) and Wennerstrom and Heiser (1992), there is no research on the linguistic suitability of teaching evaluation forms for NNSs in American universities in the United States or abroad.

Background Literature

Despite the importance and seriousness of the issue of NNSs and SET, we found no attempts made to establish the reliability and validity of specific instruments to be used by English as a second language (ESL) or English as a foreign language (EFL) students to evaluate teaching. Ratings instruments used in American universities were designed to be completed by students whose native language is English. The suitability of the language used in these forms has rarely been assessed for comprehensibility by NNSs. As pointed out by Pennington and Young (1989), evaluation instruments which have been tested for validity and reliability among native speakers are not necessarily appropriate for ESL students. They recommended that "the instruments and procedures [be] constructed by evaluation specialists sensitive to the nature of the ESL context" (p. 630).

The validity of SET has been continually debated in the academic community. As Theall and Franklin (2001) asserted, "Few issues in higher education are as sensitive, decisive, and political as faculty evaluations and in particular the quality and value of the information provided by students in their evaluations of teachers and courses" (p. 45). The literature on SET is substantial, and we make no attempt to review this body of research (for comprehensive reviews of the literature, see Aleamoni, 1981; Cashin, 1988; Germain & Scandura, 2005; Kolitch & Dean, 1999; Marsh, 1984, 1987; Theall & Franklin, 2001). Instead, in this chapter we concentrate on an area of SET that has been ignored: the validity of SET by NNSs.

The existing literature on SET has focused on other important issues concerning the reliability and validity of student ratings. Reliability studies, for example, looked at whether students' ratings were consistent over time and from rater to rater, and validity studies examined whether students' ratings actually measured teaching effectiveness, and whether these ratings were biased by noninstructional factors. Among the factors that have been identified are the level of the class being taught (Marsh, 1987), students' interest in the subject matter (Marsh & Dunkin, 1992), the size of the class (Greenwald & Gillmore, 1997), gender (Hobson & Talbot, 2001), grades (Greenwald, 1997; Tang, 1999), the rigor of the course (Best & Addison, 2000), and the instructor's warmth-inducing behaviour (Best & Addison, 2000).

Furthermore, Martin (1998) and Chen and Hoshower (2003) provided a detailed discussion of the noninstructional factors that have been found to influence SET based on the research they reviewed. They found that SET can be influenced by students' characteristics (e.g., motivation for taking the course or disposition toward the instructor and course), instructor characteristics (e.g., rank, experience, or personality traits), course difficulty (e.g., grading and leniency), and other environmental characteristics (e.g., physical attributes and the ambience of the classroom).

Moreover, related to the issue of validity, many studies in the area of SET (e.g., Ahmadi, Helms, & Raiszadeh, 2001; Crumbley, Henry, & Kratchman, 2001; Sojka, Gupta, & Deeter-Schmelz, 2002) investigated students' perceptions of faculty evaluation (i.e., how seriously students take teaching evaluations). In general, findings in this area show that students' perceptions of the value of faculty evaluation influence their responses when evaluating teaching. Students with positive views of the evaluation process are more likely to take the evaluation more seriously than those with negative perceptions.

Although the research just mentioned provides significant insights into the validity and reliability of SET, it has not addressed the question of whether NNSs understand the language (i.e., English) of the rating forms. Pennington and Young (1989) were first to specifically call for linguistically appropriate rating forms to be used by students whose native language is not English. In their article "Approaches to Faculty Evaluation for ESL," which appeared in *TESOL Quarterly*, the authors argued that "Because of limitations of language or cultural inhibitions, [ESL and EFL] students may be unable or unwilling to communicate as freely as native speakers would in written or oral forms of faculty evaluation" (p. 629). They also argued that the rating scales "frequently used for faculty evaluations, are of questionable validity when employed by those whose exposure to English . . . is limited" (p. 629). The same authors warned that if administrators continue to use these ratings for summative and punitive purposes only, the faculty will be unfairly represented. They concluded the following:

> Because of the importance of faculty evaluation to TESOL as a profession
> and to individual programs, and because of the sensitive issues that surround
> the evaluation enterprise, it is critical that those charged with evaluating
> ESL teachers or future teachers be aware of the many and varied sources
> of error, negativity, and unproductivity associated with faculty evaluation.
> (pp. 642–643)

Wennerstrom and Heiser (1992), in an article also published in *TESOL Quarterly*, investigated questions of bias and SET instrument development. They found that, among other factors, the level of English was a biasing factor in ESL students' evaluations. They pointed out that their ESL participants had varying degrees of difficulties in understanding the language of the instrument used in the study. As they explained, "We found that parts of our instrument, even in its simplified state, were being misinterpreted, especially by low-level students" (p. 285).

To summarize, SET is widely adopted in American universities in the United States and abroad as part of their quality assurance systems; however, little research has been done on the linguistic suitability of evaluation forms for NNSs. In most of these universities, student ratings are used as one (and sometimes the only and most influential) measure of teaching effectiveness. The increasing number of ESL and EFL students attending American universities in the United States and abroad calls for a closer look at the linguistic suitability of the rating forms. We argue that those in charge of SET have a responsibility to make sure that NNSs can understand the language of these rating forms. Therefore, the purpose of this chapter is to expand the scope of research on SET by addressing the following question: Do NNSs understand the questions to which they respond on the rating form used at AUS? In other words, does their proficiency in English limit their understanding of the various items or questions presented to them on the teaching evaluation form?

Procedures

To find out whether our students understood the questions to which they responded on the teaching evaluation form used at AUS, we decided to test their comprehension of some questions or items used on this particular form. We also were interested in learning about the demographic variables that could influence students' comprehension. Therefore, a multiple-choice comprehension test was designed to assess students' understanding of some of the items or questions presented to them on the actual evaluation form used by the university (see Appendix A). Thus, all seven questions used in the test were taken directly from the teaching evaluation used at AUS. These specific questions were chosen based on our belief that our students would have difficulty understanding some of the intended meanings of the words within the questions.

For each question, one word was underlined and participants had to choose the best alternative meaning for that word. Students were given five different alternatives, and only one of them was correct (see Appendix B). To make sure that only one alternative captured the exact meaning of each underlined word, four independent raters checked the test's accuracy: two professors of linguistics and two American administrators working for the university. The level of agreement was 100%.

Once the test was ready, we selected some summer courses from a convenient 2004–2005 list classified by college. We then contacted the individual instructors teaching the selected courses, and they all volunteered to administer the test in their classes. They were asked to administer the test at the beginning of their classes, and to instruct participating students to work on the test individually and not use any type of dictionary. Students were also told that the purpose of this study was to improve the quality of the teaching evaluation form used at AUS, and that participation in this study was voluntary. Participants were assured that all data would be treated in the strictest confidence. A total of 819 students (482 males and 337 females) completed the comprehension test and biographical data.

Inspection of the biographical data showed that participants in our study came from the four schools and colleges at AUS: College of Arts and Sciences, School of Business and Management, School of Architecture and Design, and School of Engineering. Furthermore, participants represented four different geographic origins: the Gulf (students from the UAE, Kuwait, Bahrain, Oman, Qatar, Yemen, and Saudi Arabia), the Levant (students from Syria, Jordan, Palestine, and Iraq), Africa (students from Egypt, Sudan, Morocco, Algeria, Tunisia, and Nigeria), and the Indian subcontinent (students from India and Pakistan). The sample reflected the cultural and linguistic diversity of the AUS student population. Table 1 summarizes the demographic information about the respondents.

Table 1. Profile of Respondents

Variable	Respondents (N = 819)
Region of Origin	
Gulf	396
Levant	243
Africa	64
Subcontinent	116
Gender	
Male	482
Female	337
Language of Instruction in High School	
Arabic	434
English	350
Asian languages	35
School/College at AUS	
Arts and Sciences	122
Architecture	79
Business	261
Engineering	357

(continued on p. 28)

Table 1. Profile of Respondents *(continued)*

Variable	Respondents (*N* = 819)
Grade Point Average	
3.50–4.00	120
3.00–3.49	223
2.50–2.99	223
Below 2.50	253
Academic Status	
Freshman	214
Sophomore	231
Junior	201
Senior	124
Graduate	49

Results

In analyzing the data, we first looked at the percentages of correct and incorrect answers for each item on the test (see Table 2).

For example, in response to item 1, about 80% of the students in the sample provided the correct answer, and about 20% provided incorrect answers. However, for item 4, about 59% of the sample failed to choose the correct meaning for the word *supplemented,* and only 41% managed to do so. The equivalent meaning for the word *supplemented* was *complemented*; however, the majority of the students chose other words such as *dated, colored, completed,* or *covered.* Moreover, in response to item 6, about 28% of the students selected words like *demoted, demolished, denounced,* or *admitted* instead of *displayed* as an equivalent to the word *demonstrated.*

Second, we considered the outcome of interest to be the number of correct answers on the seven questions (ranges from 0 to 7). Table 3 shows the resulting distribution of the number of correct answers. As shown in Table 3, about 2% of the students in the sample (*n* = 15) were unable to give the correct answer to any of the items on the test, and only about 17% (*n* = 136) answered all seven questions correctly. The average number of correct answers in this study is about 5.

Third, and further to the earlier analysis, we performed a chi-square analysis to test the homogeneity of the proportions of correct answers across the differ-

Table 2. Percentage of Correct and Incorrect Answers

Item	Incorrect (%)	Correct (%)
1. The course grading scheme was clearly defined.	20.5	79.5
2. The course was demanding compared to other courses.	31.4	68.6
3. The course objectives were accomplished.	19.7	80.3
4. The textbook(s) and supplemented material were useful to your understanding of the course content.	58.9	41.1
5. The course had high standards compared to other courses.	41.3	58.7
6. The instructor demonstrated a thorough knowledge of the subject.	27.8	72.2
7. The classroom interaction helped you learn and understand the material.	23.1	76.9

ent demographic groups of the students. Our objective was to test the theory that the distribution of the number of correct answers would be the same for different subgroups of students defined by a particular demographic variable. For example, considering the demographic factor gender, we tested the hypothesis that the breakdown of the proportion of correct answers by male students would not differ significantly from the corresponding breakdown for female students. To improve the power of the test, the number of correct answers was categorized as 0–2, 3–4, 5–6, and 7. Table 4 shows the observed breakdown of

Table 3. Distribution of the Total Number of Correct Answers

Number of Correct Answers	Students	
	Number (N = 819)	Percentage
0	15	1.8
1	39	4.8
2	59	7.2
3	88	10.7
4	101	12.3
5	153	18.7
6	228	27.9
7	136	16.6

the proportions of students who gave a certain number of correct answers classified by demographic factor, the value of chi-square statistic, and the corresponding degrees of freedom and probability.

Using a significance level of 5%, the results show that all demographic factors, except for the school or college, exhibited significantly different proportions of students in the four categories of correct answers. Below, I examine the significant demographic factors in more detail.

Origin. The percentages of African and Indian Subcontinent students who provided seven correct answers were significantly higher than those provided by Gulf and Levant students (11% Gulf, 16% Levant, 28% Africa, 29% Subcontinent). Also, significant differences can be seen in the 0–2 and 3–4 categories, which show that Gulf and Levant students had significantly higher percentages (16% from each group in category 0–2, and 27% of the Gulf group and 22% of the Levant group in category 3–4) compared to African (8% in the 0–2 category and 16% in the 3–4 category) and Subcontinent students (7% in the 0–2 category and 16% in the 3–4 category). This finding suggests that Gulf and

Table 4. Chi-Square Analysis of the Number of Correct Answers

Factor	Students Answering Correctly (%)				n	Chi-Square Calculations		
	0–2 Questions	3–4 Questions	5–6 Questions	7 Questions		Test Value	df	p Value
Origin								
Gulf	16%	27%	46%	11%	396	37.5	9	0.000
Levant	16%	22%	46%	16%	243			
Africa	8%	16%	48%	28%	64			
Subcontinent	7%	16%	48%	29%	116			
Gender								
Male	15%	27%	45%	13%	482	13.3	3	0.004
Female	12%	18%	49%	21%	337			
Language of Instruction in High School								
Arabic	20%	28%	43%	9%	434	68.1	6	0.000
English	6%	17%	52%	25%	350			
Asian languages	17%	26%	34%	23%	35			

(continued on p. 31)

Table 4. Chi-Square Analysis of the Number of Correct Answers *(continued)*

| Factor | Students Answering Correctly (%) | | | | n | Chi-Square Calculations | | |
	0–2 Questions	3–4 Questions	5–6 Questions	7 Questions		Test Value	df	p Value
School/College								
College of Arts and Sciences	11%	15%	50%	24%	122			
School of Architecture and Design	12%	22%	52%	14%	79	16.4	9	0.058
School of Business and Management	11%	25%	47%	17%	261			
School of Engineering	17%	25%	43%	15%	357			
Grade Point Average								
Above 3.50	6%	20%	47%	27%	120			
3.00–3.49	15%	19%	48%	18%	223	33.0	9	0.000
2.50–2.99	12%	25%	44%	19%	223			
Below 2.50	19%	26%	46%	9%	253			
Academic Status								
Freshman	19%	37%	37%	7%	214			
Sophomore	20%	19%	47%	14%	231			
Junior	8%	20%	51%	21%	201	86.6	12	0.000
Senior	7%	17%	52%	24%	124			
Graduate	2%	10%	49%	39%	49			

Levant students in this study had inadequate language skills compared to the African and Subcontinent students. The language of instruction in high school could be a factor in these results. Based on biographical information provided by the students, 65% of Gulf students and 62% of Levant students attended Arabic schools; whereas 61% of African and 70% of Subcontinent students attended English schools.

Gender. The female students in this study were significantly more capable of answering the comprehension questions correctly compared to the male students: 21% of the female students answered all items correctly, while only 13% of male students answered them all correctly. A possible reason for such a significant difference between the two genders could be the differences in their grade point average (GPA) standings. In this sample, 34% of the male participants had a GPA below 2.5 compared to 25% of the female participants. The chi-square analysis of the GPA standing in Table 4 clearly shows that students with a GPA below 2.5 are significantly less likely (only 9%) to answer all questions correctly and are the most likely to provide two or fewer correct answers (19%). It should also be mentioned that about 49% of the female students in the sample had attended English-instructed high schools compared to about 38% of the male students.

Language of instruction in high school. The results clearly show that fewer English-instructed students scored in the lower range for the number of correct answers (0–2 and 3–4 categories) than did Arabic- and Asian-instructed students, and more English-instructed students scored in the higher range (5–6 and 7 categories) than did Arabic- and Asian-instructed students. It is interesting to note that only 9% of the Arabic-instructed students answered all the questions correctly compared to 25% for the English-instructed students and 23% for the Asian-instructed students, indicating that the Arabic-instructed students suffered the most from inadequate language skills.

GPA. As mentioned above, in discussing the gender differences, students whose GPA was below 2.5 were the most incapable of answering all questions correctly compared to the other GPA standings. Further, the percentage of students with a GPA above 3.5 who provided complete correct answers was significantly higher than the corresponding percentages in the other GPA groups. This finding is not surprising given that the language of instruction at AUS is English and that the achievement of a good GPA standing is partially and positively linked to students' ability to understand the language of instruction. We also noted that about 56% of students with a GPA below 2.5 were in the Gulf and Levant groups and 64% were freshmen and sophomores.

Academic status. Results show that the percentage of students answering two or fewer comprehension questions correctly decreased significantly for juniors, seniors, and graduate students. The percentage of students answering all of the questions correctly increased significantly as academic status improved. These findings suggest that as a student became more academically proficient, he or she became more able to understand the questions on the SET form. It is clear from Table 4 that the percentages of freshmen and sophomores who were unable to answer more than two questions correctly was almost equal; however, 14% of sophomores managed to provide seven correct answers compared to only 7% of freshmen. This result could be attributed to the better language skills that some sophomores obtained in high school and then improved while attending AUS for about 1 academic year. We should note that although the 14% figure is significantly higher than that for freshmen, it is still significantly less than those for junior or senior students.

Reflection

Our findings clearly show that participants had inadequate English language skills for comprehending our instrument. These findings are in line with those reported by Wennerstrom and Heiser (1992). Participants in this study demonstrated varying degrees of linguistic understanding of the instrument of the study, which was generated from the actual rating form they typically filled out at the end of each semester. Although some groups (i.e., those who had attended English-instructed high schools as well as those with a GPA of 3.00 and above) performed better than others, none of the different groups was able to fully understand all questions or items on the instrument. In fact, even graduate students in this study had a problem providing correct answers to the test items. As seen in Table 4, only 39% of our graduate students provided correct answers to all seven questions.

Those with the lowest English language proficiency level, according to our findings, were students from the Gulf and the Levant. As mentioned earlier, the majority of those students attended Arabic-instructed high schools, where the emphasis was on the Arabic language and all subjects were taught in Arabic. Interestingly, however, all students in our sample, like all AUS students, had met the university admission requirement by scoring a minimum of 510 on the TOEFL. We have found that a TOEFL score is not necessarily an indication of one's English-language proficiency level as much as an indication of one's test-taking skills. Finally, it was clear in this study that freshmen and sophomores, regardless of their other demographic factors, were the weakest compared to juniors, seniors, and graduates in comprehending the meanings of items on the test.

The findings of this study raise two very important issues. The first issue concerns the validity and reliability of the feedback provided by nonnative English speakers using rating instruments. Based on our findings, we conclude that unless students fully understand the meanings of the questions presented to them on the evaluation forms, their responses are invalid, unreliable, and misleading when used for informative or summative evaluations. The second issue concerns whether or not ESL and EFL students should evaluate the effectiveness of their teachers and courses by responding to rating instruments that are written in English. We believe that NNSs attending American universities should be part of the evaluation process and are capable of providing feedback to improve teaching practices and course effectiveness. However, administrators must take into consideration students' proficiency in English. We therefore suggest that, because the main purpose of SET is to provide valid information for formative and summative purposes, the entire rating form should be translated into the students' native languages. This tactic would ensure that students understand the questions when they rate the effectiveness of teachers and course content. Naturally, however, understanding the questions does not mean that students would not be biased by other factors.

If translating the form should prove logistically impractical for any reason, we suggest providing equivalents for some of the English words that might prove difficult for some ESL and EFL students. These equivalents could be placed in brackets on the English form. Another suggestion—possibly the easiest—would be to give students the freedom to ask questions concerning words they do not understand. The person administering the evaluation could then clarify the meaning—not necessarily in the student's native language but in English. In other words, our findings indicate that university officials need to rethink the practice used now in administering the evaluations. At AUS, as well as other American universities with which we are familiar, students cannot ask any questions during the evaluation.

It is also important to mention here that most evaluation forms consist of two sections (see Appendix A). The first is a Likert scale, requiring students to read a number of statements, like those we used in our test, and rank their level of agreement on a five-point scale (1 = strongly disagree, 2 = disagree, 3 = neutral/not sure, 4 = agree, and 5 = strongly agree). The second section, which is even more linguistically challenging, is the comments section. In this section, students have to read a number of statements (e.g., please enter below any comments on how the course should be improved; please provide your instructor with helpful suggestions for improving his/her effectiveness) and respond to them in writing. Based on the findings of this study, as well as on our personal observations and knowledge of ESL and EFL students, we are certain that these students would have great difficulty in expressing themselves in writing in English. This might explain why students in this university do not write very much, if anything, in the comments section. Once again, for the sake of quality of feedback, students should at least be given the option to use their native language when responding to the comments section.

We hope that the findings of this study will motivate more research into the issue of nonnative English speakers and SET. For example, it would be interesting to interview some ESL and EFL students who are attending American universities in the United States and abroad about how they feel about the rating forms used in their universities from a linguistic point of view. Another study might look at the correlation between quality of feedback and the language of response. For example, researchers could investigate a particular two-section course taught by the same instructor, using the same textbook, providing the same assignments, and using the same grading criteria. At the end of the semester, students in the first section would be given the rating form in English, and students in the other section would be given the same form translated into their native languages. Of course, it is probably impossible for a teacher to perform exactly the same in two sections; therefore, the same experiment could be conducted in one section. In other words, students would rate their teacher first by responding to the English rating form, and then a week later the same students would rate the instructor using the translated form.

Finally, with the increasing number of nonnative speakers of English—whether foreign or second language learners—attending American universities in the United States and abroad, where SET is a common practice, more attention should be given to the linguistic suitability of the rating instruments. This is an important issue to investigate because universities, including ours, use students' input to improve the quality of education in the university in general and teachers aim to use such input to improve their own teaching methods. However, if students with low-level English proficiency misunderstand the intended meaning of an item or question on the teaching evaluation form, the validity and reliability of their input will certainly be questionable and at worst misleading.

The findings of this study were definitely an eye-opener, perhaps not so much for those of us conducting the research as for those who learned about the study when we presented our findings. When we first obtained our results, we presented them to our university as a whole. We further shared our findings with colleagues from various departments on campus. Results were also discussed in university evaluation committees, and colleagues made many suggestions during these encounters, including simplifying the instrument, allowing students to ask questions about the meanings of difficult words, and translating the instrument into students' native languages.

We have learned through this process that we must be more sensitive to students' linguistic needs in their second language. We should never assume they understand everything that they read or hear in English, and this includes even simple words we use in the classroom. In order to become more sensitive, it is important that we encourage our students to ask whenever they do not understand a word or phrase we are using. We must monitor students' reactions to comments in the classroom and their expressions, and we must be especially vigilant about how we present oral and written assignments in order to ensure comprehension. In terms of the research itself, we discovered that students require more elucidation of the instrument and what is expected of them when completing surveys for this type of inquiry. It would be beneficial to have an instruction sheet for colleagues distributing the surveys, to ensure that students completely understand the language used and the purpose of the survey. Furthermore, follow-up should occur with any type of research, but it is especially important in an EFL environment to ensure the validity and reliability of the instrument.

The significance of this research cannot be overlooked for several reasons. First of all, many American-style universities are currently operating in the Gulf region, and all employ some form of SET. We are also aware that even in Arabic-medium universities, English programs specifically use SET instruments written in English. Therefore, this is another area in which student comprehension should be ensured. Further, individual teachers who wish to collect data on their own teaching practices in the classroom need to ensure that the information they gather is valid. Finally, because university officials make vital decisions about teachers and curriculum development based on these data, they should be certain that when students respond to these surveys they have full comprehension of the questions they are being asked.

Ahmad Al-Issa and Hana Sulieman teach at the American University of Sharjah in Sharjah, United Arab Emirates.

Appendix A: AUS Teaching Evaluation Form

American University of Sharjah
College of Arts and Sciences – Course Evaluation Form
Fall 2004

PLEASE READ: This questionnaire is designed to help the University and its faculty to know the degree of your satisfaction with the course you are currently taking, and to assess the quality of teaching at the University.

Correct	Incorrect
■	⊙ ⬡ ⊠ ☑

NOTE:
MUST use a 2HB pencil only

Course
Code: _____

School or College
O College of Arts and Sciences
O School of Architecture and Design
O School of Business and Management
O School of Engineering

Credits Completed
O 0–30
O 31–60
O 61–90
O 91–120
O 121–150

	Strongly Agree	Agree	Neutral	Disagree	Strongly Disagree

I. Your Evaluation of the course content, design and management

1) The course was well organised .... ○ ○ ○ ○ ○

2) The course objectives were carefully and
   clearly defined .... ○ ○ ○ ○ ○

3) The course grading scheme was clearly defined ..... ○ ○ ○ ○ ○

4) The textbook(s) and supplemented material were
   useful to your understanding of the course content .. ○ ○ ○ ○ ○

5) The assignments and reading material were helpful
   in improving your understanding of the subject ..... ○ ○ ○ ○ ○

6) The classroom interaction helped you learn
   and understand the material .... ○ ○ ○ ○ ○

7) The course made you want to learn more
   about the subject .... ○ ○ ○ ○ ○

8) The course was demanding compared to
   other courses .... ○ ○ ○ ○ ○

9) The course had high standards compared
   to other courses .... ○ ○ ○ ○ ○

10) The course objectives were accomplished .... ○ ○ ○ ○ ○

11) Overall, this course was excellent .... ○ ○ ○ ○ ○

II. Your Evaluation of the Instructor

12) The instructor started and finished the
    class on time .... ○ ○ ○ ○ ○

13) The instructor was ready to answer
    your questions .... ○ ○ ○ ○ ○

14) The instructor evaluated your work fairly .... ○ ○ ○ ○ ○

15) The instructor evaluated your work on time .... ○ ○ ○ ○ ○

16) The instructor's comments on your work
    were clear, specific, and helpful .... ○ ○ ○ ○ ○

	Strongly Agree	Agree	Neutral	Disagree	Strongly Disagree
17) The instructor was very effective in helping you understand the course material	○	○	○	○	○
18) The instructor demonstrated a thorough knowledge of the subject	○	○	○	○	○
19) Overall, the instructor was excellent	○	○	○	○	○

American University of Sharjah
College of Arts and Sciences
Course Evaluation – Comments Sheet
Fall 2004

Instructor's Name: _____

Course and Sections: _____

- Please enter below any comments on how the course should be improved:

- Please provide your instructor with helpful suggestions for improving his/her effectiveness:

- Please enter specific comments, if relevant, on the role that Information Technology plays or could play in this course:

- Other comments:

Appendix B: Comprehension Test

Please circle the one alternative (a, b, c, d, or e) that gives the best meaning of the underlined word.

1. The course grading <u>scheme</u> was clearly defined.
   a. Portfolio
   b. Assignments
   c. System
   d. Scam
   e. Behavior

2. The course was <u>demanding</u> compared to other courses.
   a. Boring
   b. Challenging
   c. Relaxing
   d. Exciting
   e. Monotonous

3. The course objectives were <u>accomplished</u>.
   a. Achieved
   b. Disappointing
   c. Failed
   d. Fundamental
   e. Useful

4. The textbook(s) and <u>supplemented</u> material were useful to your understanding of the course content.
   a. Dated
   b. Colored
   c. Completed
   d. Covered
   e. Complemented

5. The course had high <u>standards</u> compared to other courses.
   a. Grades
   b. Means
   c. Rates
   d. Quality
   e. Inferiority

6. The instructor <u>demonstrated</u> a thorough knowledge of the subject.
   a. Displayed
   b. Demoted
   c. Demolished
   d. Denounced
   e. Admitted

7. The classroom <u>interaction</u> helped you learn and understand the material.
   a. Students' popularity
   b. Teacher's popularity
   c. Diversity
   d. Exchange of ideas
   e. Practicality

Biographical information

Gender: _____

Country of origin: _____

Language of instruction at the high school you graduated from: *Please circle one of the letters below:*

   A. Arabic   B. English   C. Asian

Major at AUS: _____

Current GPA: _____

Academic status: *Please circle one of the letters below:*

   A. Freshman   B. Sophomore   C. Junior   D. Senior   E. Graduate

Spelling Errors of Arab Learners: Evidence for Intergraphemic Mapping (*Saudi Arabia*)

Maher Bahloul

Issue

During my years of teaching in the Arabian Gulf, I have been observing learners of English struggle with the spelling of English vocabulary from the least complex to the most complex lexical items. Anecdotal as it may be, the following incident tells much about the significance of English spelling in a learner's life. One of my students stopped me in one of the corridors of the College of Languages and Translation at King Saud University in Riyadh and confessed that his failing in English was due to his extreme failure in understanding English spelling. Having been involved in teaching upper level courses, initially I did not react appropriately to the student's statement and I did not take the student's concerns seriously enough. However, when I started teaching English language skills in an evening program at the Institute of Banking in the same city, I started noting the high frequency of learners' spelling mistakes. In addition, the mistakes tended to fall within categories that went beyond the scope of particular groups or individuals. More importantly, students' grades tended to be affected by the poor spelling exhibited in their writing. Having noted the magnitude of the spelling dilemma, I initiated a small research project which identified the spelling errors, the possible causes, and the possible remedies with a hope to solving these spelling problems.

In this study, I examined the spelling errors of male adult learners of English as a foreign language to gain an understanding of how these adult learners construed and misconstrued the graphemic structure of their second language (L2). In addition to a number of intralingual and developmental errors, I found that the peculiarities of the first language (L1) writing system, Arabic in this case, accounted for almost one-third of the learners' spelling errors. Although Arabic phonology relies on the consonant-vowel (CV) template, the writing system gives more prominence to the consonant and much less importance to the vowel, especially the short one. Such a spelling gap appears to play a thwarting role in learners' acquisition of English spelling.

Background Literature

The spelling errors of English as a second language (ESL) and English as a foreign language (EFL) students result from a number of interrelated factors. The research has noted such factors as the nature of the writing system (Jimenez-Gonzalez, 1997), persistent and intractable difficulties (Moats, 1996), differences in sound systems (Nyamasyo, 1994), mispronunciation and lack of awareness of spelling rules (Haggan, 1991), difficulties in phonemic awareness (Treiman, 1991), word familiarity (Cooksey, Freebody, & Bennett, 1990), and unstressed grammatical words (Morris, 2001). However, a few studies have attributed spelling errors to the L1's graphemic systems. Arabic, for example, contains 28 letters, all of which are consonants. Words, sentences, and texts are vowelized during the early stages of learning, but soon unvowelized. Thus, verbs, nouns, adjectives, adverbs, and particles are realized through a succession of two or more graphemes. These graphemes are a combination of consonants and long vowels. Short vowels, on the other hand, are typically unrealized. Readers rely on acquired linguistic knowledge and context to elucidate their nature (Abu-Rabia & Siegel, 1995).

Procedures

In this study, the data consisted of 4,872 words collected during 1999 and 2000 while I was teaching in the evening Intensive English Program at the Institute of Banking in Riyadh, Saudi Arabia. Study participants were 88 male students. Most were in their early to late 20s, were college graduates, had taken English in high school and college as part of the general education requirements, and had already completed two 8-week sessions within the Institute of Banking. As such, their level was classified as low- to mid-intermediate EFL learners. The spelling activity used for data collection was incorporated in a listening task in the textbook series. Before collecting the data, I administered practice activities so that learners had ample exposure to the target words. To maximize learners' motivation, I collected most of the data during the course's learning and achievement assessments. Of the 4,872 target words, 1,003 were misspelled, which accounts for 20.59%, or one out of every five words. Given the amount of time devoted to practice activities, that percentage appeared to be quite significant.

Results

A closer examination of the corpus revealed myriad mistakes from three major sources: (1) intralingual errors, which stemmed from the spelling system of the target language, (2) learner-language errors, which were a result of learners' L2 developmental stages, and (3) interlingual errors, which were attributed to the interference of the mother tongue, or Arabic, spelling system.

INTRALINGUAL ERRORS

Arab learners of English, and possibly most other learners including native speakers, find it quite challenging to utter the same letter *a* in eight different ways and to spell the high front vowel /i/ in 11 different ways according to the lexical item and the phonological environment in which it appears, as shown in Table 1. The examples in Table 1 show two closely related spelling rules, namely, the lack of correspondence between graphemes and phonemes and vice versa, and other cases are abundant. Lesetar (1997), for example, compiled 115 rules to capture all different aspects of the English spelling system; such a high number testifies to the inherent complexity of the language.

In line with the spelling discrepancies Lesetar identified, we found the following in our data: the process of monographicization, in which a digrapheme is

Table 1. Grapheme Versus Phoneme Discrepancies

Letter	Sound	Phoneme	Spelling
a	dame any pan father ball pillage lunar opera	/i/	feet me Caesar people beat deceive amoeba relieve ravine key quay

reduced to a single grapheme; the process of graphemic unification, in which the same grapheme is used in similarly pronounced units; and the process of matching phonemes with corresponding graphemes. Table 2 gives examples of these errors.

As Table 2 shows, Arab learners tend to simplify English spelling in three different ways. Words containing clusters of graphemes with only a single one pronounced tend to be simplified in their written forms accordingly. Thus, words such as *know, really,* and *school* are realized as *now, relly,* and *scool,* without the phonologically unrealized *k, a,* and *h,* respectively. Other words containing the letter *c* pronounced with a voiceless alveolar fricative appear with the corresponding letter *s,* and words appear with the voiced palato-alveolar affricate *j* when it is realized in the letter *g.* A third revealing case appears with vowels when similarly pronounced units are similarly transcribed independently of their accessibility, syllabic structure, and simplicity. A word such as *now,* for example, is likely to be familiar to such students. Nevertheless, its spelling appears with

Table 2. Types of Intralingual Errors

English Spelling	Learners' Spelling
Monographicization	
know	now
foreign	foren
building	bilding
guard	gurd
really	relly
school	scool
Graphemic Unification	
choice	choise
placement	plesment
college	calleje
Phoneme/Grapheme Matching	
other	ather
studies	stadies
something	samething
mother	mather
hall	holl
bikes	baix
talking	token
now	naw
South	Sauth
foreign	foren

the diphthong /aw/ instead of /ow/, simply because it sounds correct. Hence, the phonemic representation is much more prevalent than the graphemic one.

To conclude, in this study, Arab learners tended to make a number of spelling mistakes that could be traced to the inherent discrepancies of the target spelling system; hence their intralingual status. Beyond this study, such errors may be equally observed among other learners of English and possibly among native speakers as part of their spelling maturation process.

LEARNER-LANGUAGE ERRORS

A second major source of spelling errors appears to stem from the linguistic developmental stage, which conditions what learners are capable of producing, and vice versa. Such errors are shown in Table 3.

Table 3. Learner-Language Errors

Regular Spelling		Learners' Spelling
Metathesis		
	first	frist
	ethnic	ethinc
	relative	raletive
	problem	broplem
Cluster Simplification		
	island	ilan
	tourist	toures
	used	use
	bridge	brige
	school	chool
Epenthesis		
	mine	mined
	guess	guesst
	prison	presind
Syllable Simplification and Truncation		
	depends	apants
	excellent	ecslant/exlend
	incredible	credebel
	commuter	comut
Assimilation		
	neat	need
	great	graid

On closer examination, the error types in Table 3 show a striking similarity with those made by native English speakers as part of the internal linguistic dynamics of language either at the acquisition stage or during the internal language development. Metathesis, for example, occurs when two phonemes exchange positions in a particular word. Metathesis is widely observed in baby talk, language of the elderly, and slips of the tongue. In addition, it is a process with which new words are formed. Such cases are illustrated in the learners' misspelled examples of the metathesis type in Table 3. *First* and *ethnic,* for example, are spelled *frist* and *ethinc* when the adjacent graphemes *ir* and *ni* are conversely realized *ri* and *in,* respectively. Another case of metathesis involves nonadjacent graphemes. For example, with the words *relative* and *problem,* students permuted the first and second vowels in the former and the *p* and *b* consonants in the latter, yielding the misspelled words *raletive* and *broplem.*

A second well-attested spelling error in this study was cluster simplification. Words that end or start with two adjacent consonants tended to be simplified so that the last or the first one was omitted, respectively. The word *island,* for example, consists of two syllables, the second of which ends with the consonant cluster [*nd*]. Learners tended to simplify the cluster by eliminating the final consonant, yielding a VC syllable [*in*] instead of a VCC syllable [*ind*]. Such cluster simplification was similarly observed at the syllable onset level. For example, with *school,* the CC cluster [*sk*] was reduced to a single consonant [*k*], yielding the misspelled word *chool.*

Another major spelling error which occurred was epenthesis. In these cases, learners tended to add a final consonant to a word, resulting in a cluster in most cases. Thus words such as *mine, guess,* and *prison* are realized with a final *d* or a final *t,* depending on the voicing status of the preceding sound or syllable.

Syllable simplification and syllable truncation were also widely observed in my Arabic learners' spelling errors. For example, a two-syllable word such as *depends* [*de pants*], where each syllable contains an onset and a coda, is simplified so that the first syllable loses its onset, yielding the misspelled word *apants.* Syllable truncation results when the entire syllable is omitted. This was clearly observed in the misspelled words *ecslant/exlend, comut,* and *credebel,* which were reduced versions of multisyllable words. Thus, the trisyllabic words *excellent* and *commuter* were reduced by the omission of medial and final syllables, respectively, and the quadrisyllabic word *incredible* was reduced by leaving out the first syllable.

A final common spelling error in my study involved assimilation, which occurs when sounds are colored by preceding and following phonological environments. As the examples in Table 3 indicate, the final voiceless sounds in words such as *neat* and *great* were produced with their voiced counterparts, yielding the misspelled words *need* and *graid.* Such voicing is a result of the effect of the prevocalic context. In other words, learners also appeared to spell what they uttered.

In sum, Arab learners of English in this study showed consistency in their misspellings, which involved a number of linguistic processes such as metathesis, cluster simplification, epenthesis, syllable simplification and truncation, and assimilation. Such consistency was reminiscent of their level of learner-language proficiency and hence appeared developmental in nature.

INTERLINGUAL ERRORS

In addition to the intralingual and learner-language spelling errors, Arab learners in this study exhibited a number of misspellings that appeared to stem from the interference of the mother tongue spelling system. A brief background on the Arabic spelling system is informative here. Although the phonology of Arabic (either standard or dialectal varieties) shows a predominant CV template with rare consonant clusters, the Arabic spelling system exhibits an opposite behavior, in which all short vowels are omitted and words include a succession of consonants and long vowels. Therefore, with a word such as *kataba* (he wrote), in which each consonant is followed by a vowel using the CVCVCV template, the Arabic spelling system gives much more prominence to the consonants and much less to the vowels. Thus, such a word is typically spelled with a succession of consonants *ktb* and no visible vowels. Learners of Arabic are introduced at an early age to the vowelized spelling system, but a few years later, they are expected to guess the vowels on the basis of context. The unvowelized script is the norm in all varieties of Arabic, ranging from the formal written media to informal personal letters. In short, Arab EFL learners come from this background without vowels to face a much more articulate English vowel system.

Therefore, this gap between the English and Arabic systems can be expected to have a negative effect on the spelling performance of Arab learners of English. My data supported this prediction because learners' spelling errors included consonant replacement, vocalic transfer, nativization, epenthesis, and graphic mapping.

Consonantal Replacement

A number of Arab learners' spelling errors in our data appeared to stem from the unavailability of sound units in the mother tongue and the systematic reaction of replacing them with their available counterparts. As such, the unavailable voiceless bilabial stop /p/ is systematically replaced by its available voiced counterpart /b/; hence the misspelling of words such as *places* and *groups* with *blices* and *groubs*. Table 4 shows such spelling errors. In addition to the voiceless bilabial stop /p/, Arabic does not have a voiced labiodental fricative /v/. Therefore, learners tend to replace /v/ with its voiceless counterpart /f/, an existing

Table 4. Consonantal Replacement

Regular Spelling	Learners' Spelling
Places	Blices
Groups	Groubs
Invite	Infait
University	Unfersty

phoneme in Arabic, yielding such misspellings as *infait* and *unfersty*, where the phoneme /v/ is replaced by /f/.

Vocalic Transfer

The Arabic spelling system includes three short vowels and three long vowels. As mentioned earlier, although the former vowels are optionally realized because of their diacritic nature, the latter are mandatory for inclusion in the spelling system. An Arabic word such as *kitaab* (book), for example, is spelled with four graphs—the three consonants *ktb* and the long vowel represented by a vertical line and connected to the second consonant. As for the short vowel /i/, it does not need to be realized. The three short vowels in Arabic are the high front vowel /i/, the high back vowel /u/, and the midcentral vowel /a/, which amounts to a three-vowel system reminiscent of early primitive phonological systems. Leaving aside the exact phonetic features of each of the three vowels, we noted that Arab learners tend to make abundant use of these three vowels as they spell English words in a way so that all English front high and mid vowels appear with /i/, all back high and mid vowels appear with /u/, and all midfront and central vowels appear with /a/, as summarized in Table 5 and exemplified in Table 6.

As the examples in Table 6 show, words such as *much*, *possible*, and *college* on the one hand, and *tempting* and *yes* on the other, with midcentral and midfront vowels, respectively, are all spelled with a central vowel /a/, yielding the misspelled words *mach*, *pasboll*, *callge*, *tanting*, and *yas*. Similarly, the two high

Table 5. Vocalic Transfer Rules

Types of Vowels	Vowel Assimilation
High front vowels (tense and lax)	/i/
Midfront and central vowels and low-back vowels (tense and lax)	/a/
High and midback vowels (tense and lax)	/u/

Table 6. Vocalic Transfer

Regular Spelling	Learners' Spelling
Much	Mach
Possible	Pasboll
College	Callge
Tempting	Tanting
Yes	Yas
Also	Alsu
Restaurants	Resturants
Beginning	biginning
Relatives	riltives
Family	famli

and midback vowels in *also* and *restaurants* are misspelled with the back vowel /u/. Finally, the words that include high vowels as in *beginning* and *family* are misspelled, and high vowels such as *relatives* are also misspelled with the high vowel /i/.

Nativization

Another common spelling error of our Arab EFL learners related to words that have been borrowed from English and have become part of the local dialect or standard vocabulary. Such words tend to be spelled not on the basis of how they sound, but rather on the basis of how they are locally pronounced. The examples in Table 7 show this type of transfer.

Epenthesis

As mentioned earlier, Arabic phonology relies heavily on the CV template. However, consonant clusters are abundant in English, especially in the derivation of plural nouns and the past tense. When faced with such clusters, Arab learners tend to decluster them by inserting a vowel between the adjacent consonants. Examples can be seen in Table 8.

Table 7. Nativization

Regular Spelling	Learners' Spelling
Mexican	Maxican
America	Amreca/Amirca/Ameirca

Table 8. Epenthesis

Regular Spelling	Learners' Spelling
Tempting	Tempiting
August	Agesit
Hills	Hulis

Vowel Deletion and Intergraphemic Mapping

A much more salient spelling error that Arab EFL learners exhibit relates to some sort of image mapping, which may be called intergraphemic mapping. In such a case, learners tend to visually map the Arabic script into its corresponding English spelling. Misspelled words such as *Glbreth*, *aftrnon*, and *flowr* instead of *Guilbreth*, *afternoon*, and *flower*, exhibit an intriguing omission of vowels which render unutterable each of the aforementioned words.

Reflection

The writing of Arab EFL learners at the intermediate level exhibits a relatively high frequency of spelling errors—one in five words. This study shows that such spelling errors stem from three major sources: intralingual, developmental, and interlingual. The intralingual spelling errors stem from the spelling discrepancies of the target language, English. The developmental errors, on the other hand, stem from the learners' current spelling performance gap as part of their linguistic maturation stage. The final and most salient source is the native language, Arabic. Here, we argue that in addition to a number of obvious negative transfer cases, learners resorted to the graphemic representation of the L1 to reproduce the spelling of the L2; hence the systematic intergraphemic mapping.

These conclusions have consequences on the teaching and learning of English spelling to Arab learners. ESL and EFL teachers should be aware of the opaque nature of English spelling, including the myriad discrepancies which appear to constitute real challenges to native and nonnative learners alike. Such awareness should result in developing materials that specifically target such spelling features through, for instance, heavy and systematic drilling activities in interactive and meaningful ways. These activities should lead students to notice the English spelling gaps, an effort that should assist greatly in learning the target forms and patterns. As for errors that are developmental and thus part of the learners' language, a high degree of understanding and tolerance is necessary. Given the systematic nature of such spelling errors, they represent signs of a learning system at work. Language teachers should therefore assess such spelling errors with much more comprehensibility. Finally, the interlingual spelling errors appear to call for teachers' awareness, if not knowledge, of both the phonological and graphological systems of the L1.

Given Arabic's lack of vowels, as shown in its spelling and graphemic systems, appropriate spelling teaching methodologies ought to foster learners' awareness of the different English graphemic system with a particular focus on vowel realization. In other words, ESL teachers of Arab students should be aware of the fact that such students are not quite familiar, if at all, with realizing short vowels in the written form of a word given the fact that the graphemic system of their L1 lacks such a feature. It is thus necessary to foreground learners' exposure to short vowels through, for instance, heavy practice of relevant minimal pairs (e.g., met/mat, meet/met). Moreover, students' use of the L1 to write out words in the L2 is extremely counterproductive, and teachers should discourage this practice. Arab learners tend to write out in Arabic the English word so as to remember its pronunciation. In doing so, not only do they misrepresent the English word, they also draw a visual picture of the English word where short vowels are not at all attested, which can hinder their learning of spelling and result in frequent deletions of English vowels. In addition, ESL teachers should devote more time to focusing on the learning of phonemes—vowels and consonants—of L2 that are not attested in L1, such as /e/, /o/, /p/, and /v/. Arab learners tend to substitute these phonemes with the closest corresponding ones in their native language repertoire. Finally, raising learners' awareness of the graphemic system of their L1 might prove quite effective.

In conducting this study, I considered what actions I would take as a result of my findings. Based on my research, I would say that I will never teach English spelling to Arab learners the same way I would to other EFL learners. The results of this research are extremely informative and helpful. It is quite revealing to find out that interlingual spelling errors go way beyond the phonology of the L1 and extend to its graphological system. Future spelling lesson plan objectives should therefore clearly state learners' awareness of systematic graphological differences between Arabic and English scripts. In addition, the use of the Arabic script to transcribe English words by instructors and students alike, especially in elementary and secondary institutions, to either facilitate the learning of particular words or assist in pronouncing them, should be discouraged. Such practice can only deepen Arab learners' spelling gaps, as shown in this chapter. Thus, there is no doubt that research of this nature nurtures classroom practice and renders teachers' pedagogical choices much more supportive and cooperative vis-à-vis Arab EFL learners.

Maher Bahloul teaches at the American University of Sharjah in the emirate of Sharjah, United Arab Emirates.

CHAPTER 5

What Makes a Good Teacher? Investigating the Native-Nonnative Speaker Issue in the Arabian Gulf (*Kuwait and United Arab Emirates*)

Christine Coombe and Mashael Al-Hamly

Issue

Aspects of teacher effectiveness have been studied for many decades in various educational contexts. Personal and professional characteristics as well as teaching techniques seem to be the categories most commonly cited by researchers when discussing qualities of good teachers. At a recent conference, the lack of awareness of one of the authors, Christine Coombe, came to light when several colleagues were discussing the qualities of effective teaching. In this enlightening exchange, the issue of nativeness or lack thereof was put forth as a possible characteristic of an effective English language educator. Native speakers at the table were surprised and rather shocked that the idea of whether or not the teacher is a native speaker of the language would have an impact on how students judged the quality of their instruction. Nonnative speakers were fairly insistent that nativeness did make a difference, not only in the judgment of teacher effectiveness but also in employment and salary issues as well. Still skeptical, Christine Coombe, a native speaker of English, set out to explore this issue in more depth with Mashael Al-Hamly, a nonnative speaker of English. The resulting qualitative study presented in this chapter investigates English as a foreign language (EFL) students' attitudes toward native-English-speaking teachers (NESTs) and nonnative-English-speaking teachers (NNESTs) in two major Arabian Gulf institutions of higher education, in Kuwait and the United Arab Emirates (UAE).

THE EDUCATIONAL CONTEXT

This study was conducted at two government-funded universities, Dubai Men's College in the UAE and Kuwait University in Kuwait. The student population was about 2,300 students at Dubai Men's College and more than 20,000 at Kuwait University. The institutions in which the data collection took place had several commonalities. Both institutions were primarily English medium and admitted only locals (i.e., Emiratis at Dubai Men's College and Kuwaitis at Kuwait University).

One major difference between the institutions concerned the teacher population. At Dubai Men's College, NESTs constituted the majority of English faculty. In fact, of the total number of English teachers at Dubai Men's College, more than 95% were native speakers coming from Canada, the United States, the United Kingdom (UK), and Australia/New Zealand. At Kuwait University, the distribution of NESTs and NNESTs was much different. In the English Department and Language Center, nonnative speakers of English made up 11% of the teaching staff. Kuwaitis constituted the majority at 88%, and teachers from countries as diverse as Canada, the United States, the UK, and Australia made up the remaining teacher numbers.

PARTICIPANTS

A total of 266 university students (55 from the UAE and 211 from Kuwait) participated in the study. Students from Dubai Men's College were male and were enrolled in the higher diploma/bachelor's program, majoring in business and information technology. Kuwait University students were split between males (12%) and females (88%) and were majoring in English language and literature and education. In total, 185 females (70%) and 80 males (30%) participated in this study.

Background Literature

Much research has been done on the characteristics of effective teachers. Various groups within education cite different requisite qualities when they talk about effective teaching practices. A useful way to examine these qualities is from a variety of different stakeholder perspectives: administrators, educational researchers, teachers, and students.

STAKEHOLDER PERCEPTIONS OF EFFECTIVE TEACHING

Seymour Ericksen (1984) carried out a survey among education administrators. His research found that "an outstanding teacher should be an inspired instructor who is concerned about students, an active scholar who is respected by discipline peers, and an efficient organized professional who is accessible to both students and teachers" (as cited in Williams & Burden, 1997, p. 3).

In another survey (Rosenshine & Furst, 1973), educational researchers listed the ideal characteristics of a good teacher as follows:

- Possessed clear presentation skills.

- Used a variety of activities during the lesson.

- Encouraged achievement-oriented behavior in classrooms.

- Provided students with an opportunity to learn criterion materials.

- Acknowledged and stimulated student ideas.

- Did not criticize.

- Used structuring comments at the beginning and during lessons.

- Guided student answers.

Teachers themselves identified several characteristics of effective instructors in a study conducted by Bress (2000). Qualities they found essential included treating each student as an individual, being enthusiastic and inspiring, and having caring qualities.

Students also had much to say in this area. Brown and McIntyre (1992) surveyed students age 12 to 13 in the UK and found the following qualities to be desirable in good teachers:

- Creates a relaxed and enjoyable atmosphere in class.

- Retains control of the class.

- Presents work in an interesting and motivating way.

- Provides conditions for students to understand the work.

- Makes clear what students are expected to do and achieve.

- Judges what can fairly be expected from each student.

- Helps students with difficulties.

- Develops mature personal relationships with students.

- Demonstrates personal knowledge of and talent for the subject.

- Helps and encourages students to raise expectations of themselves.

Similarly, Hassett (2000) defined good teachers as those having a sense of purpose with expectations of success for all students. Other teacher characteristics he identified were someone who can tolerate ambiguity, demonstrates a willingness to adapt and change to meet student needs, is comfortable with not knowing, is reflective about his or her own work, learns from a variety of models, and enjoys his or her work and students.

TEACHER CHARACTERISTICS

A large number of factors relating to the characteristics of effective teachers have been proposed and studied, assessing such issues as gender, minority status, physical appearance, and reputation of the teacher (Anderson & Siegfried, 1997; Tatro, 1995; Wachtel, 1998; Worthington, 2002, as cited in Brown, 2004). Other factors important to the determination of quality teachers are communication, personality, and professional factors, which we will discuss in more detail in the following sections.

Professional Factors

A number of professional qualities, such as knowledge of the subject (Ogden, Chapman, & Doaks, 1994; Shaw, Partridge, & Gorrell, 1990), could characterize a good educator. Many attempts have been made to investigate these characteristics. In one study, Fisher, Alder, and Avasulu (1998) found that providing clear explanations and presenting materials in an interesting way were important attributes of an effective teacher. Establishing an effective learning environment, which includes an understanding of what is going on in the classroom, is another important characteristic of a good teacher (Gordon, 1997).

Many studies indicate that other professional characteristics are important in the determination of teacher effectiveness (Goodgame & McCoy, 1997). Teaching techniques and methods rank highly on the list of effectiveness indicators for high-quality teachers. Other professional characteristics such as the ability to bring real-life and practical examples into the lesson are deemed to be very important (Shaw et al., 1990). Researchers have also recognized the ability to organize classes to meet student needs (Isaacs, 1994) and the ability to create opportunities for student success (Cimarolli, 1993) as important characteristics for long-term and short-term success.

Communication Factors

Sensenbaugh (1995) reviewed studies of teacher communication and focused his research on teaching immediacy factors, which are defined as verbal and nonverbal communication such as smiles, nods, use of inclusive language, and eye contact. Studies show that students experience increased motivation if taught by teachers with high immediacy skills (Frymier, 1993).

Elton (2003) studied empathy with students as a requisite for teaching competence. Findings indicate that teachers must speak at a level of understanding that is close enough to that of their students for them to be able to follow what is being said.

Personality Factors

Approachability and willingness to answer questions have been shown to be important. In a study done with college students in the United States and Sri Lanka, Shaw et al. (1990) found that for both groups of students, characteristics of kindness, friendliness, and a caring attitude were of the utmost importance. A teacher needs to have a personality that appeals to students in order to keep their interest (especially important for subject matter that is of low interest). Sense of humor, fairness, and positive attitude were also mentioned as important characteristics (Goodgame & McCoy, 1997). It is clear that as a whole, personality is an important factor in determining teacher effectiveness.

RESEARCH ON EFFECTIVE L2 TEACHING

Analysis of a good second language (L2) teacher indicates that classroom practice is oriented toward the development of the whole student and of appropriate affective states that enable students to learn more effectively. The salient features of good teacher behavior include treatment of students as persons whose needs are both intellectual and emotional.

Much of the research has been taken from content-based instruction and classroom observations. Richards (1990) queried whether information arising from studies of instructional practices in content-based subjects could help "identify what it takes to be an effective second language teacher" (p. 7). He suggested that the goals of instruction in language classes are different and therefore strategies to achieve them may vary. He recommended a dual approach to teacher education. In his thinking, a macro approach addresses the issue of "clarifying and elucidating the concepts and thinking processes that guide the effective second language teacher" (p. 14). A micro approach looks at teaching in terms of directly observable characteristics.

Richards and Rogers (1986) argued that techniques which "engage the whole person, including the emotions and feelings as well as linguistic knowledge and behavioral skills" (p. 114) are important ones for teachers to have in the L2 classroom.

In a publication entitled *Anatomy of a Good Second Language Teacher: What It Has to Say About L2 Teacher Education*, Mangubhai (1993) studied an effective teacher and made several generalizations about the reasons for her effectiveness. Based on evidence from her videotaped classes, he concluded that an effective teacher has qualities that fall under two categories: affective characteristics and teaching techniques.

He identified three noticeable qualities under the affective characteristics.

First, the teacher showed a strong interest in her students as individuals. This was noticed through her concerns for her students' health and the focus on the correct pronunciation of their names. Another attribute of this teacher was her politeness to her students. In the transcript of her videotaped sessions, *thank you* and *please* were very commonly heard. Because she was polite in class and concerned for her students' well-being, many might think that she lacked classroom control. On the contrary, evidence from her videotaped classes indicated that she set very definite standards and ground rules for student behavior and was able to enforce them.

As far as teaching techniques are concerned, this teacher displayed what Mangubhai (1993) called qualities of a "communicatively oriented" (p. 11) teacher. The teacher displayed a number of techniques for involving the whole class, which in turn, transformed the class into a cooperative group. Also present among her repertoire of teaching techniques was timing, particularly as it related to student response. A common problem in L2 classrooms is the time span allotted to students for question responses. Many teachers expect immediate responses from their students when involved in a question and answer activity. Alternatively, teachers who give students time to respond often move on to another student when they fail to get a response after a few seconds' pause. Mangubhai noted that this teacher had high expectations that all her students would speak. When failing to get a response, she rephrased the question several times until students were able to respond. A third characteristic of her classroom teaching was a focus on more learning and less teaching. To this end, she focused on getting answers from her students rather than providing them. Finally, this teacher insisted on clear explanations so that students in her classes knew exactly what was required of them.

Conspicuously lacking in all of these studies was mention of the nativeness factor as a requisite quality of effective teaching. To date, there are only a few studies in the literature of students' perceptions and preferences for nativeness in a teacher (Cook, 2000; Liang, 2002, as cited in Mahboob, 2004; Mahboob, 2004). In a study related to hiring practices, Cook (2000) came to the conclusion that "nowhere is there an overwhelming preference for NESTs. Being a native speaker is only one among many factors that influence students' views of teaching" (p. 331). Therefore, we decided to conduct a study investigating whether nativeness or nonnativeness of the teacher made a difference to our students.

This study examines the following research questions:

- Do Gulf Arab students prefer NESTs or NNESTs as English language teachers in their classes? Or does this variable not make a difference?

- What reasons do Gulf Arab students give in support for their teacher preferences?

Procedures

Students were asked to write essays on one of three different base prompts to investigate their attitudes toward NESTs and NNESTs. Base prompts were selected because, as Kroll and Reid (1994) indicate, they are one of the most common forms of writing prompts and they state the entire task in direct and very simple terms. The following prompts were used:

1. "Students learn languages better when their teacher is a native speaker." Do you agree or disagree with this statement? Support your answer.

2. "Students learn languages better when their teacher is a nonnative speaker of the language." Do you agree or disagree with this statement? Support your answer.

3. Some students think that only native speakers can be good language teachers. Others think that nonnatives can also be efficient teachers. What is your opinion about this issue? Support your answer.

The third base prompt was a replication of one used in the Mahboob (2004) study, which provided both sides of the issue in the same prompt. The other two prompts were one-sided in that they asked students to express their opinion and support it on the issue if they would learn better if their teacher were a native speaker (Prompt 1) or a nonnative speaker (Prompt 2). The directions for the prompts gave students a suggested word count of 250 words. This target replicated the type of tasks used in the International English Language Testing System because many of the students were preparing for this international benchmark. Teachers who agreed to distribute this task to their classes had the option of using it as part of the students' writing portfolio. All essays were written in class. Students were given 30 minutes to respond to the task.

Results

The first step to analyzing the data was to do a global read of all essays and classify them into three categories of response: NEST preference, NNEST preference, no preference. Once these numbers had been established, we divided the essays into prompt type (1, 2, or 3) and did similar counts (NEST preference, NNEST preference, no preference).

The student responses to each of the three writing prompts were then analyzed using an approach similar to the one used in the Mahboob (2004) study, which was based on a discourse analytic technique put forth by Hyrkstedt and Kalaja (1998). Two researchers then read and coded the student responses on

Table 1. Breakdown of Students' Teacher Preferences (*N* = 266)

Prompt Response	Number	Percentage
Preference for NEST	127	47.7%
Preference for NNEST	45	16.9%
No preference	94	35.3%

Note: Percentages do not equal 100 because of rounding.

266 essays. Using a grounded theory approach to research, we then classified student comments into logical categories that emerged from the data. In the event that a difference of opinion occurred and could not be settled with a discussion, a third arbitrator was brought in to classify the comment.

Table 1 shows the breakdown of students' preferences in the study. The results show that 47.7% of the students expressed a preference for a teacher who was a native speaker of English, and 16.9% showed a preference for a nonnative speaker teacher of English. The remaining 35.3% of the students who participated in this study had no preference with regard to the nativeness or nonnativeness of their English teachers.

In order to investigate whether the wording of the writing prompt had an effect on student preferences, we analyzed the papers according to the writing prompt they answered (see Table 2).

One-way analysis of variance tests found no significant differences to exist between the three prompts and the three groups under study (NEST preference, NNEST preference, no preference).

Four broad categories of comments emerged from the qualitative data. Under each broad category a number of subcategories were found, as shown in Table 3.

Table 2. Breakdown of Students' Teacher Preferences According to Prompts (*N* = 266)

Prompt	Preference for NEST	Preference for NNEST	No Preference
1 (*n* = 127)	87 (68.5%)	11 (8.7%)	29 (22.8%)
2 (*n* = 79)	33 (41.8%)	18 (22.8%)	28 (35.4%)
3 (*n* = 60)	7 (11.7%)	16 (26.7%)	37 (61.7%)
Total (*N* = 266)	127 (47.7%)	45 (16.9%)	94 (35.3%)

Note: Percentages do not always equal 100 because of rounding.

The first category, professional factors, included the subheadings teaching style, communication/explanation strategies, and experience and qualifications. Linguistic factors was the second category of comment that emerged. This category had the subheadings grammar, first language (L1) knowledge, pronunciation/accent, spelling, oral skills/fluency, vocabulary, error-free language, and knowledge of English. The third major category of comment, personality factors, included the subcategories dedication, tolerance/patience, encouragement,

Table 3. Distribution of Positive and Negative Comments for NESTs, NNESTs, and No Preference

Characteristic	NEST		NNEST		No Preference
	Positive	Negative	Positive	Negative	
Professional Factors					
Teaching style	16	0	7	0	15
Communication/explanation	9	1	15	1	2
Experience/qualifications	6	0	4	0	23
Linguistic Factors					
Grammar	14	1	4	0	1
L1 knowledge	0	2	19	1	2
Pronunciation/accent	53	3	4	5	8
Spelling	5	1	0	0	0
Oral skills/fluency	30	0	5	1	7
Vocabulary	14	0	2	1	2
Error-free language	26	0	0	0	1
Knowledge of English	20	0	0	0	4
Personality Factors					
Dedication	1	0	2	0	4
Tolerance/patience	3	0	2	0	3
Encouragement	22	0	2	0	0
Confidence	1	0	0	0	0
Cultural Factors					
Knowledge of English culture	16	0	0	0	0
Sharing L1 culture	0	0	5	0	0

and confidence. Culture was the final category that emerged, and it was largely divided into the subcategories knowledge of the L2 culture and sharing the L1 culture. We discuss each of these categories with sample statements from the data.

NEST PREFERENCE

Of the 244 total comments made by those students preferring NESTs, 236 comments were positive and in support of NESTs and only 8 were negative. The percentage of comments that fell into the linguistic factors category was 69%, followed by 13% in professional factors, 11% in personality factors, and 7% for culture. The majority of comments in support of having NESTs as teachers fell into the linguistic factors category. The most common linguistic factors subcategory in support of having NESTs was a desire to have a native-like pronunciation and accent. Many students said they felt that NESTs were more able to provide students with a native-like pronunciation. Comments such as the following support this statement and were found throughout the data: "Their pronunciation and vocabulary is quite rich." "The student could learn the pronunciation of the words as well as learning the genuine language."

The second most common subcategory under linguistic factors in support of NESTs was oral skills/fluency. Students who preferred native speakers did so because they felt their oral skills would be better developed and they would become more fluent in the language. Comments included the following: "The student is obligated to have conversations in English." "Native speakers encourage students to communicate in English because the teachers will not understand the students' native language."

After linguistic factors, professional factors came second, drawing 13% of the comments. Students who had a preference for NESTs identified the teaching style or methodology as an important reason for their preferences, as shown by the following comments: "Native speakers are more creative in trying to deliver the information of their own language." "Have better methods which can improve the student's language faster."

NNEST PREFERENCE

Not surprisingly, a significantly fewer number of comments were made about NNESTs. Eighty comments were put forth by students, 71 of them in support of having nonnative speakers as teachers and 9 against. The two most frequently mentioned categories in support of NNESTs were linguistic factors (48%) and professional factors (37%). The most significant comments were made in knowledge of the L1. Of the comments made in support of NNESTs, 27% were focused on their ability to speak the native language of the student and use it in class when necessary. Comments such as the following were found in the data:

"When a student is first learning a foreign language, they need to communicate with their teacher in their native language to explain difficult things." "Can explain things in Arabic if the students don't understand."

It is interesting to note that hardly any comments were made under personality factors for NNESTs as compared to their NEST counterparts.

NO PREFERENCE

For those students who had no stated preference for whether their teacher was a native speaker, the most frequently cited comment here was under the professional factors. Those with no preference placed a high premium on whether the teacher had the experience and qualifications for the job as evidenced in these comments: "If the teacher is good, it doesn't matter if he is a native or not." "It all depends on the qualifications. First and most important is the teachers' ability to interact with the students."

Reflection

An important reason for conducting this study was to find out if our students had a preference for a NEST or a NNEST. Based on the results of this study, we can say that our students had a definite preference for NESTs (47.7%) as opposed to NNESTs (16.9%) or no preference (35.3%). We found this result surprising because most of the literature on effective teaching in content-area classes and L2 classes does not mention the nativeness factor.

WHAT WE LEARNED ABOUT THE ISSUE

We found a definite preference among students in favor of NESTs in both Kuwait and the UAE. However, this preference was less prominent in Kuwait, probably because there were more NNESTs working as teachers in institutions of higher education there. Our data clearly show that our students preferred NESTs because of linguistic and professional factors such as pronunciation/accent and teaching style. However, an important factor in favor of NNESTs was the fact that they shared their students' L1. Overall, we believe it will be beneficial for institutions and students to recognize the valuable characteristics that each kind of teacher brings to the classroom.

WHAT WE LEARNED ABOUT OUR STUDENTS

Students considered shared L1 knowledge a big advantage and a plus for NNESTs. Therefore, perhaps NESTs ought to make more of an effort to learn the L1 or learn about the language of their students.

WHAT WE LEARNED ABOUT
THE QUALITATIVE RESEARCH METHODOLOGY

Both researchers come from a predominantly quantitative background. The collection and study of qualitative data gave us a greater insight into our students' perceptions on this issue. However, the quantitative data also contributed a great deal to this study. Consequently, we are convinced that a mixed-method approach is the direction that we would both like to take in further studies. This was our first attempt at grounded-theory research, which required letting the categories evolve from the data instead of categorizing responses based on pre-defined, established categories. We found this approach to be extremely valuable and one that we would like to explore in further studies.

WHAT WE WOULD HAVE DONE DIFFERENTLY

While reading over some of the student responses, we found ourselves wanting to know more about certain issues that were mentioned. In future studies, we would like to conduct follow-up interviews with students to delve more deeply into certain issues. A future study on this topic should also collect demographic information on the students to investigate whether background or personal factors make an impact in student preferences.

CONCLUSION

Study after study confirms that students who have high-quality teachers make significant and lasting learning gains and that those with less-effective teachers constantly play a game of academic catch-up. A number of factors have been found to influence students' perceptions of what makes a good teacher. Sad to say, results of this study indicate that nativeness or lack thereof is one of those factors for Gulf Arab students. We hope that this awareness will bring change. Now that we as teachers are conscious of this perceived bias on the part of our students, we can try to effect change and make students aware of the special attributes that all teachers (whether they are native speakers or nonnative speakers) bring to the language classroom.

Christine Coombe teaches at Dubai Men's College in Dubai, United Arab Emirates.
Mashael Al-Hamly teaches at the University of Kuwait in Kuwait City, Kuwait.

CHAPTER 6

Multicultural, Coeducational Group Work Experiences: Creative Collaboration or Problematic Partnership? (*United Arab Emirates*)

Cindy Gunn

Issue

The American University of Sharjah (AUS) is one of a very few coeducational higher education institutions in the United Arab Emirates with a multicultural student body. In a classroom at AUS, it is not unusual to see a mix of casually dressed men and women sitting and working alongside partially or completely veiled women or men wearing traditional dress. Outside the classroom, however, there are numerous examples of segregated activities. There are separate times for men and women to use the swimming pool and the exercise gymnasiums. The dormitories for the men and women are completely separate, and in fact, they are fenced off from one another, unlike some dormitories in universities in North America that have men and women in the same building but usually on separate floors. At honors' convocations and other student ceremonies, many young women choose not to shake the hands of the male deans or their male teachers. It is not uncommon at the ceremonies to hear an announcement that men will only shake a woman's hand if she offers her hand first. It is important, therefore, for instructors at AUS to be aware that tensions, many of them derived from cultural norms, exist between the genders.

When I first came to AUS in 2001, I was pleasantly surprised by how motivated and hard working many of my students were and how well the men and women seemed to work together. I was expecting to face the challenges pointed out by Syed (2003) that are common in the Gulf area, namely, "student motivation, literacy, underachievement, reliance on rote learning and memorization" (p. 337). Of course, I do experience some of these issues with some students, but most of the students are very cooperative and participate in collaborative group work and other class activities. Although at first I thought there might be some problems with mixing the young men and women together in groups, in reality it seemed that the students did not mind who they worked with. However, as Schulz (2001) noted, foreign language educators "need to keep [students'] beliefs or perceptions in mind when planning classroom activities, given that teaching activities need to be perceived in the learners' minds as conducive to learning" (p. 245). Subsequently, I wanted to check that I was meeting my students' sociocultural needs in the classroom, and therefore I asked the students to fill out a midsemester feedback form.

I asked the students general questions about what was helping them learn in class, what was not helping, and what could be done to help them more. Because one focus of this survey was to help me see whether or not group project work was viewed by my students at AUS as conducive to learning, I also included some questions directly related to group work. In this initial investigation, 80 students from four different 1st- and 2nd-year writing classes participated. Through this informal feedback form, the majority of the students told me that they felt they benefited from working in groups. However, five female students noted that they wanted me to pick the groups. One student wrote that although she did not mind working with men or women in a group she did not want to look like she was actively choosing to work with either men or women. In response, I did another follow-up survey and found that approximately 10% of the students did not want to work in mixed groups and that some wanted me to pick the groups. This survey was anonymous, so I did not know who made the comments. Eight of the respondents were women, and four were men.

The results of this survey were important to me because they reinforced my belief that collaborative group work was viewed by my students as helping them learn in the class. The results also pushed me to think about how I tend to form groups in class. In general, there are times when I feel it is necessary to pick the groups, but I also believe that some activities are better suited to students picking their own groups. For the most part, I had been letting the students pick their own groups. However, these results challenged my perspective. In addition, based on my previous teaching experience, I had usually found that interaction between males and females in group work was beneficial. I, therefore, began questioning how I could continue to incorporate group work productively into my classes while better meeting my students' sociocultural needs and addressing their concerns. I felt that it was necessary for me to investigate this issue further with more of my classes at AUS.

Background Literature

Group work is often used in English for speakers of other languages classes, both large and small, to help facilitate the learning process. Through collaborative activity with peers, especially in multilingual classes, students are given the opportunity to negotiate meaning in English while fulfilling the requirements of a set task. Regardless of the content area, group work includes the following advantages pointed out by King and Behnke (2005): "increasing student motivation; development of individual responsibility; coconstructing knowledge as a result of member interactions that produce new viewpoints; improving democratic skills and citizenship education; and improving skills for communication, organization, presentation, leadership, and so on" (p. 58).

The use of groups in English as a second language (ESL) classrooms is not new. In 1985, Long and Porter stated that "the use of group work in classroom second language learning has long been supported by sound pedagogical arguments" (p. 207). Bejarano also found in his 1987 study that there was a "link between the communicative approach to foreign language instruction and cooperative learning in small groups" (p. 483). In 1993, Hoekje announced that, based on her experience, "it is fair to say that group work is, in the terms of Philips (1972) the *participant structure* of choice in the ESL classroom today" (Hoekje, 1993/1994, p. 4). Many others, for example Kinsella (1996) and Leki (2001), supported the notion that group work is widely used in ESL classrooms.

There are drawbacks to the use of groups in educational settings. One is that students have acknowledged that they do not always see the value of working in groups (Hoekje, 1993/1994; Slimani-Rolls, 2003). In fact, in 1981 Sorensen introduced the term *group-hate* "to indicate the negative attitude that many students have about group work" (as cited in King & Behnke, 2005, p. 58). Another problem is freeloading, which involves some students relying on others to do the required work. Raven (2005) found that freeloading can lead to a complete group breakdown. In several studies cited by Leki (2001), ESL students had difficulty working collaboratively in groups and therefore did not truly benefit from the experience. Leki's study also showed some of the difficulties nonnative English speakers (NNES) experienced in group work situations with native English speakers. She noted that, "this study has shown how power differentials, exaggerated by linguistic limitation in English, variously prevented the [NNES] learners from managing social/academic interactions to their own advantage" (Leki, 2001, p. 62). The results of Leki's study are applicable to the students at AUS because of the varying levels of English language abilities among the students and the possible tension between the men and women.

Do the drawbacks of group work projects outweigh the benefits? I think not and agree with Leki (2001) when she acknowledged that, despite the disadvantages, "many researchers and teachers remain convinced of the value of group work and continue to explore the conditions that lead to either satisfying or negative group work experiences" (p. 41). However, in my opinion, one of the specific conditions that needs to be addressed when using group work activities in the Middle East in a coeducational institute such as AUS is the issue of gender, which may or may not lead to power struggles.

The differences in male-female communication patterns and the different treatment of males and females in class is an important research area, regardless of where in the world one is teaching. For example, Drudy and Chathain (2002) noted that "there is substantial evidence internationally that teachers—even those well disposed to the question of equal opportunities—interact differentially with their male and female pupils and that this may operate to the disadvantage of female pupils" (p. 37). However, roles for men and women seem to be more defined in the Middle East. An understanding of the culture and its influence on male-female relationships is imperative, especially when the teacher asks students to work together in groups. Slimani-Rolls (2003) pointed out that "pre-existing negative (or positive) relationships among students outside the class can interfere heavily with the group dynamic and exert an enormous pressure on its socio-emotional climate; thus preventing 'expected' interactive events, perhaps events crucial to the teacher's lesson plan, from happening at all" (p. 230). This raises the issue of who should form the groups—the teacher or the students.

Pitt (2000) noted that "any method of selecting groups and allocating projects, whether random or systematic, in general will give some groups an advantage and some a disadvantage" (p. 239). Clearly, the makeup of the group will affect the outcome. Regardless of who forms the groups, some of the literature suggests that "teachers are led to believe that automatic adhesion to the group can be expected to happen unproblematically when groups are put together" (Slimani-Rolls, 2003, p. 225). This is most often not the case. A group must work hard to function well together. When putting groups together, the different needs, expectations, and cultural influences must be taken into consideration. Sullivan (1996) found that a "lack of [cultural] knowledge may result in teachers making inaccurate judgments about their students' classroom interaction behavior" (p. 32). At AUS, the reason that a group may not appear to be functioning appropriately may have nothing to do with the task or the students' abilities but may have everything to do with men and women being reluctant to work together.

Procedures

In response to my initial, smaller-scale investigations described earlier in this chapter, I surveyed seven of my classes in the 2004–2005 academic year. The two main foci of the survey were to determine, first, how the students wanted the groups formed (whether they wanted to pick their own groups or have the teacher pick them) and, second, who the students preferred to work with in groups (a mix of men and women or single-sex groups).

I believed that these preferences were important because AUS instructors, regardless of their background training and the type of courses being taught, should address the ESL issues that occur at all levels. All of the students involved in the survey had attained a minimum score of 500 on the Test of English as a Foreign Language, or TOEFL, and had matriculated into regular university programs, which used English as the language of instruction. However, a quick perusal of the students' placement tests showed that for many of the students English was clearly their second (or third) language. The total number of students who completed the survey was 132—61 men and 71 women, representing 24 different nationalities. The breakdown by gender, nationality, and whether the students attended a coeducational high school or an all-male or all-female high school, is available in Appendix A. The survey itself is provided in Appendix B.

The classes surveyed in fall 2004 were two sections of the English course titled Introduction to Language and two sections of the communications course titled Public Speaking. In spring 2005, the classes surveyed were two sections of the communications course titled Advanced Academic Writing and one Public Speaking class. The total number of students in these classes was 161, consisting of 61 in Introduction to Language, 63 in Public Speaking, and 37 in Advanced Academic Writing. The participants represented a mix of students from all majors.

Even though some of the students had been at AUS for almost 4 years, I felt it was relevant to my study to know about their high school location to determine if they were educated in a coeducational or all-male or all-female high school. Of the participants, 86 students were educated in the UAE: 31 in Dubai, 26 in Sharjah, 18 in Abu Dhabi, 4 in the other emirates, and 7 from unspecified cities or emirates. A total of 34 students were educated in the other five Gulf Cooperating Countries: 2 in Oman, 15 in Saudi Arabia, 3 in Kuwait, 4 in Bahrain, and 10 in Qatar. Of the remaining 12 students, three went to high school in Iran; one in Singapore; one in Syria; one in Dublin, Ireland; one in Lebanon; one in Switzerland; one in Texas in the United States; two in Pakistan; and one in India. It is interesting to note that regardless of the number of nationalities represented, 120 of the 132 students went to high school in the UAE or in one of the five other Gulf Cooperating Countries, which further illustrates the need to have an awareness of the influences of the Middle Eastern values and cultural norms and expectations.

Another background question I asked to help assess the profile of my students was whether AUS's coeducational status was an important factor in the students' decision to attend. The answer *yes* came from 70 students, *no* from 57 students, and 5 students did not answer the question. Some students felt it was an important factor because they acknowledged that the world is made up of both men and women and working together is inevitable. Students also referred to the importance of the social side of learning at university, and some students said they had not worked with the opposite gender before and wanted that experience. Table 1 highlights some of the comments given by students.

The two main reasons students said it was not an important factor that AUS was coeducational were (1) They had based their decision to attend AUS on educational expectations, and (2) they were used to a coeducational environment from their high school. For example, a Saudi male student said, "I attended this school to get a good degree, not to have classmates of different gender." A Pakistani female student wrote, "It was not an issue for me. I have studied in both coeducational and all-female institutions."

Table 1. Reasons Students Chose a Coeducational Institution

Nationality	Gender	Unedited Answers
Bangladeshi	Male	Women have as much opportunity today as men and working later with women professionally. So studying in a coed university might make it easier.
Emirati	Male	To gain new experience. I have never worked with other sex before.
Iranian	Male	Breaking down the barrier of sex.
Pakistani	Male	Opposite sex attraction.
Palestinian	Male	Because I studied in an all male school, so I wanted to experience something new.
Syrian	Male	Community and social experiences with opposite sex especially during university period is essential and important for good character and personality building.
Egyptian	Female	That's the way it should be. It's healthier and it prepares you for the real world later on.
Emirati	Female	I need the experience. I never work with men in school.
Iranian	Female	Because I did not experience that.
Kenyan	Female	This will benefit you in the workplace. You don't want to leave university being wary of the opposite sex.
Kuwaiti	Female	I believe segregation is abnormal. Society consists of both males and females and they must interact with each other.
Syrian	Female	Important for social life, social education.

Results

The students were asked two fixed-alternative questions and two open-ended questions. The questions and an analysis of the answers for all four questions are outlined in this section.

The first question asked students if they preferred to pick their own groups for group work or have the teacher divide them up. Most students said they would prefer to pick their own groups (see Table 2). Not many of the students answered why they preferred to pick their own groups or why they preferred to have the teacher decide the groups. For those who did explain, the main reason for wanting to choose was that they could work with their friends. The reason given by a number of students for why the teacher should choose the groups was clearly stated by an Emirati female when she wrote, "It's the teacher's responsibility."

The next question asked whether students preferred to work in groups with students of the same gender or a mixture, and the results are shown in Table 3. Of the 22 who answered that they preferred to work in groups of the same gender, 10 were men and 12 were female. Breakdown by gender and nationality is shown in Table 4.

As noted in Table 5, the responses from students include references to cultural norms and expectations which prevent some of the students, males and females, from wanting to work with the opposite gender.

Table 2. Preferences for Student-Picked or Teacher-Assigned Groups

Question	Answer	No. of Students
1. In your classes here at AUS, if you are asked to work in groups, do you usually prefer:	to pick your own groups?	78
	to have the teacher decide the groups for you?	47
	did not answer the question	7

Table 3. Preferences for Same-Gender or Mixed-Gender Groups

Question	Answer	No. of Students
2. In your classes here at AUS, if you are asked to work in groups, do you usually prefer:	to work in a group with the same gender as you?	22
	to work in a group with a mix of men of women?	97
	did not answer the question	3
	said it does not matter	10

**Table 4. Nationality and Gender of Students
Who Preferred to Work in Same-Gender Groups**

Nationality	Number and Gender
Afghan	1 male
Australian	1 male
Bahraini	1 male
Emirati	4 males, 3 females
Indian	1 female
Iranian	1 female
Jordanian	1 male, 1 female
Palestinian	2 males, 2 females
Qatari	4 females

Students gave a variety of reasons for preferring to work in mixed groups, but the main ones were similar to why students chose to come to a coeducational institution; that is, the world is made up of both men and women and they anticipated working in a mixed environment when they left AUS for the workplace. Some students focused on the positive exchange of ideas that different genders bring to a group, and as one Lebanese male wrote, "Men and women have different, sometimes opposing opinions. It's good to have both in a group, for it would widen your scope of research and would help you cover a wider aspect of your assigned topic." A Kuwaiti female agreed and wrote, "Both have different approaches to project and group work so it is beneficial to have both." Both males and females commented on the fact that having women in a group encouraged men to work more, and a number of women commented that working in a mixed group kept women from being "mean" to each other. However, not all students wanted to work with women, but they acknowledged that they must. For example, a Saudi male wrote that he preferred to work in mixed groups but "Based on Muslim religious background and culture, interaction between different genders are preferred to be minimal." Again, the influence of culture can be seen.

Students shared some interesting viewpoints when answering Question 3: *Has your attitude toward working with the opposite gender (either positively or negatively) changed since being at AUS? If so, please explain how.* Some students who said their attitudes had changed in a positive manner indicated that they were pleasantly surprised by the input from the opposite sex and how well they were able to work together. Several students, male and female, commented

Table 5. Reasons Students Preferred Same-Gender Groups

Nationality	Gender	Unedited Answers
Afghan	Male	Because I feel more open and use an open language.
Australian	Male	It's more relaxed, easy to work, no pressure.
Bahraini	Male	I think working with the opposite gender is not effective in our world.
Emirati	Male	It's easier for talking. I can talk free and friendly. Not all "women" dress in Islamic dress so I want to avoid interacting with them.
Jordanian	Male	In groups that have a lot of meetings it's hard to meet if group is mixed.
Palestinian	Male	Some females are not that cooperative with males at AUS.
Emirati	Female	I feel more comfortable dealing with girls. I am not allowed from family to call males. I am not comfortable working with men.
Indian	Female	It's easier to initiate communication with girls.
Iranian	Female	I can push girls to work.
Jordanian	Female	We as girls have the same opinion. It's easier.
Palestinian	Female	Girls work harder. I can talk more with girls.
Qatari	Female	Sometimes I feel shy from the other gender [men] when I talk to them.

that they had never worked with the opposite sex before and no longer felt shy or nervous. The students also noted that they could see the benefits of working with the opposite sex now. Some answers from students who reported a positive change in attitude are given in Table 6.

Some of the students who said that their attitudes had changed from positive to negative after being at AUS referred to cultural expectations of behavior between men and women. For example, a Greek female wrote that, "Yes, AUS is known to be the university where people talk a lot. Considering we are living in an Arab society being close or being seen a lot with the opposite gender is considered wrong and can sometimes be perceived as totally inappropriate. Although I don't mind." An Indian male wrote that, "Yes. It has become more restrictive due to the laws of the university and the heavy presence of security

Table 6. Positive Change in Attitude Toward Working With the Opposite Gender

Nationality	Gender	Unedited Answers
Bahraini	Male	Yes, because being at AUS changed my vision or opinion about working with the opposite gender and the environment here helps me to make my attitudes positively.
Emirati	Male	Positively, because I came from an all male high school so I didn't know how to interact with females.
Jordanian	Male	Of course. It changed positively since I spent 12 years in a totally male-dominated society and school that portrayed the other gender as aliens or as a different species.
Palestinian	Male	Yes, it changed positively. Before coming to university I underestimated the other gender. The group work in university fixed that.
Egyptian	Female	Yes, I got more eased and comfortable. It made me more confident, because the school that I studied in didn't really allow that.
Emirati	Female	Yes. I am more open-minded now. I can accept anything from the opposite gender. This helps my working-job-atmosphere.
Jordanian	Female	Yes, because I was very shy from males before, because I studied in schools with female students. But now I act normally with males.
Qatari	Female	Yes, since I was in an all female school, I was really embarrassed to communicate with males here at AUS. But then I got used to it.

personnel." These comments help to illustrate that, for them at least, their behavior is somewhat controlled by the environment at AUS.

Not all students answered Question 4: *Do you have any other comments on group work, or attitudes toward the opposite gender, that you would like to make?* Those who did answer focused mostly on the positive aspects of group work. The following two quotes, the first one from an Emirati male and the second one from an Egyptian female, sum up several other students' comments as well: "Group work is mandatory since life is about working together for the better. No attitude needed just respect." "Gender doesn't matter as long as respect exists." Several students noted they felt that group work was important but also commented that some students do not do their share of the work or do not share the same enthusiasm for group work as other group members. For example, a Lebanese male wrote, "Group work is a must, but some people cannot see the benefits!!!!" A Sudanese male wrote, "As long as the group stays focused and motivated, it's all good!" This idea was shared by a Filipino female when she wrote, "Group work is great as long as everyone is committed and involved. Otherwise, it's a complete waste of time." A Saudi female further developed this idea with her comment: "I generally don't like group work because some people usually end up working more than others."

A few students addressed the issue of who should choose the groups. For example, a Qatari female wrote, "I think that the best group would be created by the teacher. The teacher has to consider the differences in the abilities of the students." An Iranian female noted that she thought, "It's good that the professor makes us to work with opposite sex even if we don't want to." She did not elaborate further, but perhaps she, like the students mentioned earlier, does not mind mixed groups but does not want to look like she actively chooses to work in a group with men.

A few students also took this opportunity to comment on the disadvantages of mixed groups. A Bahraini male wrote, "I think working with the opposite gender is not effective in our world." As noted in Table 7, there were several other references from males and females, but mostly from males, to living and working in the Middle Eastern culture and some possible problems associated with working in mixed groups.

Table 7. Problems Associated With Working in Mixed-Gender Groups

Nationality	Gender	Unedited Answers
Emirati	Male	I hope that all teachers make groups of male only or female only. It's only right.
Jordanian	Male	Due to the cultural context we live in, it is easier to work with people from the same gender as working up late, perhaps outside the AUS campus is certainly easier/more accepted.
Lebanese	Male	Yes, this is an issue here at AUS because I noticed that there are some people who have problems with working in groups of mixed genders, how will they fit into the working life? I guess this is a problem for them.
Saudi	Male	Based on Muslim's religious background and culture, interaction between different genders are preferred to be minimal.
Singaporean	Male	UAE has a religious Islamic background. Therefore men and women are not receptive to working together. Hopefully this will change due to globalization and realizing the need that men and women need to work together for themselves and for the countries' economy.
Emirati	Female	Yes. If in some classes, the professor chooses the groups. This is a bad idea. I've a married friend [female] who has men in her groups, and that caused problems b/w her husband and her.

Reflection

Reviewing the results of this study and pondering whether or not multicultural, coeducational group work at AUS results in creative collaborations or problematic partnerships does not end with a definitive answer. Indeed, the discussion of the results has revealed that it is a complex issue with a huge range of differing opinions. Although a significant number of students, 97 out of 132, said that they prefer to work in a mixed group of men and women, it is important not to discount the number of students who would rather not work in mixed groups.

The students who said they do not want to work in mixed groups and their reasons for not wanting to do so support Slimani-Rolls's (2003) observation: "Participants bring to the classroom their own relationships and expectations about how to achieve learning for themselves. Their agendas colour automatically the cognitive and socio-affective climate which underlies their interactional moves and inevitably influences classroom events" (p. 231). I believe the students in this study have shared their underlying assumptions, shaped by culture. These assumptions cannot be ignored because, although not proven in this research, my experience leads me to believe that they can significantly reduce the learning value of a group work activity.

Does this mean that we should not put men and women together in groups at AUS? I think not. The AUS mission statement says, "AUS will provide students with a rich and varied campus life that fosters their personal growth and supports their transition to responsible adulthood in a rapidly changing world." To help meet this goal, professors at AUS must also keep in mind that they "have a major responsibility to help students become more flexible learners who are prepared to succeed within a diversity of academic and professional settings" (Kinsella, 1996, p. 25). It is vital, therefore, that professors at AUS are cognizant of the concerns that some students have regarding mixed-gender collaborative activity. But still, students should be given the opportunity to work with the opposite gender and decide from the experience itself whether it was worthwhile and not completely discount the value of it based on inexperience.

Finally, the results of this study have reinforced a perspective on the particular teaching and learning environment at AUS and have confirmed the importance of social and cultural factors and the need to take them into consideration, especially when implementing social activities as part of the learning experience.

Cindy Gunn teaches at the American University of Sharjah in Sharjah, UAE.

Appendix A: Data on Survey Participants

Nationality	Male	Female	High School			
			Coed (Male)	Coed (Female)	All-Male	All-Female
Afghan	1	1			1	1
Australian	1		1			
Bahraini	3				3	
Bangladeshi	1	1	1	1		
Egyptian	4	7	2	2	2	5
Filipino		1				1
Greek		2		2		
Indian	3	5	2	4	1	1
Iranian	1	4	1			4
Iraqi		1				1
Jordanian	5	7	2	2	3	5
Kenyan		1		1		
Kuwaiti		1		1		
Lebanese	4	4	3		1	4
Pakistani	2	6	1	6	1	
Palestinian	11	6	2	3	9	3
Qatari	1	7			1	7
Saudi Arabian	3	2		1	3	1
Singaporean	1		1			
Sudanese	1	1	1	1		
Syrian	6	3	2	1	4	2
UAE	13	8	4	2	9	6
American		2		2		
Yemeni		1		1		
Total	61	71	23	30	38	41

Appendix B: Survey

This survey is being conducted for research purposes. Your participation is voluntary and anonymous. Participation, or lack thereof, will not have any bearing on your final grade. If you choose to fill out this survey, please note that I will be using the information in future presentations or possible future publications. Thank you very much for your help.

    Dr. Cindy Gunn

Demographics

    Male: _____   Female: _____

    Nationality: _____

Type of high-schooling prior to AUS: Please answer the first question and tick all other descriptors that apply.

    In which country and city was your high-school located? _____

    All Male School _____   All Female School _____   Coed _____

    Mostly male teachers _____   Mostly female teachers _____

    A mix of male and female teachers _____

    American curriculum school _____   British curriculum school _____

    Arabic curriculum school _____

    Other curriculum school (please name) _____

Was the fact that AUS is coeducational an important factor in your decision to attend?

    Yes _____   No _____

    Why or why not?

In your classes here at AUS, if you are asked to work in groups, do you usually prefer:

to pick your own groups? _____

to have the teacher decide the groups for you? _____

In your classes here at AUS, if you are asked to work in groups, do you usually prefer:

to work in a group with the same gender as you? _____

to work in a group with a mix of men and women? _____

Please explain your answer above.

When you are given the opportunity to have your work reviewed by a peer in class, who (no names please) do you prefer to have read, edit, and suggest corrections to your work? Why?

Is there anyone (no names please) that you would NOT want to review your work? Why?

Has your attitude toward working with the opposite gender (either positively or negatively) changed since being at AUS? If so, please explain how.

Do you have any other comments on group work, or attitudes toward the opposite gender, that you would like to make?

CHAPTER 7

To Mediate or Not to Mediate: Surviving in an Exam-Based EFL Context (*United Arab Emirates*)

Naziha Ali Jafri

Issue

This chapter reports on an investigation into facilitated learning conducted with English as a foreign language (EFL) teachers and students at a Pakistani community school in the United Arab Emirates (UAE). Even though Pakistani schools in the UAE are based on the English medium of instruction, teaching English as a second language (L2) is generally flavored with the students' first language (L1), Urdu, as are all other subjects expected to be taught in the medium of English.

Although L1 use might facilitate L2 learning in certain contexts, it does not necessarily promote foreign language learning in a context in which English is primarily taught as a subject. The English language curriculum in Pakistani public schools, both in the UAE and Pakistan, is based on a standard textbook prescribed by the Pakistani Board of Secondary Education. Private Pakistani schools, however, usually follow a Cambridge-approved EFL curriculum both in Pakistan and abroad.

English language teachers in Pakistani public schools encourage learners to memorize sections of text in grammar, essays, and prescribed answers to reading comprehension passages, conversation dialogues, short stories, and translation passages. Learners are then expected to retain and reproduce material on the external exams (based on a predictable pattern of questions recurring every few years).

Being an EFL teacher in this context for 2 years made me realize the following:

- Such an environment produces text-dependent learners who, though successful in their own system, lack exposure to interaction using the target language.

- The teaching methodology employed inhibits experienced EFL teachers from playing the role of mediators as described by Feuerstein, Klein, and Tannenbaum (1991), and they operate as one-way direct transmitters of knowledge.

- EFL teachers devote most of their teaching time to preparing students to get through the external examination. Foreign language learning, hence, no longer remains communicative because it does not involve tasks that encourage authentic use of L2. Therefore, learners find basic communication in everyday English difficult.

Interestingly, schools under the Pakistan Board of Secondary Education have followed the same curriculum for the past several decades. The fact that Pakistani institutions based in a professionally and academically progressive environment such as the UAE have taken no initiative to update teaching methodologies or curriculum motivated me to investigate whether noticing the lack of facilitation in L2 learning in the Pakistani context was just my assumption or a reality.

The participants in my study included four sections of grade 11 female students (16–18 years, $n = 70$) and nine EFL teachers in a Pakistani school in the UAE. Female students were chosen for convenience because the school authorities were uncomfortable with the prospect of a female (myself) working in the male wing of the school. Based on the local Ministry of Education requirements, schools in the UAE (at the time of this study) had separate buildings for girls and boys.

Background Literature

Social interactionist psychologists (Feuerstein, Rand, Hoffman, & Miller, 1980; Vygotsky, 1978) perceived individuals as social beings who learn to make sense of the world through daily interactions with other people. These psychologists perceived mediation as the part played by other significant people in learners' lives, who enhance their learning by selecting and shaping the learning experiences presented to them. Feuerstein referred to these experiences as mediated learning experiences. Hence, learning is rendered effective through meaningful interactions between people with different levels of skills and knowledge. The mediator—the individual with most knowledge (parent, teacher, or peer)—helps learners move into the next layer of knowledge or understanding (Burge, 1993; Williams & Burden, 1997).

Feuerstein also asserted that human intellect is modifiable at all ages (Blagg, 1991) as people continue to develop their cognitive capacities throughout their lives. He attributed learner failure in tests to the inability of educators to foster in learners the skills of how to learn (Williams & Burden, 1999). He introduced the concept of *dynamic assessment,* which involves the assessor and the assessed working together to find out the current level of performance on a task and then sharing possible ways to enhance that performance for subsequent learning (Williams & Burden, 1997). In such assessments the assessor or teacher is more interested in the processes by which learners attempt to solve problems rather than in their ability to obtain correct answers. This ongoing, reflexive process involves mediating more appropriate learning strategies and observing how effectively the learner is able to transfer these to other aspects of language learning. The ultimate aim of the teacher as mediator is therefore to make learners autonomous.

My study was based on the 12 features of mediation as identified by Feuerstein:

1. Intentionality and reciprocity

2. Purpose beyond the here and now

3. Significance

4. Feelings of competence

5. Control of behavior

6. Goal setting

7. Challenges and strategies

8. Awareness of change

9. Belief in optimistic alternatives

10. Sharing behavior

11. Individuality

12. Feeling of belonging

Of these, the first three are universally essential for all learning tasks to be considered mediated, and the other nine are culturally determined and in different contexts may be necessary or unnecessary (Blagg, 1991; Feuerstein et al., 1991; Kozulin, 1998). Adherence to cultural sensitivity is thus important depending on the teaching-learning context. I have described each aspect of mediation as it appears in the literature in relation to the Pakistani culture, based on my own knowledge and experience as a Pakistani student for 10 years of academic life and teaching in the context for the first 2 years of my professional life.

Intentionality and reciprocity. For effective mediation the teacher should be able to convey clear instructions for a task and check learners' understanding through reciprocation and their willingness and ability to attempt it. This makes the learning activity interactive and purposeful for learners who understand the real objective of the process as development of their thinking (Kozulin, 1998).

Purpose beyond the here and now. Teachers should be aware of and be able to explain to learners how learning experiences can hold wider relevance for them beyond the immediate time and place. To help them make spontaneous generalizations of their own, teachers should provide learners with examples in which rules extracted from abstract activities are applied to fresh learning situations (Blagg, Ballinger, Gardner, Petty, & Williams, 1988).

Significance. Learning experiences must be endowed with purpose, relevance, and excitement to make learners aware of the personal and cultural significance of activities they are expected to do in class (Blagg, 1991; Feuerstein et al., 1991).

Feelings of competence. For successful learning to take place, teachers must be able to instill a realistically positive self-image in learners so that they feel competent enough to tackle any task. Some cultures value a sense of competence and learners feel challenged to succeed without the teacher's intervention. Others value collective behavior and learners prefer working in cooperation, irrespective of whether the task requires it. Pakistani academic environments encourage a competitive culture in which learners continually try to outdo each other in getting higher grades. Feuerstein et al. (1991) maintained that mediating feelings of competence in learners can help them courageously adapt to new situations.

Control of behavior. Learners must be taught the necessary skills of being able to break down a problem, gather and assess information, process it, and express results logically. They need to learn strategies that enable them to take control and responsibility of their own learning (Dickinson, 1987; Ellis, 1991). Control of behavior in the sense of inhibiting impulsiveness and taking initiative is not the same in all contexts. Some contexts emphasize training learners to control behavior and take charge of their own learning. Others encourage individuals to respond to meaningful stimuli in an impulsive manner. Weak learners in the Pakistani context, for instance, are encouraged to resort to guesswork in solving multiple-choice questions.

Goal setting. Learners should be assisted in planning and setting up realistic and achievable goals. Research by van Werkhoven (1990) has revealed that learners are more motivated to achieve self-planned learning goals than the ones that are set for them by their teachers. Goal setting and achievement plans involve sensitization to the cultural values and capacity of individuals in the group. Pakistani public schools, for instance, refrain from spending instruction time on discussions about setting up learning goals and prefer concentrating on curriculum completion instead. Teachers in my study lamented the lack of time to indulge in interesting activities such as planning goals with learners.

Challenges and strategies. To encourage stimulation and interest in L2 learning, learners should be provided appropriate challenges and assistance in planning appropriate strategies to meet those challenges. Tasks which are just sufficiently difficult for learners encourage in them a sense of wanting to struggle with challenges and make them feel that they can always go a step further rather than feeling frustrated that their limit has been reached. Pakistani academic cultures provide learners with the ultimate challenge of succeeding in exams and help them plan strategies to score high marks.

Awareness of change. Helping learners identify ways in which they can become more aware of their own progress encourages independent pursuit of developmental goals. Learners who become adept at monitoring their own progress can recognize personal change as a lifelong process within their own power. However, if the educational aim is merely to train learners to retain important material for success in examinations, teachers might not invest time in assisting learners to become autonomous evaluators of their own progress nor encourage activities that require regular feedback to help them understand the value of self-evaluation. For instance, a teacher in my study asked her students to keep a record of library books they read, but she did not have time to keep track of what the students were doing.

Belief in optimistic alternatives. Encouraging learners to believe that every problem has a solution develops in them persistence in seeking solutions rather than giving up (Warren, 1995). Knowing that something is possible commits learners to searching for ways to turn the possible into a materialized experience. Teachers participating in my study believed that it was futile to spend time with slow learners who were unlikely to ever progress in their learning. The only way to get them through the examinations was by giving them photocopied notes to study, the teachers said.

Sharing behavior. Cooperation must be encouraged in learners to contribute to a world in which trust and mutual respect are upheld. Cooperative activities such as discussion exercises, questionnaire completion, group writing, peer assessing, and discussions encourage interaction in the target language. Generally, Pakistani institutions encourage learners to compete with each other for success in activities and exams.

Individuality. Learners must be taught to value one another as unique individuals developing at their own rates. Tasks such as diary writing, creative writing, or class discussions encourage learners to express their own opinions through the target language. Awareness of and respect for the others' views and inclinations is necessary for a smooth process of individuation and the ability to articulate views of self as related to others. Modern cultures, in contrast to traditional cultures, encourage free expression of opinions and aim to promote inner growth and the individual's self-concept. Any imposition is considered an infringement on individual rights. In the Pakistani context, differences are evident between public and private institutions. Public institutions strictly commit to the teacher's final word, whereas private institutions encourage learners to express personal opinions.

Feeling of belonging. Learners need to feel that they belong to a community— whether in the classroom or the institution—and teachers should encourage this feeling. Modern technological societies stress the individuals' rights to privacy and show limited readiness to give up on these rights in favor of becoming part of a larger entity. Traditional societies, in contrast, strongly value the need to belong and make individuals give up much of their freedom and expression of their own individuality for belonging to their reference group (Feuerstein et al., 1991). Most Pakistani institutions create a sense of belonging to the community by encouraging learning activities based on nationalism.

Different aspects of mediation are viewed in different ways, and thus it is necessary for teachers to become accustomed to their classroom cultures before finding appropriate ways to mediate learning activities.

Procedures

To investigate the absence or presence of mediation in the chosen context, I used a mixed methodology comprising a student questionnaire, a teacher questionnaire, and semi-structured interviews with the participants (see Appendixes A, B, and C). Both questionnaires were adapted from Williams and Burden's (1997) mediation questionnaire, and each one had two sections: perceived importance of mediation in the classroom and actual practice of mediation in the classroom.

Choices on both questionnaires were given on a 5-point Likert scale ranging from *very important* to *not important at all* in Part 1 and from *very often* to *never* in Part 2.

The focus of my investigation involved the following:

- High school teachers' perceptions of the importance of mediation in L2 teaching.

- High school teachers' perceptions of their own practice of mediation while teaching L2.

- High school students' perceptions of the importance of mediation in L2 learning.

- High school students' perceptions of the actual practice of mediation by their L2 teachers.

The original student questionnaire had only Part 1, and I piloted it with four sections of grade 12 students ($n = 77$) in one sitting. Following the pilot, I modified the student questionnaire by adding Part 2. The reason behind this change was that responses marked in the pilot study seemed to reflect students' perceptions about their teachers' practices instead of their perceptions about the importance of mediation in L2 learning. I then administered the amended version of the student questionnaire 4 days later to four sections of grade 11 students ($n = 70$). I included grade 11 students in my actual study because they had spent more than 10 years at the institution and could effectively articulate their perceptions about the aspects under investigation. Initially, I had planned that after administering the questionnaires I would conduct focus group interviews with grade 11 students. But I later discarded this procedure because at the time of my study high school classes were in the middle of their external examinations. Therefore, in order to be interviewed, students would have had to stay after school hours, and I deemed this request inappropriate at the time.

I piloted the teacher questionnaire with colleagues, and I used the same version in the actual study. Colleagues helped me cross-check the interview items for leading questions before I interviewed teachers. A week after administering the student questionnaire, I administered the teacher questionnaire simultaneously to four male and five female high school EFL teachers. Following the questionnaires, I made appointments with each teacher and conducted face-to-face interviews during their free hours at the workplace. For ethical and confidentiality reasons, I obtained participants' consent and informed them about their roles in a study exploring perceptions about mediated learning and teaching in L2 environments.

However, I did experience a few difficulties during my data collection. First of all, my own ignorance of the school's academic calendar caused me to discard previously planned focus group interviews with students because high school classes were in the middle of their external examinations when I started my study. In this case, I lost the opportunity to collect valuable data from the perspective of students in the context. Secondly, including classroom observations followed by teachers' evaluations of their own practices would have provided valuable reflective feedback on the topic under investigation. However, I decided against this strategy because it required training teachers to evaluate their practice with a focus on mediation, and it would have made experienced teachers feel subject to evaluation. Another problem I encountered was indifference; I found it difficult to gain cooperation from teachers who showed disinterest in reviewing interview transcripts for triangulation. Lastly, I could not include data from male students because the school authorities were hesitant to allow a female researcher to work in the male wing of the school, and I wanted to work within their comfort zone.

Results

Findings from my study were divided into the questionnaire results of students, those of teachers, and analyses of teachers' interviews. The questionnaire results revealed discrepancies between perceptions of students and teachers about the practice of mediation in L2 teaching at the school. These differences occurred despite the groups' equal perceptions of the importance of practicing mediation. Table 1 presents a comparison of teachers' and students' perceptions about teachers' actual mediation practice in L2 classrooms at the school.

All teachers reported that they clearly shared intentions of learning activities with learners, made them aware of the value of learning activities, inculcated feelings of competence, and encouraged learners to develop their individuality. Contrary to this, only 57% of the students said their teachers shared intentions with clarity. Instead, most students reported that the following aspects were not being effectively mediated by their EFL teachers: purpose beyond here and now, feelings of competence, control of own behavior, goal setting and achieving,

Table 1. Comparison of Teachers' and Students' Perceptions of Actual Practice of Mediation by Teachers

Item	Teachers Answering 5 or 4 (%)	Students Answering 5 or 4 (%)
1. Share intention	100	57
2. Significance	89	52
3. Purpose beyond here and now	100	34
4. Feeling of competence	100	45
5. Control of own behavior	67	49
6. Goal setting and achieving	56	34
7. Challenges and strategies	56	35
8. Awareness of change	56	40
9. Belief in optimistic alternatives	78	49
10. Sharing	78	59
11. Individuality	100	41
12. Sense of belonging	89	63

challenges and strategies, awareness of change, belief in optimistic alternatives, and individuality. However, most students reported that their teachers made efforts to mediate significance of tasks (52%), sharing behavior (59%), and feelings of belonging (63%).

When I interviewed teachers, they revealed that learners at the school were categorized into the arts, sciences, or commerce sections according to their levels of intelligence and not according to interest or potential. For instance, the brightest high school students were enrolled in science sections, the weaker ones in commerce, and the weakest in arts. Weaker learners were perceived to be unaffected by any kind of mediational investment (Feuerstein et al., 1991). On probing about the presence or absence of mediation in their practice, EFL teachers offered several justifications pertaining to their teaching methods. I present these findings based on each aspect of mediation as outlined by Feuerstein.

Shared intention. Most teachers said they did not feel the need to check for understanding of instructions because they followed set patterns which were familiar to students. Teachers gave what they viewed as easy notes to students, so students could photocopy them and learn from them. Teachers dictated prepared texts or used helpful guides which were easily available in the market. Generally, teachers concentrated more on course completion without indulging in other activities, as the following teacher response shows:

> In a class of 44 students . . . if I tell you that my instructions are followed by questions and all that. . . . No! We've got a pattern, our own system. (PQ)

Significance. Most teachers said they could not spend teaching time overstressing personal relevance in tasks because finishing the course was always a priority, as the following comment shows:

> However, if absolutely necessary [to explain the significance of tasks to students], the answer is simple: "Because it's in the syllabus." (SN)

Despite this constraint, all teachers agreed that understanding the purpose of activities could make students more receptive to the information given.

Purpose beyond here and now. Some teachers said they believed that learners were more interested in task completion than on seeing the wider significance of learning activities, as in the following comment:

> When they are involved in it . . . they simply enjoy doing that. (PQ)

Feelings of competence. Weak students were given extra coaching in zero periods—time set aside for special coaching as well as during lunch breaks, library lessons, and early morning hours before school. Exceptionally weak students were asked to arrange extra coaching outside school. Teachers allowed L1 communication, although it was not clear how this option encouraged learners to develop competence in L2 communication. One teacher shared the following comment:

I let them communicate in the language that they are comfortable with. After all English is not our native language. (R)

One teacher commented that verbal encouragement could foster a student's positive self-image:

I make them copy from the clever students and while correcting their copies I say, "Why didn't you have the confidence to write on your own?" (PQ)

Control of own behavior. Teachers avoided investing time in dispensing autonomous learning skills, and therefore they created a sense of lifelong dependency in learners. Teachers considered strategies such as the following a part of the system:

Difficult students . . . simply cram up the entire essay from somewhere and reproduce it for the paper or test. (SN)

Goal setting and achieving. Helping learners set achievable learning goals was impeded by offering easy achievement techniques to weak and less motivated students, as this comment shows:

I've photocopied and given them (words and meanings) to make their work easy instead of going back to the copy again and again and learning words from different units. (PQ)

You have to dictate answers in class. . . . So learning is the only job they have to do after this. (SN)

Challenges and strategies. Teachers said they instilled strategies in high school students to help them tackle the bigger challenge of scoring passing marks or higher on the external examination:

Sometimes you specify what they should learn because this will appear on the exam. This is how they pick enough to reach the level of 35%. (SN)

Awareness of change. In their exam-based learning environment, students were made aware of personal progress through a multitude of tests such as weekly, monthly, term, pre-board exams, oral tests, and graded assignments.

Belief in optimistic alternatives. Generally teachers were not informative about how they helped learners develop persistence, especially because most teachers said they believed that weak learners would always be weak and that the teacher's job was to help them get through the exam. This attitude reinforced

Feuerstein et al.'s (1991) assertion that some people view mediational investment in weak learners as a waste of time.

Sharing, individuality, and sense of belonging. Teachers said they believed that students disliked group or pair work. Yet teachers felt inclined to expose students to cooperative work such as debates, discussions, language practice games, or class projects. At the institutional level, a weekly culture period was included in the schedule for students to exchange views over a topic under discussion.

Reflection

Teachers who participated in my study perceived the importance of mediation in L2 learning environments as much as their students did. But their preoccupation with course completion for exam preparation overtook all initiatives. However, students held their teachers responsible for the students' inability to communicate in the target language even after they had spent 12 years in an English-medium institution.

Teachers did, however, acknowledge the lack of mediation in their practices and gave several reasons. One was that high school students lived under the constant threat of external exams, and the teacher spent the academic year training them to pass these exams, which took the teacher's focus away from facilitating the development of communication skills in English. Another reason teachers mentioned was time constraints in completing the assigned course, which hindered their initiatives to include any kind of task-based English language learning.

Despite giving lip service to making learning more interesting, teachers relied on an accepted helplessness and pessimism about the system to justify the lack of initiative. Teachers said that activities not dictated by the prescribed curriculum could not be included, even though they might have helped students develop L2 learning skills:

> We can take the students to watch a movie and then give them a questionnaire. But it is not required by the curricula, so why put the effort. (SN)

Teachers continually reinforced grammar concepts without realizing the effect excessive direct transmission had on students' retention capacity, especially when teachers did not pause to check whether their input had been absorbed.

Another factor was large class sizes (40 students per class), which led teachers to focus on maintaining discipline rather than on giving individual attention to help students develop autonomous learning strategies. Hence teachers resorted to strategies which increased learners' reliance on others to succeed.

High school was viewed as an exam preparation camp, and experienced teachers expressed the necessity of using teaching methods that would get students through the exam:

Professionally my first aim is to get them through the examination. (R)

Clearly, exam survival is a crucial element in the Pakistani context, and students graduating from English-medium institutions still lack the capability to make authentic use of the target language. The existing national curriculum and classroom instruction do not provide students with the problem-solving skills that will allow them to succeed in modern-day occupational contexts.

In my investigation of the presence or absence of mediation in the Pakistani EFL context, I learnt that a one-way direct-transmission approach deprived learners of a facilitated learning environment flavored with task-based learning activities. I also discovered that achievers in this context were those students who had a better retention level and not necessarily the potential to learn a foreign language. Whereas most teachers blamed the curriculum pressures for their lack of initiative, they acknowledged that integrating communicative tasks in the target language would enable learners to communicate effectively in authentic L2 situations.

During the period of investigation, I experienced fluctuating motivation as I engaged in the exhausting process of trying to get information that was being blocked out for fear of revealing too much. However, I managed to get through by persistence and the desire to illuminate a real issue that I felt was depriving Pakistani students of opportunities to develop their L2 in the UAE. The process of thinking, planning, investigating, and analyzing information educated me about the beneficial role that semi-structured interviews can play in valuable data generation.

An important aspect of teacher education that surfaced for me through the whole process was a stronger awareness of the crucial role that nontraditional facilitation techniques can play in learning and teaching a foreign or second language in a monocultural context. I communicated the revelations from my investigation to an audience hailing from public and private institutions at an international conference in Pakistan and returned much more informed about similar situations existing in public institutions in the country, as well as the perceptions of local teachers about the situation. My experiences researching this subject have led me down a path of self-development in the L2 training context. Since then, I have started to look on EFL teaching as a process that requires facilitation to accelerate learning, which means helping L2 learners develop important strategies that allow room for lifelong autonomous learning.

Naziha Ali Jafri is a language training and development officer at Emirates Aviation College (the vocational training wing of Emirates airline) in Dubai, United Arab Emirates.

Appendix A: Student Questionnaire

Part 1

Below are 12 things that your English teacher might do when she teaches you English. Decide whether they are <u>important</u> or <u>not important</u>. Please circle the number that best describes <u>your views</u>.

How important do you think it is (for your teacher) to . . . ?

	Very Important	Quite Important	Neutral	Not Very Important	Not Important at All
1. Give very clear instructions when she gives us a task.	5	4	3	2	1
2. Tell us why we are going to do a particular activity.	5	4	3	2	1
3. Explain to us how a learning activity will help us in the future.	5	4	3	2	1
4. Help us feel that we are good at learning English.	5	4	3	2	1
5. Teach us how we can learn English better.	5	4	3	2	1
6. Teach us how to set our own goals in learning.	5	4	3	2	1
7. Help us to set challenges for ourselves.	5	4	3	2	1
8. Help us to develop strategies to meet our challenges.	5	4	3	2	1
9. Teach us how to check our own progress.	5	4	3	2	1
10. Help us see that there is always a solution to a problem.	5	4	3	2	1
11. Teach us to work together with other students.	5	4	3	2	1
12. Help me to develop as an individual.	5	4	3	2	1
13. Make me feel that I belong to the class.	5	4	3	2	1

Part 2

	Very Often	Quite Often	Sometimes	Hardly Ever	Never

How often does your English teacher . . . ?

	Very Often	Quite Often	Sometimes	Hardly Ever	Never
1. Give very clear instructions for a task.	5	4	3	2	1
2. Tell you why you are going to do a particular activity.	5	4	3	2	1
3. Explain to you how a learning activity will help you in the future.	5	4	3	2	1
4. Make you feel confident about your leaning ability.	5	4	3	2	1
5. Teach you the techniques you need to learn effectively.	5	4	3	2	1
6. Teach you how to set your own goals in learning English.	5	4	3	2	1
7. Help you to set challenges for yourself and teach you how to meet those challenges.	5	4	3	2	1
8. Help you to monitor changes in your learning English.	5	4	3	2	1
9. Help you to see that if you keep on trying to solve a problem, you will find a solution.	5	4	3	2	1
10. Teach you to work cooperatively with your classmates.	5	4	3	2	1
11. Help you to develop as individuals.	5	4	3	2	1
12. Make you feel part of the class.	5	4	3	2	1

Appendix B: Teacher Questionnaire

Below is a list of some things that teachers might do when they give their students activities to do in language lessons. The questionnaire is in two parts.

Part 1

For each of the questions please circle the score that best represents your view of how <u>important</u> that item is.

	Very Important	Quite Important	Neutral	Not Very Important	Not Important at All

When you teach a language, how important do you think it is to . . . ?

1. Make your instructions clear when you give a task to your learners.	5	4	3	2	1
2. Tell your learners why they are to do a particular activity.	5	4	3	2	1
3. Explain to your learners how carrying out a learning activity will help them in future.	5	4	3	2	1
4. Help learners to develop a feeling of confidence in their ability to learn.	5	4	3	2	1
5. Teach learners the strategies they need to learn effectively.	5	4	3	2	1
6. Teach learners how to set their own goals in learning.	5	4	3	2	1
7. Help your learners to set challenges for themselves and to develop strategies to meet those goals.	5	4	3	2	1
8. Help your learners to monitor changes in themselves.	5	4	3	2	1
9. Help your learners to see that if they keep on trying to solve a problem, they will find a solution.	5	4	3	2	1
10. Teach your learners to work cooperatively.	5	4	3	2	1
11. Help your learners to develop as individuals.	5	4	3	2	1
12. Foster in your learners a sense of belonging to a classroom community.	5	4	3	2	1

Part 2

For each question, please choose the score that you think best represents <u>how often</u> you yourself carry out this particular activity.

How often do you . . . ?	Very Often	Quite Often	Sometimes	Hardly Ever	Never
1. Make your instructions clear when you give a task to learners.	5	4	3	2	1
2. Tell your learners why they are to do a particular activity.	5	4	3	2	1
3. Explain to your learners how carrying out a learning activity will help them in the future.	5	4	3	2	1
4. Help learners to develop a feeling of confidence in their ability to learn.	5	4	3	2	1
5. Teach learners the strategies they need to learn effectively.	5	4	3	2	1
6. Teach learners how to set their own goals in learning.	5	4	3	2	1
7. Help your learners to set challenges for themselves and to meet those challenges.	5	4	3	2	1
8. Help your learners to monitor changes in themselves.	5	4	3	2	1
9. Help your learners to see that if they keep trying to solve a problem, they will find a solution.	5	4	3	2	1
10. Teach your learners to work cooperatively.	5	4	3	2	1
11. Help your learners to develop as individuals.	5	4	3	2	1
12. Foster in your learners a sense of belonging to a classroom community.	5	4	3	2	1

Appendix C: Interview Questions

1. How do you make sure that your instructions for a task are clear?

2. How do you check that students have understood what to do?

3. Do you ever tell your students why they are doing a particular activity? Do you think it is important to do so?

4. How is it evident that learners find personal relevance in the task assigned?

5. Do you ever explain to your students the value of the activity to them in the future? How do you do this? Do you think it is important?

6. Do you provide them with learning strategies in L2 lessons that might be helpful in other situations? Could you give an example?

7. To what extent do you think that the language skills that you teach in class will be of practical use to learners in real life? If not, what amendments would you suggest?

8. How do you deal with learners who lack confidence in their ability to learn the language?

9. Do you ever try to enhance your learners' beliefs in themselves? How do you do this? Is it important? Why?

10. How do you help your learners foster self-confidence?

11. Do you ever help your learners to set goals for themselves? How do you do this? Do you think it is important?

12. Do your students set their own learning objectives? How do they do this?

13. Do you help learners to set challenges for themselves? How do you do this? Do you think this is important?

14. Can you describe any obstacles that you face in completion of the pre-scribed course? How do you try to overcome these?

15. Do you teach learners strategies that help them learn effectively on their own? Can you give me an example? Do you think it is important?

16. Do you teach learners to be aware of their own progress? How do you do this? Do you think it is important?

17. Do you assist learners in understanding that persistence can help solve problems? How do you do this? Is it important? Why/Why not?

18. How do your learners feel about working in groups or pairs? Why?

19. How do you encourage learners to

    a. Help each other

    b. Take others' feelings into consideration

20. Do you think it is important for learners to develop as individuals? Why? How do you encourage them to develop as individuals?

21. Do you feel the need to foster in learners the sense that the classroom is a community and that they are part of this community? How do you do this? Do you think it is important?

22. What changes would you recommend in the foreign language learning environment in your institution? Why?

CHAPTER 8

The Effectiveness of Learning Contracts With Arab Learners of English (*United Arab Emirates*)

Paul MacLeod

Issue

This investigation took place at the University of Sharjah during spring semester 2005. The University of Sharjah (UoS) is a relatively new (established in 1997) English-medium university located in the University City complex on the outskirts of Sharjah City in the United Arab Emirates (UAE). It offers a wide variety of degree options to a mixed population of students. The majority are Emirati, with a large minority of Arab expatriates and a small number of scholarship students from Sudan, Turkey, Cameroon, Mauritania, Somalia, and Chad. The university consists of one main campus segregated into men's and women's sections with a faculty of fine arts and a medical, dental, and health science complex located nearby.

As part of the admission process, all students must take the Institutional Test of English as a Foreign Language (TOEFL). Students who score less than 500 are assigned to Levels 1–4 in the Intensive English Program (IEP) run by the English Language Centre. The university, as a relatively new entity, has been making changes to policy to better meet the needs of students and to enhance the reputation of the UoS. In summer 2004, in response to criticism from degree program faculty and the public and private sector, the UoS Board of Governors changed the program structure and exit criteria of the IEP effective in fall 2004. The number of contact hours for students was increased from 18 to 25 hours per week, and the exit criteria changed from gaining a passing grade (70%) in Level 4, or passing the exit exam given at the end of every semester, to getting a score of 500 or better on the TOEFL.

Although students who had previously been in the IEP were allowed to complete their studies under the previous criteria, new students in fall 2004 had to meet the more demanding exit criteria. Unfortunately, most of these new students failed to understand that the new guidelines applied to them; they expected to be able to exit under the old system. The misunderstandings that resulted from the rapid implementation of this change caused a great deal of anger and resentment among the students.

In spring semester 2005, I requested to teach a 2-hour block (two consecutive 50-minute classes) with a Level 4 class of Listening/Speaking and TOEFL, in the mistaken belief that with one semester to gain the requisite 500 TOEFL score, Level 4 students would be hard working and self-motivated. Unfortunately, by spring 2005 the students who were new in the fall semester (who constituted more than 95% of my class) were demotivated by the stress of 5 hours of English language instruction 5 days a week, demoralized by the difficulty of their task, and angered by their perception (correct in my view) that their opinions, problems, and ideas were being ignored by their teachers, the IEP administration, and the university administration. The few students new to the university in January 2005 were quickly influenced by the negative attitude of the majority.

PARTICIPANTS

The students in this study were members of my Level 4A Section 1 class on the men's campus. I was responsible for teaching them for 10 hours per week (5 hours of listening/speaking and 5 hours of TOEFL preparation). The class originally consisted of 20 students, but 4 dropped out, leaving 16 at the conclusion of this study. Of the original students, 6 were Emirati nationals, 12 were expatriate Arabs living in the UAE, and 2 came from other Arab-speaking countries. All of the students were male, native speakers of Arabic who had studied English since elementary school (on average 12 years), and they ranged in age from 17 to 21. Their TOEFL scores at the beginning of Level 4 ranged from 442 to 490. All had taken the TOEFL at least three times, and many had had four or five attempts at it. One extremely frustrated student told me that he had written the TOEFL more than 10 times!

THE PROBLEM

We suffered through a very trying first half of the semester, with the students' mantras alternating among "We're bored," "It's not fair that we have to pass the TOEFL," and "We have too many hours of English." Meanwhile, I was tearing my hair out to find some way to interest them in anything to do with learning the English language. The demands of the curriculum, the syllabus, and the rules of the IEP seemed incompatible with making any changes that would allow me to implement some of the students' suggestions. These ranged from the ridiculous ("Don't have classes on Wednesdays") to the quite reasonable ("We don't want to take notes from the listening/speaking book. We hate that book, and we need more TOEFL listening practice, not note-taking").

This situation strikes me as the essential dilemma of teaching language in the Middle East: Upper and middle administrators pay homage to phrases and concepts such as learner autonomy, creativity, and critical thinking while imposing a syllabus and curriculum which leaves no scope for the teacher to give the learners the autonomy necessary to foster critical and creative expression. In other words, in most institutions of higher learning, students are told what, when, where, why, and how they will study in English, and their opinions or objections are ignored. Teachers and administrators then bemoan the students' lack of motivation to study a subject that both parties know they need. The problem of lack of motivation is, to a great extent, a function of students feeling that they are still in high school and are still being treated like children.

Fortunately, the sweeping curriculum and policy changes had left me with a loophole. The new system required Level 4 students to write a midterm examination, but the TOEFL was considered their final exam. In practical terms, this meant that few, if any, skills or other elements supposed to be gleaned from the prescribed listening text formed any part of their post-midterm grade. Any student who achieved a score of 500 or higher on the TOEFL would exit. The midterm examination would be used only as part of the calculation of the grade point average. Failure to achieve a score of 500 on the TOEFL would earn the student an incomplete grade until he or she received the requisite TOEFL score. Therefore, I decided to conduct guided interviews to gather student opinions about changing the way the class was run. As I saw it, the class was already dysfunctional, and any changes might give the students a chance for success which, up until then, I hadn't been able to provide. I believed that a learning contract of some kind would be helpful to keep the students focused on their goal. Therefore, I conducted research into the use of learning contracts with Arab learners of English.

Background Literature

A preliminary Internet search yielded several discussions of learning contracts which featured the ideas of Malcolm Knowles (1987), an iconic figure in the field of adult education and learning contracts. He defined a learning contract simply as "a plan for acquiring specified knowledge, understanding, skills, attitudes, or values by a learner" (p. 62). Further, he stated that a typical learning contract contains what the participants will learn (the learning objective), the methods for accomplishing the objectives, the evidence that will be required to demonstrate that the objective has been reached, how the evidence will be evaluated, and the completion date. As Frymier (1965) stated, "Allowing students to decide which grade they wish to strive for, which activities they will engage in, and how they will demonstrate that they have satisfactorily completed their studies permits a teacher to seize upon powerful motivating forces within individual students. . . . This notion shifts responsibility for learning from the teacher to the student, but at the same time offers an incentive by insuring success under known conditions. Students are challenged without being threatened" (pp. 263–264).

Codde (1996) offers a good summary of the major research into the effectiveness of the learning contract with adult learners. Among the benefits he lists—with reference to Knowles (1986) and Newcomb and Warmbrod (1974)—are the following:

- The learner has choice and voice in selecting alternatives for meeting learning objectives. Learners are more likely to become totally involved in projects they have helped select and plan.

- The learner has opportunities to exercise responsibility by making commitments to complete his or her personal learning goals.

- Individualized and independent learning activities stress personal involvement in learning.

- The teacher refrains from giving excessive direction because too much can result in students showing apathetic conformity, defiance, scapegoating, or withdrawal.

- The teacher considers the differential learning styles of students when providing learning alternatives.

- The teacher stresses competition with oneself over competition with others, and cooperation with others becomes an acceptable peer learning activity.

- The learner feels a sense of freedom from the threat of failure.

- The learning task falls within the learner's range of challenge—the task is neither too easy nor too difficult and the probability for success is good but not certain.

- Students have opportunities for novel and stimulating learning experiences.

- At least some of the purposes, objectives, and expectations of the course are defined in behavioral terms which clarify the learning task.

- Progress in learning depends largely on how the learner perceives (as a result of reinforcement or encouragement) the appropriateness of his or her efforts to accomplish the learning objectives. Students are more likely to repeat behaviors that the teacher rewards.

- The learner receives feedback on the appropriateness of his or her efforts through increased self-evaluation skills.

- Learning is generalized to other life situations. Generalization is most likely when the learner achieves the intrinsic reward of feeling self-satisfaction for reaching his or her objectives.

Obviously, with my students, motivation was a key issue. The literature review confirmed my instinctual beliefs that a learning contract could be an effective tool. If it worked, it would help my students take at least some responsibility for their own learning while enhancing their motivation and morale.

Although my initial literature review proved helpful in establishing the parameters of this research, it also confirmed my belief in its relevance. There are innumerable articles about learning contracts in books and periodicals, on databases such as ERIC, and on the Internet; nevertheless, I could find almost no reference to the use of learning contracts with Arab learners of English. In fact, the only such work I located was "Classroom Democracy—Letting the Students Choose" by Rosalind Buckton (2001), which was based on a presentation originally given at TESOL Arabia 2000 Conference and was subsequently published in the conference proceedings. In this article, she lamented how tertiary education in the Arabian Gulf encouraged the same teacher-centered style used in secondary schools and that "students approach their learning with a secondary-school mentality, wanting to be told exactly what pages to study for a test and which items are most important" (p. 81). If the focus changes to give students the opportunity to determine at least part of what they study, she said, then "students will feel that they are being treated like adults and will look forward to lessons as events where they can make an active contribution" (pp. 81–82). Buckton did not, however, use a learning contract per se. Rather, she used questionnaires to elicit student feedback and tried to incorporate their stated needs and desires into the work of the class whenever possible. Curriculum and other program restrictions prevented her from allowing students the free rein that a traditional learning contract would offer, but I was intrigued by her assertions and determined to see if the more formalized process of using a learning contract would produce the results that the students and I desired.

Procedures

The first step I took was to give the students a two-part questionnaire that I developed (see Appendix A) to determine whether my observations and intuitions about the students' attitudes were true.

Once I had collated and transcribed the questionnaire responses, I analyzed the data. Not all of the information proved to be relevant to this study, but responses to the questionnaire did clarify some issues. Of the 14 students who completed the form, 10 of them said 25 hours a week of English class was terrible, 3 said it was the same as 18 hours per week, and only 1 said it was helpful. Nine students said the textbook was poor or very poor, and 4 considered it average. Their opinions about the TOEFL's validity varied widely: 8 considered it unfair, 4 considered it a fair measure of their ability, and 2 remained neutral. The additional comments they made were along the following lines: "change the rules" and "we don't need TOEFL."

The most significant finding was the discrepancy between their expected results and their study habits. I noted that 79% of the respondents (11 students) rated their chances of exiting the IEP as "excellent" or "very good—if I work hard I will exit," and yet 79% also rated their study habits as fair (5–7 hours per week) or poor (less than 3 hours per week), which equates to 1 hour or less per day. Only one student stated that he studied 8 hours per week or more. This disconnect between low student effort and high expected results is, as Buckton (2001) noted, a carryover from secondary school culture, which holds the teacher solely responsible for learning. The results of the questionnaire confirmed my impressions of class members' attitudes; thus, I had every reason to believe that changing some of the class elements that they did not like would be motivating. My hope was that the process of developing and agreeing to a learning contract would, as the research indicated, stimulate students to take more responsibility for their own learning and results.

REVISING CLASS PROCEDURES

Unfortunately, I could not give the students complete autonomy to choose how, where, and what we would study. The rules of the IEP are very clear. Teachers must teach every scheduled class period, and students must attend. If a student misses 10% of his classes, he is given a written warning; at 15%, he gets a second warning; if a student reaches 20% absences, he fails and is withdrawn from the course.

After tabulating the results of the questionnaire, I took one class period to explain to the students the new way in which the class would move forward. I explained that I wanted to give them more freedom to determine what we would study and that I would no longer use the listening textbook or the assigned

TOEFL preparation text in class. They could, and should (especially in the case of the TOEFL text), use these materials for reference and self-study. After their initial shock and jubilation, students asked the following questions:

1. Will there be attendance? *Answer:* Yes, you must attend. If you miss 20% of your classes, you fail. (The attendance issue and class procedure changes produced an interesting and somewhat unexpected side-effect, which I will discuss in detail in the results section.)

2. Why are you doing this? *Answer:* I realize that you are bored, hate the textbooks, and dislike being forced to go to class for 25 hours per week. I hope that this approach will give you a better chance at getting the TOEFL score you need and exiting the IEP.

3. What are we going to do in class? *Answer:* You are going to get together in groups now, discuss the issue, make a list of what you want to do in class, and then we will negotiate a solution.

4. When will the new procedure start? *Answer:* Tomorrow, instead of regular classes, you are going to meet with me individually in my office according to the schedule I'm going to post and discuss a learning contract for the rest of the semester. (Here, I explained to the students what a learning contract was.)

I expected at least some of the groups to come up with some frivolous or unrealistic ideas for what we should do for the remainder of the semester. I also suspected that there might be some conflict between different groups wanting to do different things. Much to my delight, however, the students took the process very seriously, and their ideas were all variations on a theme. Not unsurprisingly, given that a TOEFL score of 500 was their primary goal, my students wanted me to concentrate on TOEFL preparation, particularly practice tests. I had to convince them that a TOEFL practice test every day would be impractical, not to mention extremely boring. Eventually, we hammered out a schedule that featured a different aspect of TOEFL preparation every day, culminating with one practice TOEFL test per week. The schedule was flexible and subject to change, given the approval of 60% of the class members. The only caveat was that the students proposing changes would have to address the class and explain why or how the changes would improve the learning experience.

The students were excited by these changes, and thrilled to finally have some input into what and how they were going to study. As the class broke up, amid the pledges to show up on time for their appointments, there were many cries of "We have the best teacher in the world." This just made me wonder all the more if I had done the right thing by abandoning the prescribed texts and approaches.

THE LEARNING CONTRACT INTERVIEW

With the learning contract in hand (see Appendix B), I conducted a 10- to 15-minute semistructured interview with each student to discuss their progress in the class. I talked with each student about his feelings about his level of commitment to his studies, his attendance level, the amount of study he was doing independently, and how much, if any, additional study he felt he needed to do on his own to get a TOEFL score of 500.

A typical interview went something like this (numbers correspond to the items in the learning contract in Appendix B):

1. T: So, how is your attendance?
   S: I'm at 17% [absences], Teacher.
   T: That's pretty high. Do you think you will be able to attend all of the classes for the rest of the semester? If not, what percentage will you be able to attend? You're close to 20% so you have to be careful.
   S: I will attend all of them teacher. I don't want to fail on attendance.

2. T: Now, what about homework and class work? How much of it do you think you'll do?
   S: I can do 90% of it, Teacher; I think that is enough.

3. T: [Reads Statement 3 in the learning contract.] Do you agree that you will give your complete attention and energy to the lesson?
   S: Yes, Teacher. I will do my best.

4. T: OK, how many hours do you study English outside of class now?
   S: I usually try to study 1–2 hours per day, Sir, but it is so hard with 25 hours of classes per week.
   T: Do you think that that is enough to help you score 500?
   S: I'm not sure, Sir.
   T: Can you do more?
   S: I will try, Sir.
   T: How much will you try every day?
   S: I can do 2 hours every day.
   T: OK, if you do that it will be a big help, but if you don't study on your own it will be very difficult for me to help you. Do you understand?
   S: Yes, Teacher. As you said, the semester is half over so I need to work hard.

5. T: What about homework or other things I need you to do outside of class? Do you plan to do all of it, some of it, none of it?
   S: Oh no, teacher. I will do it all. I need to work hard to pass the TOEFL.

6. T: All right, now. If you do all of these things, what do you expect will happen? What score on the TOEFL do you think you will earn?

S: I think I will get a 500 teacher . . . do you think it is possible?

T: Yes. If you do everything that you say you are going to do here, then I think you can score a 500.

I then explained items 7 and 8, asked if they had any questions, invited them to come back if they felt the need to amend their contract or had any questions, and asked them to sign it.

Question 6 on the learning contract (see Appendix B) produced the greatest variety of responses. Several students put down a number below 500 (most of these students chose 490) and there were some students who I had to tell that their numbers in the previous statements were not high enough to help them get a 500.

Results

I had hoped that the students' poor attitude and motivation for English language learning would be improved. What, if any, effect there would be on the students' learning (as measured by their results on the end-of-semester TOEFL) I had no idea. My feeling was that if the attitudinal factors were improved, then they would study more outside of class and I would be able to help them learn more inside the classroom. The combination of these factors would presumably result in an improved TOEFL score.

In the weeks after the contract signing, the students' morale and effort remained high, and I waited to see if they could maintain their momentum. They did maintain strong attendance, and I had almost no behavioral problems. As the semester drew to a close, I was happy that the students had worked so hard, hopeful that they were doing the extra work they claimed to be doing when I inquired, and cautiously optimistic that many of the class might actually get the 500 TOEFL score and exit the program. There was one phenomenon that I found interesting, as noted in the discussion of attendance during the interview process. Many of my students were slowly but steadily creeping toward the 20% absence level. Many were attending my class faithfully, occasionally going to their reading and grammar classes, and ignoring their writing class completely.

As shown in Table 1, most students were absent from the other classes 2–3 times more than from my Listening/Speaking or TOEFL classes. I wish that I could claim that this was because of my superior teaching ability, but actually I believe it was a combination of the learning contract and the students' becoming more aware that my class was concentrating only on the TOEFL and TOEFL-related activities. The exit interviews corroborated my intuition on this trend.

In end-of-class informal interviews, I asked the students for their impressions of the class and whether the changes had helped them. They were very confident and eager to take the TOEFL and were highly positive about the experience,

Table 1. Total Class Hours Missed in Level 4 Section 1

Student No.	Grammar	Listening/ Speaking	Reading	Writing	TOEFL
1	18.65	7.33	16.66	19.31	7.00
2	13.31	6.64	14.64	14.65	11.33
3	18.00	5.33	14.33	16.33	5.00
4	11.94	2.65	10.96	16.30	7.00
5	4.00	6.99	7.33	32.33	6.00
6	9.00	7.00	13.66	13.66	8.00
7	25.29	12.63	30.31	22.63	7.00
8	9.33	8.32	10.66	20.00	6.00
9	16.00	14.33	18.33	10.00	11.00
10	15.00	7.66	15.33	18.97	4.00
11	20.95	6.66	19.31	17.65	5.00
12	6.65	3.33	15.65	26.65	3.66
13	6.33	8.00	5.33	11.32	7.00
14	4.00	2.33	3.00	2.00	3.00
15	9.32	8.32	4.66	10.98	6.33
16	17.98	7.99	21.33	15.97	3.66

saying, "You didn't treat us like children," "I am happy you listened to our complaints," "We appreciate your changing the class," and so on. When I asked about the attendance issue, most replied, "the other classes were not helping us."

Although the attendance figures and shifts in attitude were interesting and gratifying, the TOEFL scores proved most gratifying (see Table 2). Three students earned a 500 and exited the IEP. Scores increased for 13 out of 16 students. Of these 13, 10 students' scores went up by 23 points or more. Five students showed an improvement of 40 points or more. Three students scored lower than previously, and one of those declined a precipitous 53 points. Note that students who did not complete the course or take part in the learning contract process have been deleted from the attendance and results list. Of these students, two exited the program.

Would the students have achieved this level of improvement without the learning contract? I believe they would not have because the students' attitudes

Table 2. TOEFL Results From Level 4A, Spring Semester 2005

Student No.	TOEFL Score		Gain
	Beginning of Semester (January 29, 2005)	End of Semester (May 28, 2005)	
1	453	490	37
2	443	483	40
3	487	**520**	33
4	440	450	10
5	450	480	30
6	470	493	23
7	450*	**500**	50
8	453	470	17
9	440*	387	−53
10	487	477	−10
11	440	463	23
12	473	467	−6
13	433	490	57
14	450*	490	40
15	463	**503**	40
16	477	483	6

Note: Boldface indicates satisfied required TOEFL score. *No date.

and motivation toward their studies were extremely poor before we undertook this project. Unfortunately, I was not able to use a control group. I had only one Level 4 group of students, and it was not possible for me to split them into control and experimental groups to compare the results.

Reflection

Completing this project allowed me to reflect deeply on what I was doing and why I was doing it. I found that giving the students some ownership of their learning was a powerful motivational tool, and that most students rose to the challenge of taking more responsibility for their own learning and seemed to learn more. That should be evident. Unfortunately, the paradox of English language teaching in the Arabian Gulf is that teachers and administrators constantly bemoan the students' lack of motivation and autonomy while at the same time building such prescriptive systems of course delivery—to overcome these perceived weaknesses—that students' and teachers' initiative and autonomy are often stifled. Student motivation and autonomy will always be a problem here for as long as institutions of higher learning perpetuate the teacher-centered failings of the secondary school system in their attempts to ameliorate the problems caused by such a top-down system.

Perhaps the most important lesson I learned from this project is that action research is important for me to question my own assumptions about what my students can and cannot do. The process was crucial to gaining a fresh perspective about what is going on in my classroom and why my students act the way they do. I also learned, or relearned, that research does not always have to be complicated, difficult to conduct, or take place over a period of years to have situational validity. That said, I am proud of myself as an educator for establishing the facts behind my assumptions and acting on my findings to provide a more positive learning experience for my students and myself. I believe this experience has added a powerful tool to my teaching repertoire.

Some educators might read this and think: "Proud of himself?! He committed the cardinal sin of education: he abandoned the curriculum, caved to student pressure, and taught to the test. What could he possibly be proud about?" First, the TOEFL is a proficiency test. It is intended to measure the proficiency or the ability of the students to use English in academic situations. There are many different ways of achieving proficiency. Second, I believe that Arab learners of English need specific instruction and test practice on the TOEFL because they are not familiar with many of the cultural references it contains. Some research has concluded that there is no cultural bias in the TOEFL. Angoff (1989) stated, "There is no support for the hypothesis that TOEFL items that make reference to American people, places, institutions, customs, etc., tend to advantage TOEFL candidates who have lived in the United States for a year or more over those who have spent little (one month or less) time in the country" (p. 6). Nevertheless, one of the stated reasons for revising the TOEFL (Educational Testing Service, 2003) was to "provide more information than the paper-based TOEFL test about the ability of international students to use English in an academic environment" (p. 2). My experience has been similar to that of Lanteigne (2004): "English proficiency tests—such as the TOEFL . . . are problematic when applied to EFL learners in developing countries whose use of English is vastly different than the English used in American universities" (p. 32). By using a learning contract and an approach that the students believed would help them, I was able to enhance motivation without sacrificing instructional quality or integrity.

As a result of this study, I plan to continue the use of learning contracts with my students even if the contracts are limited by curricular factors to areas such as homework and independent study. Any sense of autonomy I can foster in the learners under my tutelage will be beneficial for them as they continue their academic studies. Further, research is now part of my professional portfolio—it is not just something done by outside experts and authorities. Periodic action research will inform my teaching practice and require me to continue formally examining what I do and why I do it. I, like many other teachers, sometimes fall into the prescribed curriculum trap and continue to use the same old materials or activities because I feel I have to. It is worthwhile to seek ways to break out of the curriculum bind without upsetting the system too much. When I do this, my teaching practice and my students' learning opportunities are enhanced.

Paul MacLeod teaches at the Petroleum Institute, Abu Dhabi, United Arab Emirates.

Appendix A: Student Questionnaire

Part 1

1. Where are you from?

2. How many years have you been studying English?

3. When did you start studying in the IEP?

4. Why are you studying English?

5. Why did you choose the UoS?

6. How often do you read English books, newspapers, or magazines outside of class? (not homework)

7. How often do you read Arabic books, newspapers, or magazines outside of class? (not homework)

8. If you had a choice would you study English?

9. What was your TOEFL score when you entered the UoS?

10. What was your most recent TOEFL score?

11. How many times have you taken the TOEFL?

Part 2

1. Rate your chances of exiting the IEP at the end of this semester
    a. Excellent—I'm sure I will do it
    b. Very good—If I work hard I will exit
    c. Fair—If I am lucky I might exit
    d. Poor—I have almost no chance of exiting

2. Rate your study habits
    a. Excellent—I spend 8 or more hours a week studying English
    b. Very good—I spend between 5–7 hours a week studying English
    c. Fair—I study English between 3–5 hours per week
    d. Poor—I study English less than 3 hours per week

3. If you do not exit at the end of the semester what is your plan?
    a. Study at the UoS in summer
    b. Return for L4 [Level 4] next semester
    c. Change to an Arabic major
    d. Change universities
    e. Other

4. Twenty-five hours per week of English is
    a. Very helpful—we need all of the practice
    b. Helpful
    c. The same as 18 hrs/week
    d. Terrible—it's too much and we are bored

5. The TOEFL is a fair measure of our ability in English
    a. Strongly agree
    b. Agree
    c. Neutral
    d. Disagree
    e. Strongly disagree

6. Our textbooks are
    a. Excellent
    b. Very good
    c. Average
    d. Poor
    e. Very poor

7. Overall, my teachers are
   a. Excellent
   b. Very good
   c. Average
   d. Poor
   e. Very poor

8. Overall, Sharjah University is
   a. Excellent
   b. Very good
   c. Average
   d. Poor
   e. Very poor

9. Would you recommend UoS to a friend?
   a. Yes
   b. No

10. If you could change ONE thing about the UoS, what would it be?

Other Comments (please write in English only)

Appendix B: The Student Contract

I, _____(student) have met with my teacher, Mr. Paul MacLeod, to discuss my progress in Level 4 Listening/Speaking and TOEFL Preparation.
We have agreed on the following points:

1. I will attend all classes OR I will attend _____% of classes.

2. I will complete all class work OR I will complete _____% of class work.

3. When I am in class I will give my complete attention and energy to the lesson.

4. I will study _____ hours outside of class every day.

5. I will complete all assignments or I will complete _____ % of assignments.

6. If I abide by this contract I expect to gain a 500 TOEFL or _____on the TOEFL.

7. I have read and understood this contract and I promise to abide by the conditions I have agreed to above.

8. I hereby give Mr. MacLeod permission to use and/or publish my information for educational or research purposes.

Signature Student   Signature Teacher

_____   _____

Date: _____

CHAPTER 9

Six Hats for Discussion and Writing (*United Arab Emirates*)

David Palfreyman and Fran Turner

Issue

This chapter reports on research the two authors conducted using de Bono's Six Thinking Hats model (de Bono, 1999) to develop thinking, discussion, and writing skills with our shared class (intermediate learners in the English Readiness program at Zayed University in Dubai). The Six Hats model distinguishes six different types of thinking and discussion, and suggests ways of using these different types to help us think and talk about real-life issues. David Palfreyman led six lessons with our shared class to introduce and apply the Six Hats model, and he and Fran Turner collaborated to gather data about the progress of this experiment.

First, we briefly describe our teaching context and how this shaped our inquiry. We then review some key concepts from the literature on thinking, discussion, and writing. The main part of this chapter describes the series of lessons and associated work using the Six Hats model, the data which we gathered from these lessons, and what these data show about the progress of the learners' awareness and skills. We then review the overall outcomes of the research for our professional development as teachers and as researchers.

Both of us teach in the Readiness (Foundation) program at Zayed University, Dubai. Zayed University is an English-medium university for female United Arab Emirates (UAE) nationals. Incoming students must gain a score of 500 on the Test of English as a Foreign Language, or TOEFL, and pass an institutional academic language skills exam, or else they are required to study for up to 2 years in the Readiness program. In the Readiness program, they work with an in-house course book to develop skills such as taking notes, writing academic essays, and participating in academic discussions. The aim of the Readiness program is to increase the level of students' language and also to induct them into a university setting, where they are expected to seek and understand information, to synthesize information from different sources, and to apply it in making decisions and solving problems.

Teachers in the Readiness program have often commented that students have problems with critical thinking; they tend to take a black-and-white view of situations and issues, paying insufficient attention to detail and analysis. This may be partly because of their educational and family backgrounds: students' experiences in state secondary schools seem to involve more memorization than analysis or creativity; at home, their elder relatives (and perhaps siblings) may well have no experience of higher education; and students' social roles as young women in Gulf Arab society also may not encourage the development of critical thinking skills. Students tend not to show an ability to abstract from particular situations, to produce a variety of ideas, to make connections between ideas, and to develop their own or others' ideas.

These are important skills in any Western-oriented academic setting, and any student needs to develop these skills during the early months or years at university. However, in our context the issue is particularly salient, for several reasons. First, our student population is fairly homogeneous. Second, their social backgrounds and norms are quite distinct from the kind of Western academic culture promoted in the university. Third, these young women are pioneers in the UAE's efforts to extend higher education for women beyond the elite, who traditionally had such access.

Background Literature

The term *critical thinking* applies to a range of skills for analyzing and discussing issues and situations. Ennis (1987) identified skeptical reflection and reasoned thinking as key elements of critical thinking. Information gathering is another key element, related to information literacy (Grassian & Kaplowitz, 2001). Thinking skills are also often associated with open-endedness. Resnick (1987) characterized *higher order thinking* as nonlinear, complex, and leading to multiple solutions. Hudson (1967) discussed the importance of *divergent thinking*, which explores the multiple possibilities inherent in a situation, as opposed to *convergent thinking*, which homes in on the correct solution for a problem.

There is some debate about how accessible these thinking skills are to students from certain cultural or ability groups. Zohar and Dori (2003) critique the notion that higher order thinking skills are attainable only by very academically minded students: their research shows that students of low academic ability can develop their higher order thinking skills, and indeed make greater gains than higher ability students, if engaged appropriately in a program of case-based instruction. Atkinson (1997) and others suggest that students in the West are socialized into critical thinking by their cultural background, and that students from other backgrounds do not exhibit critical thinking. However, Stapleton's (2001) research suggests that Japanese students may possess critical thinking skills but express them in culturally based ways that are not immediately recognizable to observers from other cultures.

As noted, our students seemed to lack some of the thinking skills described. For example, they often jumped into a discussion without factual background knowledge, and based their arguments on their own or others' ideas and opinions. However, there are models and strategies available to guide teachers in developing these skills. Barell's (2003) KWHLAQ strategy guides the student in asking questions such as "What do we want or need to know about this topic?" and "How will we go about finding answers to our questions?" (p. 137). For brainstorming ideas, Fobes (1993) emphasized the importance of writing down ideas and concentrating initially on generating different ideas rather than evaluating the ideas as they come. Fobes suggested writing down all ideas, no matter how useless or impractical they may seem at the time. A seemingly useless idea might be used as part of another idea, or it might reveal insights which can prompt a new, more-useful idea. In other words, Fobes observed, "ideas that are useless as solutions are not necessarily useless in the thinking process" (p. 65).

DE BONO'S SIX THINKING HATS

De Bono (1999) offers a model of thinking called the Six Thinking Hats. These are metaphorical hats, which are associated with six different types of thinking, as follows:

- **White Hat**—gathering information. White Hat thinking involves identifying the factual information available, then deciding what further information is needed and where to get it.

- **Green Hat**—creating new ideas and new approaches. Green Hat thinking emphasizes creativity.

- **Yellow Hat**—looking for opportunities (positive possibilities) and benefits (positive results). Yellow Hat thinking is positive in outlook; however, it must be realistic, and should be supported with logical reasons.

- **Black Hat**—being careful. Black Hat thinking focuses on pitfalls and potential problems and disadvantages. Although it is skeptical in outlook, it must still be logical and provide reasons.

- **Red Hat**—feelings and intuition. Red Hat thinking allows people to express their emotional or intuitive ideas, without needing to support them with logical arguments.

- **Blue Hat**—overview and planning. Blue Hat thinking considers the discussion as a whole, including the contributions of the other hats. In a business meeting this is the chairperson's role; in a classroom situation this is the teacher's role.

De Bono developed the Six Thinking Hats to facilitate group thinking in business contexts. A key principle is that only one hat is used at a time: for each stage of the discussion everyone agrees to use one hat only. For example, everyone focuses on possible benefits (Yellow Hat), then everyone looks for possible threats (Black Hat), and so on. This is to allow some space in the discussion for each type of thinking and to avoid mixed-thinking situations, for example, when some people are attacking and others defending an idea for purposes of their own. The hats do not need to be used in any particular order, but one common pattern begins with white (gathering information), moves on to green (brainstorming interpretations or responses), then yellow (looking for the benefits of each idea generated), black (considering the possible dangers), red (airing gut reactions to the various proposals), and then blue (summarizing the discussion and deciding on next steps).

The advantage of the Six Hats model for our purposes was that it is simple and memorable. It allows us to distinguish a range of types of thinking and bring all of these into a discussion situation.

DISCUSSION, WRITING, THINKING, AND TECHNOLOGY

Why should language teachers be concerned with developing thinking skills? One answer is that we see our role as readying students for university study not only in terms of language, but also in other academic skills such as information literacy and critical thinking. In addition, the thinking skills outlined in de Bono's model are intimately linked with language skills: Engaging in academic discussions, for example, has a linguistic dimension but also a cognitive one. Stapleton (2001) focused in particular on how to assess students' critical thinking skills by looking at their writing. He identified the following as key indicators of critical thinking in academic writing: presenting arguments (claims supported by logical reasons); using evidence (from personal experience, research, or other sources); and recognizing and addressing viewpoints other than one's own. He also identified linguistic expressions of these functions (e.g., the use of conjunctions or phrases such as "Some people claim that . . ."").

Thinking and discussion are intimately linked. Sociocultural theorists including Vygotsky (1978) and Bruner (1985) see thinking as developing from interaction: ideas first are discussed and develop between people, then develop within the individual mind, so that thinking is in fact internalized discussion. Thus one way to improve students' thinking skills could be to improve the quality of their discussion. De Bono's Thinking Hats are in fact discussion hats. De Bono himself writes in terms of groups thinking aloud through their discussions. The Six Hats model helps make us more aware of different types of thinking, and stimulates us to explore different types of discussion; the principle of everyone putting on the same hat at the same time makes this a collaborative enterprise. All of these developments can contribute to the quality of discussion and thinking.

Interactive discussion and writing are also closely related. A quality discussion can feed into students' writing, by generating ideas which the student can use, refute, develop, or otherwise respond to, and by activating lexis and grammar to be used in writing. From taking part in a discussion, the student can also become more aware of how the ideas can be related to each other and organized. Indeed, any writing may be seen as a one-sided interaction on paper. Bakhtin (1984) views writing as a hidden dialogue, with the writer responding to other opinions and thoughts. In our study we were interested in developing students' writing by developing the quality of their discussions.

In the modern age, the processes just described are linked to another element—technology. Computer-mediated communication offers new ways for students to write and discuss (for example, in chat rooms, blogs, or wikis), and these media highlight the connections between writing, discussion, and thinking. Even though the Six Hats model is not necessarily linked to technology, one of us (Palfreyman) was interested in using computer-mediated communication to apply the model more effectively. Note, however, that the other (Turner) viewed technology as a possible distraction for the students and associated it more with social chit-chat between students using instant messaging.

Procedures

Our action research inquiry (Kemmis & McTaggart, 1982) involved trying out a particular kind of intervention (using the Six Hats model) to address a perceived gap in the curriculum, and we gathered data about the student outcomes in thinking, discussion, writing, and motivation. As the experiment unfolded, we also learned about ourselves as teachers and researchers.

During the 9-week course, Palfreyman led a series of six lessons using concepts from the Six Thinking Hats model, and Turner (the main teacher for this class) observed these lessons and took notes, as well as assisting with the lessons, doing some lead-in and follow-up work relating to the Six Hats theme, and observing the class in the rest of the course. We discussed the project regularly, both face-to-face and by e-mail, in order to compare data, assess progress, and plan our next steps at each stage. In this section, we will explain the procedure and rationale for each lesson, the data gathered, and what we learned from these data. Sample materials are available from the authors on request.

LESSON 1—INITIAL INPUT ABOUT THE MODEL

We felt that the students needed to start with an overall view of the Six Hats model, and to become aware of the variety of thinking and discussion styles involved. Palfreyman introduced the model using a lecture and note-taking format familiar to students from coursework. After briefly outlining the topic, *discussion*, he gave a 10-minute lecture on the Six Hats model, describing its purpose (in de Bono's work and in this course), explaining the significance of each hat, and outlining how the model might be applied to a discussion. The lecture included examples relating to discussions with students' friends and family. The students took notes on the lecture, then they worked in pairs, first to compare their notes and then to complete a summary of the lecture and match examples in a worksheet to the different hats. In the next lesson, Turner asked students to write a summary of what they had learned from the Six Hats lesson. For homework, students were asked to give an example to illustrate how one of their acquaintances or family members used each hat.

During the lesson, students seemed familiar with the idea of a discussion as opposed to an argument, and with the idea of successful and unsuccessful discussions. Palfreyman mentioned that in discussions people sometimes call out comments without listening to what others say, and the students agreed that they had seen this happen. The *thinking hat* as a cultural concept, unsurprisingly, did not strike a chord with the students, but the simple clarity of the hats as symbols appealed to them.

The reflective paragraphs which students wrote in the following lesson expressed a positive response to the lecture, to the Six Hats model, and to the idea of using it in their own discussions. Students found the lecture comprehensible and organized, and they saw the model as offering rules for participating effectively in discussions.

Students showed evidence of understanding the concept of most of the Six Hats. In general, they were able to complete the worksheet. They were unsure (as was Turner, as a newcomer to the Six Hats model) about which color was best for a couple of the examples, but this led to useful discussion. In their homework, students were generally able to name an acquaintance or family member who often used each style of thinking and discussion, and to give a convincing example. For the White Hat, one student wrote, "My mother helps me to find what information is missing in my project," and for the Green Hat another wrote, "Reem thinks about what will happen with new cars without petrol."

The hat which most students did *not* relate convincingly to their own experience was the Blue Hat. Blue Hat thinking takes a *meta*-perspective on the discussion (e.g., summarizing or evaluating progress in the discussion), and this seemed to escape the students, who focused instead on the examples given in the lecture, of a chairperson or a teacher using this hat. One student, for example, wrote "Alanood always likes to tell others what to do," and another wrote "my teacher suggests to work a lot to pass this course."

LESSON 2—PLANNING A WORLD TRIP

The students' first opportunity to apply their understanding of the different hats was a discussion to plan a group trip. They were to imagine that they had won a 3-week holiday in which they could visit one or more of five countries. The students were not familiar with most of the countries and began to ask about their location. This was our opportunity to relate the task to the Six Hats, and Palfreyman asked: "If you want to know something about the places on the board, which hat do you put on?" They immediately recognized this as a White Hat activity. Each group chose a leader and a note taker, and they were given 5 minutes to come up with questions about the countries, which would help them in planning their trip. They then used a map of the world and Wikipedia (or another online information source) to seek the answers to these questions.

We then moved on to the Green Hat. Students brainstormed ideas about what to do on the trip, focusing on suggesting and noting ideas, rather than discussing each idea (which comes later with the Yellow and Black Hats). In order to promote this focus, and to remind the students of the link with the Six Hats, each group had a Cuisenaire rod of the appropriate colour (white in the previous stage, green at this stage) sitting on the table in front of them as they talked, and group leaders were asked to remind the group of this if they strayed onto other kinds of discussion.

After this stage, we began to discuss their ideas as a class, using first the Yellow Hat (thinking of advantages and possible benefits) then the Black Hat (focusing on disadvantages and potential dangers). As part of the next lesson with Turner, students wrote down Yellow and Black Hat issues with regard to each country and what to do there. For homework, students wrote a reflective paragraph about the activity.

The idea of using the Six Hats is to force participants to focus on one kind of thinking at a time, so as to facilitate a richer and more balanced discussion. This strategy both restricts students and encourages exploration. For example, at the Green Hat stage, students need to resist discussing each option, and instead focus on producing a variety of suggestions. We noted that several groups had difficulty keeping this focus, and started to evaluate or comment on the suggestions made: a natural reaction, but one which tends to produce fewer and less varied suggestions. A similar problem is found in many students' essays; they tend to think of one idea and expand on that, rather than presenting a range of ideas.

The students' reflective paragraphs tended to focus on enjoyment of the lesson (which is gratifying, but less useful for assessing their understanding) and on the lesson's content (e.g., learning information about Tanzania). Out of 15 paragraphs, 5 referred to the Six Hats model, but only 1 referred to individual hats and their use in the discussion. Apparently, the students had engaged in the process but did not have explicit awareness of the relevance of the Six Hats model. Timing was an issue in the lesson, which attempted to bring in as many hats as possible. One student commented on this challenge, and another said that we should sit and discuss the topic rather than writing down ideas.

LESSON 3—DEALING WITH SHOPPING ADDICTION

We next applied the Six Hats model to a key course topic: shopping addiction. We decided to use a case-based discussion, which would expose students to an individual with a shopping addiction, and discuss the best way to deal with this addiction (building on information from the course book). To make this seem more realistic, Turner played the part of a person with a shopping addiction, and the students acted as therapists trying to help her.

The students first used the White Hat, interviewing the "addict" to gain information about the problem. They then applied the Green Hat; individually, they thought of possible solutions to the problem and posted their suggestions on an online class discussion board. Next, the class was divided into two groups: Yellow and Black. All students logged on to the discussion board, read each suggested solution, and posted an individual response to each solution. Students in the Yellow group thought of advantages or benefits of each suggestion, and students in the Black group pointed out its disadvantages or dangers. Students began this work in class and finished it for homework. Finally, students read through all the messages on the discussion board, decided which they thought was the best solution, and wrote a paragraph explaining their choice. This activity was intended to introduce Blue Hat thinking (reflection on the content of their discussion) and to start bridging from discussion into writing.

In their final summarizing paragraphs, most students fulfilled the basic aim of explaining which of the solutions they thought was best. Some had difficulty in supporting their choices in the terms we required, but compared with the early messages on the discussion board, most paragraphs were more clearly and logically expressed. It seemed that taking part in the online discussion had given the students a better grasp of the issues involved and enabled them to better express causal and other relations in their paragraphs.

LESSONS 4 AND 4A—GREEN, BLACK, AND YELLOW PRACTICE

At this point, we decided that students could benefit from focused practice in specific kinds of thinking, particularly the Green, Yellow, and Black Hats. In particular, the online discussion had revealed a weakness in students' generation and support of Yellow or Black Hat responses to ideas, so we provided some short slots in two lessons to focus on these kinds of thinking.

The Green Hat practice involved asking the class to brainstorm uses for everyday objects, including a laptop (each student has one), a lemon, and a paperclip. Students (initially as a class and then in groups) suggested different things which they could do with each object, no matter how unusual. With the laptop, for example, they first suggested uses such as writing an assignment or playing a game; with prompting, they started to think of less obvious uses, such as using it as a paperweight, or hitting a thief/attacker with it in self-defense. Students enjoyed this exercise and produced imaginative suggestions.

For the Yellow and Black Hats, we wanted students to practice considering other points of view. Rather than supporting ideas which they agreed with or attacking ones they disliked, we required them to think, for example, of disadvantages of having a holiday the next day (e.g., they would miss useful input for their upcoming exam) or of advantages of their laptops not working (they would spend less of their free time playing computer games and more time socializing with their family).

LESSON 5—ADVERTISING A PRODUCT

The course topic at this stage was advertising, and students had learned about different forms of advertising. In this lesson, students used different kinds of thinking to work out an advertising strategy for a product. Each group of three or four students had a piece of realia such as a mobile phone or a tube of hand cream, and they discussed their plan in a series of online chats in a virtual classroom. Like the discussion board, this medium made the ideas available on record for analysis and discussion afterward, but like a face-to-face discussion, it offered the potential to bounce ideas off each other in real time.

Students' first task was to establish basic information about their product (White Hat), such as the features of the mobile phone. They then brainstormed ideas (Green Hat) for advertising their product. After a break to review the ideas in the transcript of their interaction, they discussed the advantages (Yellow Hat) and drawbacks (Black Hat) of each idea. Finally, as a group they looked at the advantages and disadvantages they had discussed, and wrote a paragraph summarizing their ideas, using linkers to show, for example, where the paragraph moved from the idea itself to the advantages and then to the disadvantages.

The transcripts of the students' interactions show that they were broadly on task but still had some digressions from the hat assigned for each section of the lesson. For example, Extract 1, from a brainstorming discussion, is annotated to show which kinds of thinking were used. Although Green Hat is used more than any other hat, the majority of the interactions consist of various kinds of reactions (Red, Black, or Yellow) to the suggestions, so the range of ideas is reduced. Thanks to the archiving feature of the virtual classroom software, we were able to use this and similar extracts in a follow-up lesson to raise students' awareness of the thinking in their discussions.

> **Extract 1:**
> Alia: ok why we don't put ads in street [Green]
> Alia: why don't we put the ads in the tv and we let a famous person to to it for us [Green]
> Hind: it will cost to much money [Black]
> Alia: but maybe we will get a high profit [Yellow]
> Hind: I don't think so [Red]
> Alia: why?
> Hessa: what about puting new option ?? [Green]
> Hind: may be some people do not like this famous person [Black]
> Hind: lik what?
> Alia: but maybe the people will like the ads and will like the phone so they will buy it [Yellow]

The quality of these interactions varied. Some consisted mainly of social chat or off-task comments (sometimes in Arabic). However, the following extract from a Yellow Hat discussion shows how one student (Afra) prompted others to support her ideas.

> **Extract 2:**
> Hind: we chose also a white background
> Hind: to give a nice reaction and we will let her to sit on a red chair
> Afra: mmm
> Afra: but what is the advantagers to chose white background and red chair
> Hind: it will be atractive
> Afra: ok
> Hind: it will be in the street
> Hessa: we use aa simple shape
> Afra: but why we will do in the street what is the advantges?
> Afra: ?
> Hessa: alot of people will see it

LESSON 6—DEVELOPING AN ARGUMENT

A key objective of the course was to write a position essay arguing for or against a statement. We wanted at this stage to give the students a choice of topic, in order to engage them more, so as a class we brainstormed controversial topics and statements that interested the students. From their suggestions we selected

"Emirati men should be able to marry foreign women." For homework, students were asked to use a White Hat approach to the topic by seeking related facts from relatives, friends, and the Internet, and then determine whether they agreed or disagreed with the statement.

The students chose this topic because they had strong feelings about it, and this affected the ideas that students produced from their homework. First, much of the information that the students provided appeared to us to be opinions and emotional responses (Red Hat) rather than facts—for example, "Children of mixed marriages have language problems," or "Foreign wives are usually second wives." However, students considered that these were established facts, so they did not feel the need to research the topic. This led us to rethink, even at this late stage, how we used the Six Hats with students. It had seemed earlier that White Hat thinking was relatively unproblematic for students, who were used to thinking of questions and researching information. However, on a familiar topic that aroused their feelings, such as marriage, they needed some focus to see the role that information could play in debating the subject.

We therefore prepared a handout to help students distinguish between generalizations, opinions, and facts. The handout provided examples of factual questions and used points made by students in their homework task to highlight the following issues:

- **Degree.** For example, which degree would students choose—"all/most/some/a few foreign wives are second wives." This led to some debate among the students as to which was the most accurate description, and so to a more nuanced understanding and expression of their assertions.

- **The difference between fact and opinion.** When asked directly about this point, students showed some awareness of the distinction. There was useful discussion about whether a statement needed to be true to be factual.

- **Evidence.** The handout asked students to offer evidence for assertions they had expressed, which led to a discussion of what kind of evidence (e.g., personal experience, anecdotes from family members, statistics from newspapers) is valid in a university essay.

In the Yellow and Black sections of this handout we encouraged students to support their arguments more. Most students felt that it was dangerous for their society for Emirati men to marry foreign women, but they tended to present Red Hat arguments against it without support. On the other hand, students were able when prompted to suggest benefits of marrying foreign women, even though they disapproved of it, but they needed to provide more support for these ideas. This is, of course, a common problem in writers' arguments, even in their first language (Stapleton, 2001).

Results

It may be unrealistic to expect great gains in these particular students' thinking, discussions, and writing, considering their low skill level at the beginning of the course and the limited time which could be spared in the course for work on the Six Hats. It is also clear from our account that students' progress was not linear. However, as the course went on, there was certainly a refinement in students' awareness levels and discussions of different styles of thinking and their means of expressing these thoughts in writing.

At the end of the course, Turner asked each student to write down a question about the Six Hats for other students to answer. Then the students passed the questions around the class, and each student wrote her answer anonymously. Twelve students were present and took part in this activity. The answers were fairly brief, but they seemed honest to us.

One student wrote a question about students' affective responses: "Did you enjoy writing using Six Hats?" The response to this was fairly positive (seven students replied "yes," two "sometimes," and three "no"). Some of those who replied "yes" gave reasons, which typically involved the Six Hats being useful for organizing their ideas. Students seemed to feel more positively than negatively about the model.

Another student asked, "What did you learn from studying the Six Hats?" Ten students replied that they had learned more about writing. Many responses to this question mentioned organizing and planning ideas, and four mentioned thinking (one referred to "thinking in a different way"). As well as enjoying the Six Hats model, therefore, the students seemed also to have felt that they learned something from it. In answer to the question "Did the Six Hats help you to plan your essay?" 10 students replied "yes."

Some students asked about how classmates would use the Six Hats model in the future. The most common response was "in my studies." Another student asked specifically about whether students would use the model in their studies, to which all students replied in the affirmative, citing, for example, "organizing my ideas" and "when we write the essay." Some students also mentioned their home life (e.g., "discussions with my father") or future work. One student asked, "Will you use the Six Hats in your daily life?" and all but one of the other students responded "yes."

Two students asked about the model itself. One asked, "Which do you think is the most important hat?" In response, nearly half of the students mentioned the Green Hat, perhaps reflecting their interest in creating new ideas, but all of the hats except the Yellow Hat were mentioned by at least one student. Another student asked, "Which hat do you still have questions about?" Five students replied "none," which is possibly reassuring, and three replied "the Blue Hat," which is understandable considering the abstract nature of this type of thinking and the relatively softer focus on this hat in the course.

Reflection

Our experiment was conceived in the spirit of action research—assessing the impact of an intervention to address a perceived problem. However, as we tried out the Six Hats model in practice and gained feedback during the process, we also increased our understanding of our students, of the skills we were trying to develop in them, of our own practice, of the process of implementing an innovative approach in the curriculum, and of the research process. In this section we will reflect separately on what we learned as teacher researchers and on what we could do in the future.

DAVID PALFREYMAN'S REFLECTIONS

Using the Six Hats model increased our awareness as well as the students', helping us to understand students' competence in different kinds of thinking. I realized that our students are ready and able to engage in White Hat thinking on cold topics of only academic interest (e.g., advertising strategies or an imaginary holiday). In these cases, they can ask and research factual questions about the topic. On the other hand, with hot topics in which they are personally and socially engaged, such as marriage to nonlocals, they reach automatically for the Red Hat and find it hard to take other approaches. Students showed an aptitude greater than I had anticipated for creating new ideas and approaches with the Green Hat, and their use of the Yellow and Black Hats showed a need for practice in considering viewpoints different from their own and in providing logical support for their statements. One use of the Six Hats could be for profiling a student's thinking skills, with their use of each hat being evaluated separately.

Another effect of the Six Hats experiment was to make me think about what a discussion involves. De Bono (1999) favours using one style of thinking at a time, and also emphasizes staying on task as much as possible. Students, on the other hand, had a tendency to spend time on social interaction, whether face-to-face or in online environments. Is sticking to one hat at a time the most productive way to conduct discussions, and how strict should we be about this? Is it authentic to have a transactional, task-oriented discussion including no social interaction? These are questions which I would like to investigate further.

I started with a simplistic notion of implementing a particular model (the Six Hats); however, during the course, I began to see our enterprise more as mediating between the model, learners' skills, and course content. The Six Hats model was one piece of the evolving puzzle, but students' developing thinking skills and my assessment of these were equally important. I realized the need to break the process of learning to think, discuss, and write into stages, which did not necessarily follow one after another but had to be revisited in a cycle of awareness raising, discussion, writing, and further awareness raising. We had to relate the Six Hats model to the kinds of essays needed for the course objectives and to be specific about the language which students could use to express ideas, information, and perspectives. Conducting this research therefore enriched my view of teaching.

FRAN TURNER'S REFLECTIONS

The students liked this new approach of using the Six Hats to develop their thinking skills and then using them in their essay writing. The Six Hats approach helped them come up with ideas and use transition language to move from one point to another, which gave them better skills for expressing their ideas. I felt that with more practice they would be more able to incorporate this language into their writing, which was something they found difficult.

In future I would spend more time making sure students understand the purpose of the Six Hats as we work with the model. In this case, about halfway through the course students asked what the purpose of the hats was. We had talked about the purpose at the beginning, but at that time they had nothing to relate it to. Further along, however, having experienced the activities and discussions, they could better understand the benefit and could make sense of it. Once they understood, they were enthusiastic about continuing.

Maybe one of the reasons they had difficulty putting it all together was that they focused on the Thinking Hat skills for only an hour or two each week, so the skills seemed to be reserved just for special times. I would prefer, therefore, to do a short (10- to 15-minute) thinking skill activity on a daily basis. One such activity would be to practice connecting ideas with "if . . . then . . ." to help them focus on making such connections in their writing. As I became more familiar with the Six Hats model, I also found opportunities to refer in passing to the hats when they were relevant to other lessons.

For our study, some of the activities were done on a computer using the discussion board and a virtual classroom. The particular students participating loved to chat on the computer, so I would have preferred for them to write their ideas on paper. In my experience, if they have to write something by hand, they think about it more before responding and can see more clearly whether their idea is relevant to the current hat. Students tend to be reactive, putting down the first thing that comes into their minds, relevant or not to the issue we are working on.

I believe that teachers do need to take time to introduce and conduct activities to promote thinking and essay writing. Unfortunately, in our teaching situation the curriculum is demanding, and it is challenging to integrate such an approach. However, I feel the concept is worthwhile for improving not only students' essay writing skills but also their thinking in general. Therefore, I intend to make efforts to incorporate this approach, as far as practical, in my teaching in the Readiness program.

David Palfreyman and Fran Turner teach at Zayed University in Dubai, UAE.

CHAPTER 10

Teacher and Student Perceptions of Best Practices in Teaching (*Tunisia*)

Ali H. Raddaoui

Issue

This study aims to profile what constitutes a good teacher and what constitutes a bad teacher, in the eyes of students and teachers of English in the undergraduate program of an English Department in a Tunisian institution of higher education. Despite the publication and currency of many teaching best practices (Bangert, 2004; Bonesrønning, 2004; Emery, Kramer, & Tian, 2003; Jay & Johnson, 2002; Triki & Baklouti, 2003; Wilson, 1999), based on theoretical advances in teaching and learning, expert observation of teaching sessions, and teacher evaluation schemes, it is likely that teaching best practices include elements that are both discipline- and context-sensitive.

For the purposes of this study, I conducted semistructured interviews with eight undergraduate English majors and six English department faculty members at the College of Arts and Humanities in Sfax, Tunisia. My assumption is that teachers and students are experts in their own right and represent valid sources of knowledge whose views, disparate as they may be, are still paramount in profiling effective teaching. I like to add that the representational dimension of this study does not stand in lieu of my own interests and biases as researcher, teacher, and reflective practitioner. Following Burr's (1995) approach, I am not hereby claiming to speak on behalf of the respondents and to exclusively represent their views. As an instructor and administrator in the institution from which I have elicited student and faculty viewpoints for this investigation, I would like to emphasise the jointly constructed nature of the meanings, interpretations, and reflections that follow from this research.

As per a 2005 circular from the Ministry of Higher Education, the education system is on a reform course seeking to realign Tunisian higher education with European higher education standards emanating from the Bologne Declaration (European Ministries of Education, 1999) and the creation of a unified European higher education arena. Some of the keywords of this grand plan are accreditation, employability, entrepreneurship, and quality. The Ministry of Higher Education in Tunisia (2006) has put in place a quality quest program that involves monitoring and measurement of performance at all relevant levels, including academic program evaluation and student evaluation of teachers.

Currently, there is a process through which teachers in higher education institutions are recruited, promoted, and tenured. This requires that the applicant submit a file which will be reviewed by an academically recognized jury. However, unlike primary and secondary school teachers, for whom an initial professional development program leading to certification and career-long supervision is in place, faculty working in higher education institutions do not have an officially sanctioned professional development program to help them with career advancement. Nor does the ministry have an official body to evaluate their teaching. Additionally, student views are not formally sought by administration or other promotion and tenure juries. Absence of evaluations generates hearsay evaluations among students, such as so-and-so "is tough," "is careless," or "is nice." Lack of a recognized formula for students to evaluate teacher performance can lead to student unrest and boycott of classes. If teaching performance is to be used as one of the criteria in promotion and tenure decisions, concerned parties must be able to profile effective teaching.

Let me now give more detail on the specific context for this present study. The languages of instruction for most higher education programs in Tunisia are the national language, Arabic, or the country's second language, French. Aside from specific programs where other languages are used, English is the medium and object of instruction for English departments nationwide. In the English Department of the College of Arts and Humanities in Sfax, English is the only medium of instruction. Students graduate with a degree in English language, literature, and civilization. They take courses in grammar, comprehension, composition, oral expression, and phonetics, in addition to courses in literature, U.S. and British history and culture, and other courses in linguistics, such as phonology, syntax, semantics, discourse analysis, stylistics, pragmatics, translation, and such.

Now let me provide a glimpse into my own involvement. With a record of only 2 years of teaching in the English Department, I am naturally interested in developing an image of success. As an English as a foreign language instructor in the Kingdom of Saudi Arabia and the United Arab Emirates, my teaching performance was systematically evaluated. Because there is no such scheme at my current place of work, I allocate space during my teaching time for receiving student feedback. For reasons that deserve separate analysis, students are not wont to evaluate teachers live, directly, and publicly in an auditorium filled to capacity. When this happened one beautiful November morning in 2005, I was taken aback! One 4th-year student took the floor to say, "You told us it's okay. We're going to talk about whether your teaching is good or bad." Obviously, this meant, if anything, that the image of good teacher I was trying to cultivate did not quite collate with the image this student made of my teaching.

Background Literature

This incident points in a number of directions. First, it constituted for me an invitation to rethink how I practiced teaching. This reflection could take place at a personal and restricted level, but it should also be extended to cover the all-important notion of learning from both the teachers' and students' perspectives. Second, it was an indication of a mismatch between my and my students' perceptions of good teaching, and a motivation to investigate teacher and student views on exemplary teaching.

Let me clarify that I am not expecting that student views will necessarily produce a consensual body of thought that is accurate and valid across the board. Wilson (1999) argued that although student views may be immature, superficial, and prejudiced, their ratings of teachers have a significant impact on course effectiveness. He maintained that teaching is effective only by accident, when the teacher is unaware how students actually perceive his or her teaching. Opportunities for improvement arise from teachers' reflecting about their performance, from student evaluations, or from peer or self-evaluations. Bress (1995) qualified the differential perception in terms of entrenched views and spoke of a gap in perceptions. In an article titled "Are You Listening, Teacher? Tape Yourself and See," Wrangham (1992) described the value of one activity conducted as part of obtaining the Royal Society of Arts diploma: Teachers record on audiotape a 5-minute classroom exchange and proceed to investigate "the mismatch between what they thought they were doing as teacher and what actually happens in class." Hativa, Barak, and Simhi (2001) asserted that there is much less discrepancy between the beliefs and knowledge of good teachers on the one hand and their classroom practices on the other. For less effective teachers, the gap is much wider, and this calls for further investigative and reflective action.

Additional evidence for this lack of fit comes from research conducted by Boddy (2004) in which peer observers judged lectures to be well paced and yet students often considered the same delivery to be too fast. This finding lends further force to the argument that student views, and consequently student evaluations of teachers, outweigh the views of professional teachers because it is the students who have the task of learning.

Pace of delivery for lectures is but one of the indices of teaching behaviour. Identifying quality instructional behaviour in a formula to be applied safely and systematically is tempting, but this formula may, in the words of Brundrett and Silcock (2002), be no more than a myth. Devising "a *single* cohesive blueprint," they argued, is not feasible because "educational and social scientific theory has always supported divergent models of good practice arising in settings which make comparative assessment between teachers and schools problematic" (p. vii). Bonesrønning (2004) also attributed the difficulty of this enterprise to the fact that effective teaching is not reducible to empirical characteristics such as teacher education and experience. Lima (1981) likened the search for these empirical determinants to "searching through a haystack which simply contains no needle" (p. 1059).

With these caveats in mind, I acknowledge that some general and specific schemes for characterizing quality teaching are available. Hoyle (1980) describes one such scheme which links teacher effectiveness to professionalism, and further classifies professionalism into two types: restricted and extended. Restricted professionalism is a feature of teachers whose thinking and practice are narrowly focused on classroom experience and the academic program and are not informed by theory. By contrast, teachers in the category of extended professionalism espouse a wider view of the educational context, which sees effectiveness not as a fixed value but rather as a quantity that can be improved through research and development. In an interesting keynote speech titled "How to Be a Really Rotten Teacher," Collinson (1997) concurred with this view that the "desire to do better is one of the things that distinguishes the able teacher from the inept" (p. 7).

Finch, Helms, and Ettkin (1997) looked at the problematic nature of characterising good teaching and presented the conflicting views in terms of a spectrum. One end of this spectrum correlates good teaching with high student ratings. This view is not without its critics. Teachers can tinker with these ratings by being entertaining speakers or lenient graders, at the expense of scholarship. The other extreme is that low student evaluations, low grades, and difficulty of subject matter materials can also be considered features of high academic standards (Finch et al., 1997).

It follows from the research findings that quality teaching is a complex matter. Jay and Johnson (2002) captured this complexity by referring to three types of reflective practice teachers can conduct: descriptive, comparative, and critical. Descriptive reflection involves the intellectual disposition to set the problem, state the goals of teaching, devise ways of solving the problem, think about the extent to which the goals are or are not being met, and essentially develop a feel for what is working and a concern for what is not working. Comparative reflection is enriched with alternative descriptions and analyses of teaching—including, possibly, peer observations and student evaluations—along with an awareness of theoretical advances. Critical reflection considers the implications of these alternative perspectives in light of one's own morals and ethics as well as the moral and political dimensions of schooling with its "public democratic purposes" (Jay & Johnson, 2002, p. 77).

Over and beyond these overriding perceptions, there is no dearth of literature on what, in extra-Tunisian contexts, represents teaching best practices. Harley, Barasa, Bertram, Mattson, and Pillay (2000) captured the image of a good teacher by identifying six roles good teachers play:

1. Learning mediator

2. Interpreter and designer of learning programmes

3. Leader, administrator, and manager

4. Community, citizenship, and pastoral role

5. Scholar, researcher, and lifelong learner

6. Learning area or phase specialist

Together, these six roles draw a clearer profile of quality teaching, although they are still not translatable into characteristics that are readily observable and determinable.

Triki and Baklouti (2003) understand the pedagogical act essentially in terms of five rhetorical faculties:

1. Invention, or how to establish contact with the audience

2. Arrangement, or how to organize your lesson

3. Style, or how to select the appropriate level of language and address

4. Memory, or how to achieve long-term learning

5. Delivery, or how to manage impressions during the lesson

The previous examples show that at the most general level, features of good teaching are not difficult to formulate. They will, however, remain at a level of generality and ambiguity. Perceptions of the same lesson, even in the presence of a detailed grid, may not be convergent. Neither are quality assessors likely to adopt a single formula for unequivocally confirming a teacher to be either good or bad. Quality, like beauty, will remain in the eye of the beholder, who is informed by his or her own history, practice, readings, and theories. Further, it is possible that on an international scale, elements of teaching best practice consider culture, country, and possibly even discipline. From this standpoint, it will be interesting to describe and analyze behavioural indicators of good teaching in the Tunisian English teaching context.

Procedures

For the purposes of this research, I invited 8 of my students and 6 instructors of English in my department for taped interviews. All 8 students were 3rd-year English department students. Seven were female and 1 was male, and their ages ranged from 22 to 24. Five of the 6 teachers were at the rank of assistant professor, and 1 was a full professor. All teachers had doctorates, and their ages ranged from 35 to 55. Their teaching experience ranged between 7 and 30 years. Two were female and 4 were male.

I based my choice of the type of data collection technique on Leech (2002). Because there is abundant literature on teacher evaluation and teaching best practice, I had to exclude unstructured interviews, which would mostly be useful if I were conducting an exploratory study whose themes and contours I knew little about. Structured interviews with closed-ended questions would be useful if I wanted to systematically compare responses and come up with answers that would be easy to tabulate and quantify. Given that formal, administratively sanctioned teacher evaluations were not in practice countrywide or within the institution, I felt that semistructured interviews would produce responses that were varied enough to capture the spectrum of opinion that had not yet been sampled, and constrained enough to produce responses that could be clustered into an economical set of categories.

I divided the interview protocol into five main themes:

1. Who is a good teacher?

2. Who is a bad teacher?

3. What are student perceptions of good teaching as opposed to teacher perceptions of student perceptions of good teaching?

4. What role do grades play in student evaluation of teachers?

5. How do teachers and students view the formal introduction of teacher evaluation?

At the end of each interview, I gave each respondent the opportunity to add comments they felt were left out of the interview.

I informed respondents of the objectives of the interview, and requested and obtained their consent to audiotape the interviews and, where possible, to publish the results. I also assured them of the confidentiality and anonymity of their responses. I used an open-source software program called Audacity 1.2.4 to record the interviews (http://audacity.sourceforge.net/). The total length of the student interviews was 5 hours and 57 minutes (or 16,776 words), and the teacher interviews totalled 3 hours and 35 minutes (or 25,905 words).

For data analysis, I used a free, qualitative data analysis software application called Weft QDA (n.d.), Version 9.6. This is an easy-to-use, easy-to-learn text analysis application with the capability of organizing categories into a tree structure, adding category and document memos, text searching, highlighting coded text in document and category windows, and rearranging categories.

Results

As the literature review showed, there are different ways of categorizing teaching best practice. These form a continuum of indicators that are general and theoretical at one end and specific and practical at the other. When pursuing the type of qualitative research I conducted, it would be ideal to develop a model, a unifying principle, an umbrella notion, or a metaphor that captures the complexity of the issues being discussed. The metaphor that seemed to offer the most coverage was that of *teacher as manager*. Following Triki and Baklouti (2003), I understand management to be a large-scale, all-encompassing act that the teacher undertakes. Further, teacher versus student centeredness is but one element.

Although not all the respondents' interview comments fit under this metaphor, it aptly represented the topic of the interviews and the comments articulated. For example, one teacher made the following comment:

> I insist on the notion of management of impressions, in other words, controlling all sorts of things, such as your own appearance, your clothes, how you bear yourself, how serious you look, how friendly you are with your audience, or how formal you are, how close, how distant, and whether you give the impression of total control of the topic so that actually, you don't even look at your notes and give the impression of improvising, or, on the other hand, whether you stick too closely to your notes? Are you going to dictate, are you going to simply talk about things and summarize the main points; are you going to use data show, and so on. (Teacher 4)

In this teacher's view, preparation covers diverse aspects of teaching so that events are not seen to occur randomly but are made to unfold in a manner that is prepared, preplanned, and scheduled. Another respondent (Teacher 2) talked of the teacher "guiding the whole stage," as if in the theater, and said that success in teaching is contingent on the teacher's histrionic abilities. The following comments from Teacher 6 further support this guiding role:

These are very obvious points which can be ignored, but I think teaching has
a lot to do with management, management of time, management of sharing,
talking time, management of classroom design, management of how much
talking and writing in the classroom. (Teacher 6)

Thus, the management metaphor is extensively supported, but it will be interesting to detail what falls under this broad category. Analysis of the interviews revealed the following three acts of management:

1. Teachers manage their own image as subject matter experts.

2. Teachers manage the course content.

3. Teachers manage how this content is shared with the students.

As will emerge from the analysis of each category, these capacities are interrelated and interdependent, and they overlap on many dimensions.

TEACHERS MANAGE THEIR OWN IMAGE AS SUBJECT MATTER EXPERTS

This section looks into how teachers manage the side of them that has to do
with knowledge. A number of points are in order.

What meanings are assigned to knowledge? Students see teachers as loci of
knowledge when they have the expertise and specialization required and when
they have the information students need, ask for, and do not yet know. Teachers
assign wider definitions to knowledge. They refer to it as competence in the field.
Knowledge can be classified as enough knowledge or a lot of knowledge, being
up-to-date, resourceful, insightful, and encyclopaedic. Knowledge equates with
intellectual authority emanating from being widely read in the field. Following
from this, teachers are not judged knowledgeable when instead of addressing
a point head on or admitting that they do not know the answer they choose to
hedge and not speak to the point. One student shared this view in the following
comment:

This may even turn out to be a negative point in his teaching because when
just asking him a particular question about a particular theme or period,
this teacher deviates from the question and gives extra information which is
not needed at that time. By this, by providing extra information, that I don't
need, further information, he gives the impression that he is just showing off.
(Student 4)

When is a teacher not considered knowledgeable? Knowledge is not to be
equated with overloading students with information to give the false impression
of expertise.

A bad teacher, for instance, in terms of input is someone who overloads the students unnecessarily, focuses on content just because this person wants to display his or her own knowledge of a particular topic, and that results in the alienation of the students. (Teacher 1)

Beyond these shared meanings of knowledge, Finch et al. (1997) allude to a disturbing attitude whereby a certain cult develops around what appears as an inordinately advanced level of knowledge some teachers seem to have. In these cases, students who do not really understand what the teacher is saying are nonetheless fascinated by it, as Teacher 1 explained:

So, they [students] tell you so-and-so knows a lot. We don't know what he's talking about in class, but he knows a lot. My interpretation of it is that there is some kind of admiration: although this person is not helpful in class, but already he's someone who is knowledgeable. So they kind of rate the teachers according to *what they reflect they know* [italics added]. (Teacher 1)

What does it mean that a teacher is lacking in knowledge? Being perceived as one with a little or not enough knowledge is a dangerous thing for a teacher's image. As opposed to what happens with a knowledgeable teacher, a teacher who doesn't know enough is someone whose lecture doesn't produce a cumulative effect. Students feel this teacher does not have enough to give and does not know enough to explain, as one student commented:

Generally a bad teacher is a teacher who, when I come to his session, I go out the same as I go in, with nothing in my head, nothing new, nothing interesting. (Student 5)

A teacher and another student echoed this incremental view of knowledge as follows:

If the best thing is that they understand, the worst thing would be that they attend a lecture or attend a class and by the end of class, they feel that they haven't understand anything. . . . The most frustrating thing in class and the class you hate is the class at which end you feel that haven't gotten much. (Teacher 3)

Another teacher's area is poetry. We study poetry in 2nd year. [The teacher] can't explain very well. Not metaphor, nothing. You feel she is a secondary school teacher, a normal teacher. (Student 6)

Further, one understanding shared by many students is that inability to explain correlates with the teacher's inclination to dictate the course. A teacher who reads his or her course notes can be seen as one who doesn't understand what he is saying, as a student pointed out:

We notice that many teachers only dictate information, especially in Civilization. We notice that our teacher . . . she can't explain Civ [civilization] very well. She enters the auditorium; she takes a paper and begins to dictate, only. She can't explain. Nothing. Even the exam questions, we notice that they are only recitation questions. If someone is good at learning by heart, they can take a good mark. All questions are rote learning questions, not questions indicative of understanding. That explains the high degree of cheating in the faculty. (Student 6)

Because of the rote learning culture that students inherited and continued to work with, I noted that students had a hard time catching up with teachers as they dictated the course content. Students were trying to take verbatim notes of what the teacher was saying. More students shared their views about dictating course notes:

I don't also like teachers who bring along with them a pile of notes. You are a teacher. Come along and speak to us off the top of your head. Whenever this guy makes a mistake, I say, this is why he's bringing books [course notes] along. (Student 8)

Another student looked at dictating course notes differently, and took a utilitarian stance in favour of this kind of teaching. This student probably knew that teachers who dictate course notes usually write exam questions that refer to these notes:

I like [this teacher]. He explains very well. He simplifies things in any way. The ideal teacher is [this teacher]. The questions are to be learnt by heart in the exam. (Student 6)

What else is required beyond knowledge? There is no doubt that lack of knowledge disqualifies a teacher. More important, however, there is also an understanding expressed by Teacher 6 that "a bad teacher is not a person who doesn't know [enough] information," and Teacher 1 noted that "teaching is not just knowledge of certain topics." This is what I would summarize as the "Knowledge? Yes, but . . ." category. The *but* of it is that, as Student 4 noted, "Teaching is not simply a question of knowledge because we can all get knowledge even without a teacher. . . . I mean, the source of knowledge is not something impossible to have." What is required, beyond knowledge, is the ability to explain, expand, organize, and convey.

TEACHERS MANAGE THEIR COURSE CONTENT

This section concerns itself with what good teachers do with the course or the lesson, mostly during the preparation phase.

Good teachers primarily shoot for achieving understanding among students.

Understanding is a complex phenomenon, but teachers and students seemed to agree on the next six correlates of understanding.

Good teachers present simplified course materials. Students loathe contradictory behaviors displayed by some teachers who are in the habit of using difficult language while asking students to use easy language. Student 6 put it this way: "Teachers say, 'use easy language.' Why doesn't the teacher use easy language?" Simplicity goes beyond the use of simple, easy words. It encompasses an important content-organizing principle, which is that complex notions can be broken down into simpler, more easily understood representations and, starting with these representations, can pave the way for the more complex discussions. One of the students shared an example:

> I have a teacher in mind who is used to putting what he wants to say in simple words. He doesn't use vague words and ideas that cannot be easily understood by students. He knows how to communicate; he understands the way students think. He tries all the time to explain using simple words, sometimes everyday words and everyday concepts. He starts from concrete examples to refer to more complicated ideas. (Student 2)

Good teachers set objectives for the lesson. If the objective is a compound one, good teachers will be able to cut it down into mini-objectives that are easier to manage and achieve, as one teacher observed:

> In general, I think my teaching, is, let's say, target-oriented. In other words, I have an objective and I want to achieve it. I have learnt while working in our hard circumstances not to make too high expectations, in other words, have small objectives and reach them. (Teacher 1)

Good teachers organize their lessons. This characteristic is, by far, the most often cited feature of good teaching. Students and teachers valued organizing, planning, structuring, sequencing, outlining, and arranging ideas, and in this regard they showed high emotional involvement when relating stories of bad teachers they had:

> Pedagogically speaking, I believe he was a fiasco. Maybe he knows many things. I don't know, maybe he knows more things than we did at that time, but nothing was clear in his mind. He used to come and speak about anything. No pedagogy, no lecture, no titles, no subtitles. (Teacher 2)

> What he is saying is not interesting. Maybe he seems lost. I don't know. He doesn't know how to begin or how to move from step to another, waiting for something, I don't know. (Student 5)

Organizing material is a complex act that includes, among other practices, the systematic visual display of the lecture outline on the board. The outline is a way to classify and arrange ideas. Students like material to be presented in the form of classes and taxonomies, Teacher 2 argued. The presence of an outline can guard against improvisation and lack of transition; it is a way for students to see the complete picture.

Good teachers give a summary of their presentations. This tendency also comes with good planning. If students see the complete picture, in easy, outline form, then they will be more likely to take home a global understanding—at least the forest contours, maybe without the trees—and this is not insignificant.

Good teachers synthesize presented material. If summary refers to one presentation in capsule form, then synthesizing means that teachers consider the bulk of their presentations as separate strands and tie or knot them together to create a more global view of the whole course.

Good teachers link theory with practice. Many of the courses offered at the College of Arts and Humanities in Sfax have a theoretical component and a supervised, hands-on, practical component. Often, the theoretical class is assigned to more senior teachers, and junior teachers assist with the practical component. A minimum level of coordination must take place between the teachers. If coordination is lacking, then students are taken in diverging directions. As a result, they may have trouble grasping the relationship between the two components and understanding the relevance of the material, and this gap could lead to negative perceptions of the teachers involved.

TEACHERS MANAGE HOW COURSE CONTENT IS SHARED WITH STUDENTS

The previous section concerned how the teacher tends to process subject matter, mostly during the preparation phase. This section considers what good teachers do during the actual handshake with students. Classroom teaching is a social encounter, and learning is the goal. In the classroom, two dimensions—the pedagogical and the social—work together. In a teaching situation, it can be difficult to distinguish between the two because the players are the same. First, I will consider the human relations side—how the agents, mainly the teacher and the students, deal with each other at the human level. Second, I will consider the teaching dimension—how the actors deal with each other as people involved in a pedagogical process.

In terms of sociopedagogical best practices, the following elements emerged from the interviews.

Good teachers respect their students. Of all the behavior indicators relating to knowledge, planning, pedagogic skills, and social skills, the element of respect is first and foremost on Tunisian students' minds. When asked to reminisce about a teacher they disliked, students painted the image of someone who humiliated, ridiculed, insulted, embarrassed, blamed, threatened, or underestimated students; treated them as stupid and good for nothing; or spoke to them sarcastically. Students did not like someone who acted superior, dictatorial, harsh, stern, domineering, proud, snobbish, insincere, pitiless, military-like, police-like, or haughty. Some students expressed utter dislike for teachers who seemed to favor students on the basis of gender, social class, or place of birth. Their favorites were teachers who treated them as adults, acting in a manner that was understanding, trusting, tolerant, empathetic, caring, polite, loving, flexible, adaptable, inclusive, fair, balanced, helpful, and modest, as one student explained:

> He's very, erm, he's always shows off. Me and me! Once we didn't know the number of the room. He had on his timetable classroom 24. We were waiting for him [in another room]. He came very angry and he said he was the best teacher in the faculty and never ever students made him wait. (Student 7)

Good teachers love their subject and instil a love of their subject. Respondents used a variety of expressions to highlight this feature of good teaching: cheerful teachers who love their jobs, think of the course they teach as their cup of tea, and do not think of teaching as a burden. These teachers foster participation among students through fun, motivating, and interesting activities, leading eventually to the creation of a bond which associates love of the teacher with love of the subject and vice versa, as one student noted:

> [The role of a great teacher is] first and foremost to make them like the English language, as it was in my experience. I was fond of English because of my teacher. (Student 3)

> When I attend your lesson, I start hating civilization. (Student 3)

Good teachers do more than transmit knowledge. Interviewees viewed good teachers as sources of knowledge to students, and students as recipients of that knowledge. The transmission model in teaching was strongly present in the discourse of many interviewees. They talked of teachers *giving*, as an intransitive verb, getting the information to the students, transferring information, delivering the lecture, providing answers for students, conveying the information, and so on. An interesting question is who first implanted the dictation culture, the predisposition to listen for and record every word the teacher says? One teacher expressed his frustration with this attitude as follows:

> In a sense, a bad teacher . . . [is] someone who pretends to be the main source of knowledge. He keeps students in front of him, in the corridors, and he starts teaching some academic dogma; students keep receiving the message, take notes very, very faithfully, to return the notes by exam day, believing by doing so, they will pass. So, this kind of teaching produces a very lazy, between inverted commas, "stupid generation of students" who rely very, very much on the teacher. Academically, a bad teacher is someone who monopolizes knowledge, who transmits knowledge. (Teacher 6)

Naturally, teachers and students, and students themselves, do not always see eye to eye on this issue. For example, one respondent went to the extreme position of favoring a class where teachers monopolize the floor and keep student interventions to a minimum:

> A good teacher must be serious, and he can transmit the message to the students easily without letting them ask a lot of questions. (Student 7)

Luckily, teaching best practice is often seen to operate beyond the transmission model. The tutorial sessions in the college, which represent practical applications of the theoretical lectures, represent a phase of teaching in which students, working in pairs or in teams, will do the bulk of the work, under teacher supervision. Team-teaching, though not a common practice in the college, is mentioned as an enhancement of teaching in the sense of an individual enterprise. Helping students acquire skills and strategies is a significant addition to the transmission model. Pushing knowledge boundaries for students through the activation of prior knowledge and building on it to produce greater understanding represents a considerable advance in the direction of the partnership model in teaching.

Good teachers encourage authoring among students. Teaching with the sole task of reproducing knowledge represents a criterion for measuring whether teachers are using best practices.

> In many occasions, I feel guilty of not assisting my students get the message, or to fully understand the lesson, or to shift from the position of passive receiver to a position of a knowledge producer, of a data producer in the classroom. If I don't feel that my students, during the session, or at least, at the end of the session, shift from the position of receivers to producers of knowledge, then I consider myself as a failed teacher that day. (Teacher 6)

Reflection

Overall, this study shows areas of convergence and divergence among students and teachers regarding teaching best practice. Despite agreement on the feature of teacher as expert, neither the teachers nor the students consider it absolutely essential; knowledge is understood to be available all around, and it can be acquired. It has not emerged as being the make or break feature. In addition, teachers and students value preplanned, organized teaching, but also appreciate a measure of improvisation. Nor does organized content appear to be what is sorely lacking.

There appears to be a difference between students and teachers at the level, coverage, and detail of the course notes. Students like having substantial course notes at their disposal, and they do not seem for the most part to have broken loose from transmission as a favourite learning mode. Teachers, on the other hand, show great awareness, in principle, of the need to impart content and teach skills and strategies, and can even go as far as singing the praises of helping students become authors and generators of knowledge.

What most forcefully transpires from this Tunisian study is the need students feel for democratic teaching practices. Teachers urgently need to provide a large measure of negotiation and recognition of the student. To break the cycle of dependence on the teacher as a unique source of knowledge and pave the ground for graduating students who are capable of expression beyond mere reproduction of course notes, teachers must deal with the teaching act as a regular transaction conducted on the basis of human-to-human interaction.

Being thus sensitized to student and quality concerns, teachers should think of the teaching act beyond furnishing a class schedule and teaching slots. I am personally committed to designing a teacher evaluation sheet at my own level and asking students to exercise their natural right to evaluate my teaching; just as it is my right and duty to assess their work and progress. Also, in the hope of weakening the grip of the transmission model that still has many adherents, I have reworked the tutorial section of one of my main courses, sociolinguistics. It now includes more hands-on, practical work, which requires students to formulate answers rather than simply seek further clarification of my lecture notes. For sociolinguistics with graduate-level students, my goal this year is to do more project-based learning. Project work will give them a real chance to synthesize the material studied and experiment with it first-hand through creating, as a group, a product that is theirs.

Along with these changes to be effected in conjunction with the students, other concerns emerge, such as the need for sustained professional development and more reflective and action research, for my colleagues and myself. I anticipate that my professional development could target alternative ways of doing research, in order to double-check the validity of this particular study's findings. Other areas for further investigation include the transmission model in teaching and the worrying trend for cheating on exam among university-level students. Most important, and in view of the growing importance distance learning has acquired, new standards for teaching best practice in the new electronic or virtual medium have to be identified and publicized.

Ali H. Raddaoui teaches at the Faculty of Letters and Humanities,
University of Sfax, Tunisia.

The Effect of Group and Individual Peer Feedback on Student Writing in an EFL Gulf Context (*Saudi Arabia*)

Ali Shehadeh

Issue

Peer feedback involves students critiquing and providing feedback on one another's writing. As part of the process and postprocess approaches to second language (L2) writing pedagogies, peer feedback has gained increasing attention in the L2 writing research and instruction since the late 1980s (Berg, 1999; Matsuda, 2003; Rollinson, 2005). Indeed, it is well established now that peer feedback is beneficial in the L2 writing classroom as peers can provide useful feedback at various levels (e.g., Hedgcock & Lefkowitz, 1992; Hyland, 2000; Jacobs, Curtis, Braine, & Huang, 1998; Paulus, 1999; Rollinson, 2005). No wonder, therefore, that peer feedback is now commonplace in many L2 writing classes.

Rollinson (2005, pp. 24–25), as part of his review of the literature on peer feedback, summarizes the main advantages of peer feedback in the L2 writing classroom as follows: First, peer readers can provide valid and useful feedback. For instance, Caulk (1994) reported that 89% of the peer feedback provided by his intermediate-advanced level foreign language students was valid, and Rollinson (1998) reported that 80% of the peer feedback and comments provided by his college-level students was valid too. Second, writers do revise effectively on the basis of comments provided by peer readers. Mendonca and Johnson (1994) and Rollinson (1998) found that 53% and 65%, respectively, of writers' revisions incorporated peer comments. Third, peer feedback tends to be of a different *kind* from teacher comments. Caulk (1994) found that teacher feedback was rather general, whereas students' feedback was more specific. Fourth, becoming a critical reader of others' writing may make students more critical readers and revisers of their own writing. Fifth, peer feedback creates a sense of audience that writers seek, and they prefer more-or-less immediate feedback. At the same time, peer audiences are also potentially more sympathetic than the more distant and possibly more judgmental teacher audience. Sixth, peer feedback can encourage a collaborative dialogue in which two-way feedback is established and meaning is negotiated between the two parties. Seventh, peer feedback may encourage or motivate students to write because it operates on a more informal level than the typically one-way, formal teacher feedback. Finally, when students see the benefits of peer feedback, their positive attitudes toward writing are enhanced.

Background Literature

Previous studies on peer feedback in the L2 classroom have mainly investigated the impact of individual peer feedback on students' writing, mostly comparing it with other sources of feedback (teacher-, self-, or other-directed) using different settings, formations, and procedures (e.g., Caulk, 1994; Paulus, 1999; Tsui & Ng, 2000). The impact of group feedback as against the commonly used technique of individual feedback on students' writing, however, has not been specifically examined or explored.

Apart from three studies, most research that looked at group work in the L2 writing classroom did not investigate the impact of group feedback on students' writing. Such research examined issues relating to collaborative writing, group dynamics, various types of group formations, and how groups function in peer review tasks (e.g., Lockhart & Ng, 1995; Mangelsdorf & Schlumberger, 1992; Mendonca & Johnson, 1994; Nelson & Murphy, 1992; Storch, 2005; Villamil & de Guerrero, 1996). The three studies that explored the impact of group feedback on students' writing were conducted by Hedgcock and Lefkowitz (1992), Connor and Asenavage (1994), and Zhu (2001).

Hedgcock and Lefkowitz (1992) compared gains from teacher feedback with gains from small-group peer feedback. Their study involved 30 college-level learners of French whose first language was English. The participants were divided into two groups and each group was given two multidraft essay assignments. In the control group, the instructor alone supplied written feedback; in the experimental group, revision took place in small groups, with participants reading their own papers aloud to their group partners, who responded orally according to a written protocol. Analysis of the final versions of the two essays produced by the groups showed that essays produced by the experimental group received significantly higher component and overall scores than those produced by the control group.

Connor and Asenavage (1994) investigated the impact of peer responses on subsequent revisions, comparing comments from the teacher with self-evaluations and other sources. The revisions in essays from two groups of freshman English as a subsequent language students were evaluated over several drafts. As in Hedgcock and Lefkowitz's (1992) study, each student read his or her draft aloud, soliciting oral peer feedback from group partners. The revised drafts were analyzed to determine which revisions were made as a result of the teacher feedback, peer group feedback, or self-evaluation and other sources. The results showed that the students made many revisions but that few of these were the result of direct peer-group feedback (5% of total revisions). Of the total revisions, 35% were teacher-influenced and 60% were from self-evaluation or other sources.

Finally, Zhu (2001) examined interaction and feedback in peer response groups consisting of native speakers (NS) and nonnative speakers (NNS). He inspected participants' turn-taking behaviors, language functions performed during peer response, and written feedback on each other's writing. He found that the nonnative speakers as a group took fewer turns and produced fewer language functions during oral discussion of writing, particularly when they were performing the writer role. However, nonnative speakers were comparable to the native speakers with respect to the number of global comments provided in writing.

This review shows, first, that none of the three studies specifically investigated the relative impact of group feedback as compared to one-to-one peer feedback on students' writing in the L2 classroom. Second, two of the three studies yielded inconsistent and contradictory findings. Third, all three studies have collected data from situations that are rare in the L2 writing classroom. Specifically, Zhu's (2001) study involved NS and NNS participants, which is a rare situation in the L2 writing classroom and therefore of less interest for pedagogical practice. Similarly, group partners in the Hedgcock and Lefkowitz (1992) and Connor and Asenavage (1994) studies listened to their peer's writing read aloud to them, and responded to it orally, which is also rare in the L2 writing instruction classroom.

As stated, none of the previous studies investigated the impact on students' writing of *group feedback* (operationally defined as critiquing and providing feedback on a peer's writing in small groups) as opposed to the commonly employed technique of *individual feedback* (operationally defined as critiquing and providing feedback on a peer's writing individually). Research is needed that specifically examines the impact of group feedback against individual feedback on students' writing because we do not know yet whether and to what degree feedback provided by a group of students is different from that which is

---

provided by individual students in affecting or improving students' writing in the L2.

The interest in such research stems from both theoretical and pedagogical considerations. From a theoretical perspective, one can argue that, holding all other variables constant, group feedback is potentially more reliable and valid than individual feedback because it is logical to assume that in a collaborative and supportive peer-feedback setting, knowledge that is not available to a single reader may be available to a group of readers, who can collaborate with one another, share knowledge, pool their joint efforts, discuss different aspects of the writing, and supply the missing information (see also Hedgcock & Lefkowitz, 1992, p. 258, for a similar argument).

From a pedagogical perspective, investigating whether and to what degree group feedback can be a variable that influences writing in an L2 educational context is also important because it has a consequence for pedagogical practice in at least two ways. First, with the introduction of task-based approaches to language learning and teaching (see, e.g., Skehan, 1998; Willis, 1996), group work has become a common interaction type in many classroom contexts in the world. Indeed, the current view of language learning and teaching emphasizes task-based instruction in which collaborative group work is central to the language classroom (see, e.g., Edwards & Willis, 2005; Ellis, 2003; Skehan, 1998, 2003). There is, however, little empirical validation of task-based group work in the L2 writing classroom. For instance, in Storch's (2005) study of collaborative writing, she pointed out that "Although pair and group work are commonly used in language classrooms, very few studies have investigated the nature of such collaboration when students produce a jointly written text" (p. 153). This is especially true when it comes to group editing and feedback tasks. The findings of the current study might therefore be a step toward making principled decisions about the usefulness of group feedback in the L2 writing classroom, which would enable us, consequently, to make informed pedagogical adjustments by establishing a proper context for effective peer feedback to ensure effective writing pedagogy and instruction.

Second, the three studies that examined the impact of group feedback on students' writing collected data from situations that are rare in the L2 writing classroom. Unlike these studies, my study collected data from L2 students only, in a context in which students could read, edit, and provide written and oral feedback on a peer's writing, which is a more common situation in the world's classrooms.

Finally, from personal experience, observations of many language classrooms, and informal discussions with a number of L2 writing instructors who expressed similar concerns, my belief in the validity of these considerations was further consolidated. Involving a pretest and posttest design, this study aimed at extending research on peer feedback and set out to determine whether and to what degree L2 learners who were engaged in group feedback tasks showed more improved writing skills than those who carried out such peer feedback tasks individually.

Procedures

I conducted this study with my students at a large public Saudi university. The English program at the Department of Translation and European Languages at this university offered a variety of courses toward a bachelor's degree in English and translation, including reading, writing, listening, speaking and oral communication, grammar, vocabulary building and expansion, translation, and introduction to language and linguistics. The syllabus for the first semester included six courses (grammar, vocabulary building and expansion, listening, reading, speaking, and writing). The syllabus for the writing course investigated in this study, lower intermediate in level, included idea development, organizing skills, editing skills, critical thinking, and skill-based objectives. The assessment included two midterm exams and one final exam. Short, nongraded quizzes were administered periodically, generally every 2 weeks.

PARTICIPANTS

Thirty-six male English as a foreign language (EFL) learners participated in this study. They were 1st-year students in their first semester majoring in English at the university. They ranged in age from 18 to 21 years. They had been admitted to the English program based on their national university entrance examination scores. Prior to university, they had studied EFL in their middle and secondary schools for 6 years. The department considered them to be lower-intermediate learners. They reported infrequent use of English for communication outside class and limited exposure to English through mass media, movies, or the Internet. Their writing skills in English were very basic.

Based on insights from second language acquisition research, lower-intermediate level learners were specifically selected because feedback can be expected to be more effective when learners have achieved a reasonable level of language proficiency, whether written or spoken, than with beginning or more advanced learners (Carroll, 1995, 2001; Lyster & Ranta, 1997). Feedback can be less effective with beginning learners because their low proficiency affords them only a limited linguistic repertoire from which to draw in supplying or incorporating appropriate feedback. Similarly, feedback can also be less effective with advanced learners, partly because these learners might be less concerned about linguistic accuracy as long as their message meanings are conveyed, and partly because their language abilities might have prematurely leveled off, or *fossilized*, at a certain level (Carroll, 1995; Long, 1996).

The 36 students were divided randomly and equally into two groups. The first group of 18 students was considered the control group, and the second group of 18 students was considered the experimental group.

A writing scale originally developed by Jacobs, Zinkgraf, Wormuth, Hartfiel, and Hughey (1981) and adapted by Hedgcock and Lefkowitz (1992) was used to determine the difference in performance between the two groups on both the pretest and posttest with respect to L2 writing. The original scale defined five component areas of mechanics, vocabulary, grammar, organization, and content on a 0- to 100-point scale. The three component areas that related to language accuracy (mechanics, vocabulary, and grammar) were selected for the purpose of this study on a 0- to 50-point scale (see Appendix A).

PRETEST

Prior to instruction, the two groups were asked to write a paragraph 8–12 lines long on an assigned topic relevant to their context. The topic was, "Why do I want to study English at university?" with no other instructions or guidelines given. The paragraph assignments were collected from the two groups, randomized, and evaluated blindly by two trained raters, who used the 0- to 50-point scale. Interrater reliability was established at .93. The data were analyzed using a t test with the level of significance set at .05. As expected, there were no significant differences between the two groups for each component score or the total score because the two samples had been drawn from the same population. Table 1 shows the closeness of the totals and subscores between the two groups.

As can be seen from Table 1, the mean score for the mechanics component was 2.6 for the control group and 2.5 for the experimental group ($t = 0.47$, n.s.). The mean score for the vocabulary component was 8.5 for the control group and 8.3 for the experimental group ($t = 0.36$, n.s.). The mean score for the grammar component was 8.6 for the control group and 8.8 for the experimental group ($t = -0.43$, n.s.). As for the total score, the mean was 19.7 for the control group and 19.6 for the experimental group ($t = 0.04$, n.s.).

The instructional curriculum was identical for both groups. I taught both

Table 1. Mean Total and Component Scores on the Pretest

Portion of Test	Maximum Score	Control		Experimental		t Test
		M	SD	M	SD	
Total score	50	19.7	3.9	19.6	4.6	0.04, n.s.
Grammar	25	8.6	1.7	8.8	2.1	−0.43, n.s.
Vocabulary	20	8.5	1.7	8.3	1.9	0.36, n.s.
Mechanics	5	2.6	0.6	2.5	0.7	0.47, n.s.

groups and followed the syllabus, lesson plans, and material provided by the course textbook. Thus, all variables were held constant, including the participants' first language (Arabic), gender, age, language profiles, and instructional method. Furthermore, the format of the peer feedback sessions was also the same for both groups. In both groups, students (1) individually wrote a timed paragraph on an assigned topic, (2) exchanged paragraphs with their peers for editing and feedback, and (3) discussed their feedback and comments with the original writers.

I decided that both groups would use a combination of written and oral feedback because recent studies have found that explicit written feedback together with conference (oral) feedback significantly affects the level of accuracy in the students' writing (e.g., Bitchener, Young, & Cameron, 2005). Specifically, Bitchener et al. (2005) found that students who received direct written feedback and student-teacher conferencing after each piece written significantly outperformed those students who received direct written feedback only. The only variation between the two groups in the current study was the manner in which the editing feedback and conferencing conditions were carried out. Whereas in the control group the editing, provision of feedback, and conferencing with the original writers were carried out by students on a one-to-one basis, in the experimental group these tasks were carried out in groups of three students.

For each editing task, after all students had completed their paragraphs, control group students were divided into pairs, and experimental group students were divided into groups of three. The 18 students in the control group formed nine pairs. In each pair, students individually read, edited, provided feedback, and then discussed their feedback and comments on the paragraphs in their possession with their partners, the original writers of the paragraphs, on a one-to-one basis. Each student performed 12 such peer editing tasks throughout the course.

The 18 students in the experimental group, on the other hand, were divided into six small groups, each consisting of three students. Each group randomly teamed up with another group and exchanged paragraphs for editing and feedback. Each week one of the three compositions was selected by the instructor. Compositions were selected on a rotational basis so that the three students in each group were given equal opportunities for their compositions to be reviewed and evaluated. Students in each group jointly read, edited, and provided feedback on the paragraph in their possession. After that, the two groups took turns discussing their feedback and comments on the paragraph with the original writer from the partner group on a three-to-one basis. Hence, the editing feedback and conferencing conditions in the group format were decidedly different from those in the dyadic format.

Finally, given that training students for peer editing and feedback tasks increases their engagement and interaction and results in better quality peer feedback and peer talk (e.g., Berg, 1999; Stanley, 1992; Zhu, 1995), all students participating in this study were given a training session demonstrating the procedure for their respective tasks. Also, all students were given a complete set of written instructions (see Appendix B) and an oral explanation of the procedure.

As stated, students in both conditions performed 12 peer editing tasks throughout the course. The study was carried out during the first semester of the academic year 2004–2005 over a 14-week period, during which time both groups completed the 12 chapters that constituted the prescribed course material.

Results

In week 14, after all instruction had been completed, the two groups were asked to write a paragraph (as a posttest) 8–12 lines long on an assigned topic relevant to their context. The topic this time was "What did I benefit from learning English at college this semester?" with no other instructions or guidelines given. The paragraph assignments were collected from the two groups, randomized, and evaluated blindly by the same two trained raters, using the same scale as the pretest. Interrater reliability was established at .91. The data were analyzed also using a t test with the level of significance set at .05. Differences in performance between the two groups on the posttest are displayed in Table 2.

The results show that the experimental group significantly outperformed the control group in the three areas examined (mechanics, vocabulary, and grammar) as well as on the total score. As can be seen from Table 2, the mean score for the mechanics component was 4 for the control group and 4.5 for the experimental group ($t = -2.30$, $p < .05$). The mean score for the vocabulary component was 12.6 for the control group and 16.3 for the experimental group ($t = -8.68$, $p < .01$). The mean score for the grammar component was 12.8 for the control group and 19.5 for the experimental group ($t = -10.97$, $p < .01$).

Table 2. Mean Total and Component Scores on the Posttest

Portion of Test	Maximum Score	Control		Experimental		t Test
		M	SD	M	SD	
Total score	50	29.4	2.5	40.3	3.3	− 10.84**
Grammar	25	12.8	1.6	19.5	2.0	− 10.97**
Vocabulary	20	12.6	0.9	16.3	1.5	− 8.68**
Mechanics	5	4	0.6	4.5	0.5	− 2.30*

*$p < .05$; **$p < .01$

For the total score, the mean was 29.4 for the control group and 40.3 for the experimental group ($t = -10.84$, $p < .01$).[1]

In order to obtain a more accurate sense of how much improvement was made in the experimental classroom based on group feedback alone, I decided to further examine the data for changes that took place between the pretests and posttests in both conditions using paired t tests. As displayed in Table 3, although both groups exhibited significant improvement in students' writing between the pretests and posttests, the magnitude of improvement in the group format was notably higher than that in the individual format on the total score and the three component scores.

Indeed, we notice from data analysis that the performance of both groups on the pretest ranked 1, *poor*, on the scale on all three components. On the post-test, students in the control group progressed to Rank 2 on the scale, *fair*, on the components of vocabulary and grammar, and to Rank 3, *good*, on the component of mechanics only. A possible explanation for this within-group difference is that compared to the vocabulary and grammar of a language the mechanics of writing are more straightforward. Mechanics represents a relatively limited range of rules and conventions which can be more easily dealt with and mastered. Students in the experimental group, on the other hand, progressed to Rank 3, *good*, on all three components examined.

First of all, this investigation has shown that both feedback conditions, especially the group condition, exhibited markedly significant improvement in

Table 3. Mean Differences Between Pretest and Posttest

Portion of Test	Pretest		Posttest		t Test
	M	SD	M	SD	
Control Group					
Total score	19.7	3.9	29.5	2.5	−17.73*
Grammar	8.6	1.7	12.8	1.6	−11.52*
Vocabulary	8.5	1.7	12.6	0.9	−12.76*
Mechanics	2.6	0.6	4	0.6	−11.99*
Experimental Group					
Total score	19.6	4.6	40.4	3.3	−22.94*
Grammar	8.8	2.1	19.5	2.0	−19.89*
Vocabulary	8.3	1.9	16.3	1.5	−21.02*
Mechanics	2.5	0.7	4.5	0.5	−14.28*

*$p < .01$, two-tailed.

the students' writing between the pretests and posttests. This result provides additional support for the well-established finding that peer feedback is useful and beneficial, and that students do revise effectively on the basis of comments provided by peer readers (e.g., Caulk, 1994; Mendonca & Johnson, 1994; Rollinson, 1998). A possible reason for students' significant improvement in both conditions is that feedback, both written and oral, is more effective with lower- to middle-intermediate learners (as was the case with the present participants) than with beginner or more advanced learners (Carroll, 1995, 2001; Lyster & Ranta, 1997). It is also possible to argue that this result is in part due to the fact that only those components that relate to language accuracy (mechanics, vocabulary, and grammar) were examined in this study where progress is comparatively less demanding and more readily observable than is the case with other areas such as organization, content, communicative quality, argumentation, and language appropriacy.

The most salient result of the study, however, is that group feedback significantly improved accuracy in students' writing in the L2 in the areas of mechanics, vocabulary, and grammar, compared to individual peer feedback (Table 2). This finding provides support for past research on group feedback in the L2 writing classroom, in particular for Hedgcock and Lefkowitz (1992). They found that essays produced by the experimental group, where revision was supplied orally in small groups, received significantly higher component and overall scores than those produced by the control group, where the instructor alone supplied written feedback.

On the other hand, the findings obtained here and those obtained by Hedgcock and Lefkowitz (1992) were not consistent with Connor and Asenavage (1994), who found that only 5% of total revisions made were a result of peer group feedback. Connor and Asenavage acknowledged, however, that the effect of student peer feedback in their study was unexpectedly low, but they provided no account for this result. Indeed, Connor and Asenavage's result is surprising because several studies have shown that (a) most peer feedback (over two-thirds) is valid and useful (see, e.g., Caulk, 1994; Rollinson, 1998) and (b) students do revise effectively on the basis of comments provided by peer readers. As stated earlier (see Issue section), Mendonca and Johnson (1994) and Rollinson (1998), for instance, found that 53% and 65%, respectively, of the revisions made were incorporations of peer feedback and comments.

How can we account for the most salient finding of the current study, namely, that group feedback has a distinct advantage over individual feedback in improving accuracy in students' writing in the L2? It is possible to account for this finding in light of the two central components of the process and post-process approaches to writing and writing pedagogies, namely, intervention and awareness. To illustrate, intervention allows teacher and peer collaboration in the form of feedback during the writing process, whereby teacher and peers can read and respond to the L2 learner writing as it develops into the final product (Paulus, 1999). At the same time, intervention and collaboration help raise learners' awareness of the strategies and ways of generating and developing ideas, editing, revising, and improving their own writing, and this awareness is another important element in the process and postprocess approaches to writing pedagogies (Susser, 1994). Raising learners' awareness, in turn, helps learners notice their errors and weaknesses in the L2, and this has a consequence for L2 learning because, as Schmidt (1990) argued, "those who notice most learn most, and it may be that those who notice most are those who pay attention most" (p. 144). Similarly, Nelson and Murphy (1993) argued that paying attention to peers' feedback is important in order to make it effective and useful, especially in the areas of grammar and lexis.

It is possible to argue therefore that the reason group feedback was more successful than one-to-one peer feedback in improving language accuracy in students' writing in the L2 was because it constituted a better context for raising learners' awareness and enabling them to pay attention and notice their errors, weaknesses, and strengths in their writing than a context in which only individual peer feedback was available. This view is supported by Hedgcock and Lefkowitz's (1992) earlier conclusion that collaborative group feedback makes learners better *aware* of the structure of their own writing and an ability to self-correct errors.

One can also argue that the advantage of group feedback is partly due to the reliability of the feedback provided in the group format and students' receptiveness to peer feedback in this format. Keeping all other variables constant, it is possible to argue that collaboration in editing and providing feedback on a peer's writing is likely to produce more reliable feedback in the eye of the writer because it affords the editing group the opportunity to produce more comprehensive and trustworthy feedback than a setting where only one peer's feedback is available. It follows that students are likely to be more receptive to feedback from a supportive and collaborative group of students than from a single student.

The findings of this study suggest that group feedback can provide students with a valuable tool to improve their accuracy in the L2. From a pedagogical perspective, this is an important finding because it enables us to make principled decisions about the usefulness of group feedback in the L2 writing classroom and, consequently, make informed pedagogical adjustments by establishing a proper context for effective peer feedback to ensure effective writing pedagogy and instruction. Group feedback should therefore be encouraged as a favored and standard teaching and learning strategy in the L2 writing classroom.

Before looking at how group feedback can be encouraged in the L2 writing classroom, however, teachers should consider some of the practical advantages of group feedback. This study identified four advantages. First, unlike individual feedback, group feedback enables students to pool their joint efforts and discuss different aspects of the writing, thereby producing more comprehensive feedback. Second, group feedback boosts students' confidence in the validity and reliability of their feedback because it is a result of a joint—not a single student's—effort. Third, knowing that the feedback supplied is a result of a joint effort from a supportive group, the writer's receptiveness of this feedback is likely to be heightened. Finally, by seeing the benefits of group feedback, students' attitudes toward collaborative group work, including group feedback, are likely to be enhanced.

How can group peer feedback be used and encouraged in the L2 writing classroom? One way of encouraging group feedback in the writing classroom would be to have some especially outstanding groups discuss their feedback publicly and present it to the whole class so that other students and groups could benefit from the group's feedback, comments, and experiences. Another way is by getting some students who have incorporated a substantial amount of group feedback in their subsequent revisions to demonstrate to the class or to other groups how group feedback enabled them to produce higher quality compositions. And a third way is by getting the instructor to explain to the class the benefits of group feedback, demonstrating with real examples the main benefits and characteristics of successful group peer feedback tasks.

Reflection

On reflection, two important implications might be derived from the findings of this study: (1) Group work in the EFL classroom must be considered an important tool not just for the skill of speaking (e.g., Edwards & Willis, 2005; McDonough, 2004; Shehadeh, 2004), but also for the skill of writing. As with the skill of speaking, group work in the writing classroom emphasizes the social nature of language, learning, and knowledge making. (2) Group peer feedback should be encouraged in the classroom because it can significantly improve students' ability in L2 writing. This finding is especially important in the EFL Gulf context because it encourages student cooperation where pair or group work, especially concerning the skill of writing, is hardly employed by instructors or favored by students.

My belief in the significance of the findings and implications of this study was enhanced by follow-up informal conversations with several students in the experimental group who used group peer feedback. These students reported that they found the activity very useful, rewarding, less face-threatening, and interesting. I have therefore decided to incorporate group peer feedback as a standard classroom learning and teaching activity in my future writing classes. Indeed, by the time I submitted the final version of this chapter, I and other practitioners had further tested the activity in several writing class situations, and we all reported similar observations and found the results encouraging.

Ali Shehadeh teaches at United Arab Emirates University, Al Ain, UAE.

Note

1. It is worth noting that although the level of significance adopted for this study was .05, results of 3 of the 4 comparisons performed were significant at the level of .01 in favor of the experimental group, which means that we have highly significant results here.

Appendix A: Paragraph Rating Scale for EFL Compositions

SCORE CRITERIA

Grammar

22–25   *Excellent*: accurate use of grammatical structures; very few errors in agreement, number, tense, word order, articles, pronouns, prepositions, etc.

18–21   *Good*: simple constructions used effectively; some problems in use of complex constructions; some errors in agreement, number, tense, word order, articles, pronouns, prepositions, etc.

11–17   *Fair*: significant defects in use of complex constructions; frequent errors in agreement, number, tense, negation, word order, articles, pronouns, prepositions, etc.

5–10   *Poor*: no mastery of simple sentence construction; text dominated by errors.

Vocabulary

18–20   *Excellent*: accurate word or idiom choice; mastery of word forms.

14–17   *Good*: adequate range; some errors of word or idiom choice.

10–13   *Fair*: frequent word or idiom errors; inappropriate choice or usage.

7–9   *Poor*: little knowledge of target language vocabulary.

Mechanics

5 *Excellent*: masters conventions of spelling, punctuation, capitalization, paragraph indentation, etc.

4 *Good*: occasional errors in spelling, punctuation, capitalization, paragraph indentation, etc.

3 *Fair*: frequent spelling, punctuation, capitalization, and paragraphing errors.

2 *Poor*: no mastery of conventions due to frequency of mechanical errors.

Adapted from Hedgcock and Lefkowitz (1992, pp. 275–276).

Appendix B: Student Instructions

Instructions in the One-to-One Peer Editing Condition

1. Write a paragraph 8–12 lines long on . . . (the topic to be specified every week by the instructor as per the syllabus).

2. Exchange your paragraph with a classmate for editing and feedback.

3. Read and edit your partner's paragraph, making all necessary corrections and changes.

4. After you have done all that, discuss your comments, corrections, or any other clarifications you may have with your partner, the writer of the paragraph in your possession.

Instructions in the Group Peer Editing Condition

1. Write a paragraph 8–12 lines long on . . . (the topic to be specified every week by the instructor as per the syllabus).

2. Sit with your group partners.

3. Meet with another group.

4. Exchange your paragraphs with your partner group for editing and feedback.

5. Jointly read, edit, and provide all necessary changes and corrections to the paragraph selected by the instructor.

6. After you have done all that, discuss your comments, corrections, or any other clarifications you may have with the writer of the paragraph in your possession.

CHAPTER 12

Negotiating With Multiple Repeaters (*United Arab Emirates*)

Salah Troudi

Issue

This study was conducted within a university English language program which required students to move through three English as a foreign language (EFL) proficiency levels before moving on to an English for specific purposes (ESP) course. Some students had difficulty passing the exams at each level and therefore had to repeat the same level until they passed. This research project looks into ways of helping multiple repeaters improve their English learning to pass final exams by better understanding their educational and linguistic needs. It also seeks to challenge some of the assumptions and labels used to describe this group of students.

THE CONTEXT

Following local tradition, the university where this study was conducted had separate campuses for male and female students. This study involved female students in EFL classes. Students joining the university were required to register in a basic education program, studying Arabic, mathematics, English, and computer skills. At the time of this study in the English language program, students were placed in three proficiency levels for a one-semester course at each level: false beginner, low intermediate, and intermediate. These were officially called Level 1, 2, and 3. The courses prepared students in the four language skills—

listening, speaking, reading, and writing—with an emphasis on reading and writing. When they had successfully completed the three levels, which means passing midterm and final examinations, students would take an ESP course, according to their academic majors (Guefrachi & Troudi, 2000). Advanced-level ESP courses had become necessary because university faculties in medicine, engineering, science, and agriculture used English as the medium of instruction.

Within the English program, students who failed to move to the next level were allowed to repeat each level up to three times. This policy reflected a recent change; students previously were allowed to repeat any level as many times as needed to matriculate to the next level. The old situation brought to existence the issue or phenomenon of multiple repeaters. These were students who, for various academic and nonacademic reasons, failed to pass from Level 1 to Level 2 or Level 3 after just one semester. They needed to repeat each level at least twice to be able to pass the final examinations. Teachers tried their best to help multiple repeaters but in many cases found it difficult to achieve better results. Some teachers avoided teaching multiple repeaters and preferred more proficient students. Administrators also struggled to cope with the needs of multiple repeaters, and the students themselves had low morale and very low motivation.

MY EXPERIENCE WITH MULTIPLE REPEATERS

I must admit that when I found out that my Level 2 EFL class was a mixture of repeaters and multiple repeaters I was not thrilled, to say the least. The year before I had taught a similar class, and it was an experience in frustration and even exasperation at times. It was very hard to work with students who simply refused to study. I managed to help most of them pass their final exams, but I was not sure of their language learning progress. The common image of a multiple repeater in the English program is an unmotivated learner with low English proficiency and tardiness and absenteeism problems. I need to add here that the university has a 15% policy on absenteeism. If a student misses 15% of class hours, then she is not allowed to sit for exams, which means automatic failure and therefore repetition of one level.

Even though I thought of action research during my first class of multiple repeaters, I found it impossible to focus on anything other than responding to my students' immediate needs of coping with the syllabus and being ready for the exams. I was not entirely satisfied with my approach to their needs and problems, and I knew I could have done much better than looking for quick remedies. I did not accept the common assumption that multiple repeaters are unmotivated learners and that it is their lack of academic effort that is at the root of their very low achievement. The action research I conducted was partly to find a more efficient way to help my students and partly to challenge accepted labelling and definitions of multiple repeaters.

Background Literature

To the best of my knowledge, there is an alarming paucity of action research studies conducted in the United Arab Emirates and reported in the English language teaching (ELT) literature. This scarcity, of course, does not automatically imply that ELT professionals in the area do not engage in this form of research, but the written dissemination is missing. Teacher research in general is better represented in recent years, and an increasing number of practising teachers are writing about their studies in local publications. However, I could find nothing written about the issue of multiple repeaters and failing students.

There are different definitions and conceptions of action research, reflecting various understandings of what it entails and what it should strive for. In the past three decades, the ELT and applied linguistics literature have presented action research as one strategy or option for teachers pursuing professional development (Bailey, Curtis, & Nunan, 2001; Burns, 1999; Nunan, 1990, 1993, 1994; Wallace, 1998). What the ELT and teachers of English to speakers of other languages disciplines did was modify or tone down the critical dimension of action research to suit the fundamental philosophy of learners' unquestioned need to learn English all over the globe and teachers' need to find out the most effective approaches and techniques to support this learning. With this neutral and liberal view of ELT, the focus of action research has been on classroom-based issues. Richards and Lockhart (1994) define action research as "teacher initiated classroom investigation which seeks to increase the teacher's understanding of classroom teaching and learning and to bring about change in classroom practice" (p. 12). It is also seen as a disciplined way to reflect on practice with a focus on finding practical solutions to daily classroom pedagogical problems and challenges. It should be "systematic and entails gathering evidence on which to base rigorous reflection" (Mingucci, 1999, p. 16).

Procedures

With my past experience in teaching multiple repeaters, I started the class with some background knowledge of the nature of my students' academic problems and challenges. This knowledge, however, did not make me form a final judgment about what my students needed. My aims for the project were the following:

- To understand why my students were multiple repeaters

- To find out what teaching style and learning activities my students preferred

- To design a remedial plan to improve students' overall language proficiency as measured by the university Level 2 exams

I started the project with the firm belief that students' input and suggestions were essential to any intervention. In my previous experience with multiple repeaters I did not involve my students in the interpretation of the syllabus into daily teaching activities. This lack of involvement, I think, was one of the reasons that they showed little interest and made little effort.

For this project I used four data collection tools: classroom observation; group interview; individual, semistructured interview; and open-ended written questionnaire.

CLASSROOM OBSERVATION

To obtain a complete picture about the nature of the students' academic problems, I decided to observe my group for seven sessions and take notes of major interactional events. Burns (1999) stated, "Observation is a mainstay of action research. It enables teachers to document and reflect systematically upon classroom interaction and events, as they actually occur rather than as we think they occur" (p. 80). During observations, I focused on students' behaviour, attendance, readiness to participate in classroom talk and activities, time needed to start working on a task, and the overall atmosphere of the class. I had to juggle two roles, the practitioner and the researcher, and it was not easy to keep track of what was happening while focusing on providing help to students. Therefore, I resorted to taking more detailed notes at the end of every session. I need to add here that I also collected written samples of language problems my students had. These were mainly in the form of grammatical or functional errors.

GROUP INTERVIEW

The group interview was more like a group chat than a structured or even a semistructured interview. With 15 minutes left at the end of the fourth class session, I asked the students about their problems in English and why they were multiple repeaters. There was some hesitation at the beginning and reluctance to speak, but then one student asked if she could reply in Arabic. She was, of course, allowed to, and therefore many more were encouraged to take part in the conversation. I had to allocate turns, because many tended to speak at the same time. What the students said in this session convinced me that I needed to allocate more than just a 15-minute chat to listen to my students' stories and experiences with English. A lot was said in the conversation as the students talked about their frustration with English, but I felt they were reluctant to talk in front of their classmates about specific language problems and reasons for failing past courses. I then asked for their permission to interview them for 15 minutes after class. I was pleasantly surprised when they all agreed, and some of them even seemed pleased with the idea of talking to their teacher about their own learning problems.

INDIVIDUAL INTERVIEWS

These semistructured interviews were based on the results of classroom observation and the group interview. Every student was assured at the beginning of her interview that the purpose of the questions was to help me understand her difficulties with English and to help her cope better with her class work. I asked the students for their permission to take notes. I did not record the interviews because I was worried the students would become inhibited and I would also have needed the approval of the administration. This would have slowed me down, and I did not have much time. The course was only for 14 weeks. Data collection and analysis had to be done in a short time so that intervention could be planned in a timely manner. I took notes while the students spoke. All interviews were conducted in Arabic because it would have been impossible for my students to express themselves in English. I asked every question in English and then translated it into Arabic to make sure my interviewees understood the question. The interview was structured around three main questions:

- Why do you think you are a multiple repeater?

- What do you find difficult in English?

- How do you want me to teach you?

In addition to these three major questions, I also asked about their school experience, how they were taught English, and what their view of a good English teacher was. I felt that this last question would give me a clearer idea about how they wanted me to teach them.

OPEN-ENDED QUESTIONNAIRE

To collect the maximum amount of data about students' problems and difficulties in learning English, I decided to ask them to write in Arabic about these problems and also possible solutions to them. There were two main questions written in English and translated into Arabic to avoid any possible misunderstanding:

- What do you find difficult in learning English? Please be precise and give examples.

- What do you think you need to be better at English?

The students replied to these questions at home and had plenty of time to reflect on their language and learning problems. Some of them produced long, detailed, and well-articulated answers with clear suggestions about what needed to be done. The questions were all written in Arabic, and 17 students replied.

ANALYSING DATA

I did not wait until the last interview to look at the data. Being very interested in the students' views, I conducted ongoing data analysis by reading my notes after every interview and organizing information under the three main research questions. I managed to interview 15 students out of a total of 18, and I felt comfortable that the data I collected were representative of the whole group. I looked for patterns and emergent holistic themes in the students' responses (Holliday, 2002; Radnor, 2001). Seven main categories emerged, which also helped me make sense of my observation notes. Reading the interview notes and the written responses to the open-ended questionnaire clarified why some students were not eager to participate in activities and why others arrived late to class with no books or notebooks, while disturbing their classmates and interrupting the lessons. This was done with no apologies to me or to their classmates and apparently not much thought about the gravity of what they did. The emergent themes helped me think of my action and plan my intervention in an attempt to remedy the situation at hand. The following section discusses the seven themes that emerged from the data.

Results

SEVEN THEMES

English at school was not good. There was almost a total consensus that learning English at school was not a satisfactory or a happy experience. Students studied English for almost 4 hours per week for 9 years. The students were not happy with their teachers because, to quote one student, "they were not good and did not explain well." According to my students, there was a lot of repetition in the lessons and even throughout the years. They did grammar over and over again, studying the same rules, and there was very little speaking in class. Many teachers explained the whole lesson in Arabic because that was what the students wanted. Some students complained to the school director if the teacher would not use Arabic in her English class. One student mentioned that they "did not study how to write and for the final exam the teacher gave them a number of ready essays to learn by heart because the exam was about one of those essays." Given this situation, it is hardly surprising that many students found writing to be the most challenging skill. Another student stated that her teachers taught her to write, but it was different from what they were expected to do at the university. Students had a textbook for every year and some of them said that they were expected to learn some texts and language rules by heart.

English is difficult, or I hate English. These statements were repeated in almost every interview. Students talked about their inability to understand reading passages or to write an essay. They have ideas in Arabic but cannot put them down in English. One student said, "Sometimes I don't attend my English class because I feel it is too difficult for me and I don't understand." Students can easily feel trapped in a frustrating situation in which inability to understand the teacher and follow a lesson leads to further inability to do homework. As the course progresses through the semester, students feel worse, and some of them stop attending. The university provides additional academic help in the form of tutorials to weak students, but not all multiple repeaters make use of this assistance. It was clear to me that "I hate English" was an expression of frustration and even despair. Some of my students' confidence was very low, and some dealt with their language problems by ignoring them and assuming that they would eventually pass from one level to another after repeating each class a number of times.

I don't need English. This theme is related to the previous one. Some students expressed their frustration with the university policy requiring all students to take English. Almost all my students mentioned that they did not need English because they were going to study their subjects of speciality in Arabic, such as Arabic language and literature, history, or theology. They felt that they should be exempted from this requirement. I must say that in the case of multiple repeaters, I understood this attitude. I suggested that the administration introduce a different evaluation system for repeating students which would not require them to take the exams other students take and would allow alternative assessments on their general efforts and progress through project work. This suggestion was not considered because the university wanted conformity in evaluation.

Teachers fail us. This was the immediate response of many students to the first major question in the interview. Students thought that it was their class teachers who were responsible for failing them. When I explained that their teachers did not mark their midterm or final exams, some students insisted that the teachers should have helped them better by providing better explanations of the lesson and better exam revisions. I think that putting the blame on the teacher and not accepting responsibility for one's own failure is an expected strategy in such a situation. They did not accept the reality that they played a big role in their failure to pass their exams. For my students, passing the final exam was not within their control. I interpreted this attitude as a way of saving face and avoiding embarrassment. Talking about attribution in foreign language learning, Williams and Burden (1997) stated, "most people tend towards externalising reasons for failure whilst internalising reasons for success" (p. 106). Some students, however, mentioned that it was not the teacher's fault. "I don't study enough and I don't always do homework," remarked one student.

Boring classes. Another common complaint was about the extent to which

English classes were boring. The textbook was not interesting to the students. There was a general understanding among teachers that the content of the textbook used at that time did not relate to the students or challenge them intellectually. The themes were targeting students from Western cultures. Some students talked about using videos in class and watching movies as an alternative to using the textbook.

Patient and flexible teacher. Students were very clear about how they wanted their teacher to be. The remark "I want my teacher to be patient and nice" was put forth by more than one respondent. Students also wanted their teacher to follow their pace and to slow down when explaining grammatical points and to repeat the explanation whenever necessary. Another salient point raised by the students was the absence and tardiness policy. They wanted the teacher to ignore the university policy and not to mark them absent when they missed class. A teacher who ignores this policy was seen as a nice and friendly teacher and helpful to students. I need to add here that this perception of the teacher is not exclusive to multiple repeaters. Overall, students do not like the 15% absence policy and therefore prefer teachers who are ready to not mark them absent. Absenteeism and adherence to the policy were the cause of many conflicts and misunderstandings between teachers and students. Teachers follow the policy to make sure the university regulations are respected, but in the eyes of their students, they are being unfriendly and unhelpful.

Use Arabic to help us. This is a suggestion made repeatedly by all respondents. The students wanted their teacher, if he or she spoke Arabic, to explain some grammatical points in Arabic and translate some instructions. "Sometimes I don't know what to do because I don't understand the question," remarked one student. This is an ongoing issue in language teaching. For teachers who speak the same first language as their students, the first language can be a very helpful tool in teaching the target language. A quick translation of a word or an expression can sometimes save the teacher time and save the students frustration and even anxiety. Aware of this point, some of my Western colleagues resorted to using lists of vocabulary items translated into Arabic. The lists were given to students for reference and individual work. In fact, the insistence on the use of the target language only in EFL has long been challenged as an effective approach (Auerbach, 1993; Canagarajah, 1999; Phillipson, 1992).

HYPOTHESISING AND INTERVENING

Once I analysed the data, the next step was to think of a strategy for intervention. One major conclusion I made after listening to my students and observing them for a number of sessions was that I needed to interpret the syllabus and deliver it in view of their needs and the suggestions they made. I needed to make sure that during my teaching session I did not get too involved in covering the objectives in my lesson plans whilst forgetting to slow down and focus on my students' needs and difficulties. The intervention I planned was therefore negotiated with the students. I felt that by negotiating several points of the syllabus with the students, they would feel at the centre of teaching and in some control of what they were doing in class. Breen and Littlejohn (2000) stated that procedural negotiation is a way for teacher and students to share decision making in a process syllabus. Therefore, I embarked on a process of negotiation and shared decision making with my students. This negotiation started as soon as I finished collecting data and lasted until the end of the semester. I solicited their opinion about decisions on content, classroom rules and etiquette, teaching methodology, and extra help. During the course, I observed my own teaching while keeping in mind the planned intervention and students' reactions to it.

Content

I explained to students that we did not have a choice about the content of the textbook or the midterm and final exams and that the criteria for the exams are set by the testing committee in the department. I also added that, like them, I did not like some of these criteria and some chapters in the textbook, but we could have our own texts and materials in addition to the textbook. I asked students to write down four of their favourite topics that they wanted to read, write, or talk about in class. This activity was successful, and some students listed more than four topics. I used these lists throughout the semester to select extra reading materials, topics of conversation, or content for warm-up activities.

Individual students recognised the topics they chose, and some would enthusiastically announce to their classmates if the topic was one they had suggested at the beginning of the semester. The topics varied, and some were about local issues such as employment in the UAE, marriage, and family life. Local English newspapers were used when selecting supplementary reading passages. These were challenging, but with prereading activities to familiarize students with the vocabulary in the passages they could concentrate on the tasks and did not show signs of irritation and boredom. I believe that my students felt connected to the issues in those articles and passages, and they even asked me questions and wanted to know my opinion about the issue under discussion. This strategy might seem like common sense in teaching EFL, but many textbooks are organized around a set of generic and safe topics, such as education or the environment, which fail to attract learners' attention or challenge them intellectually. In this context, the teacher needs to be very sensitive to students' reactions to the passages in the core textbook and try to supplement them whenever possible. With the use of the supplementary texts, I noticed an increased interest in reading throughout the course. Some of these texts were used as homework tasks, and most students did their work, which was a great departure from my previous experience with multiple repeaters.

Classroom Rules and Etiquette

Students were aware that the 15% absenteeism rule was a university policy rather than a scheme that teachers developed. We openly talked about the effect of missing classes on students' grades and performance in exams. We agreed that if a student was ready to miss 15% of classes, which translates to 32 class hours, it meant that she was not interested in the course and therefore did not really care about passing the exams. We also agreed that students should not miss more than 5% of the course if they really wanted to improve their English and move on to Level 3. This was an internal decision that students adopted wholeheartedly.

In negotiating classroom rules with my students, I emphasized that my aim was to help them and that it was important to respect each other by respecting the rules we agreed on. The students wanted me to be flexible regarding tardiness, and I accepted a 10-minute late arrival rather than the 5-minute university policy. We also agreed that when late, a student should come in to class quietly without disturbing her colleagues. We talked about the importance of bringing textbooks, dictionaries, and notebooks to class and agreed that drinks and food were not allowed except during break time. I felt that negotiating classroom rules with my students allowed me to learn more about their attitudes toward learning and their eagerness to express themselves.

Teaching Methodology

The students did not want a boring class and wanted a patient, friendly, and enthusiastic teacher. They also wanted me to use Arabic to explain certain grammatical points or the meaning of some words.

In class, concentration was often short, so I resorted to short activities and to dividing up one task into mini-tasks. One of the major problems was their language proficiency. The content of the Level 2 syllabus was simply too high and too difficult for the majority of these students. To check their language abilities, early in the semester I administered a Level 1 grammar and writing test also used as a revision exercise, which most of them failed. With this realization, I decided to start from the basics. My students confused the different types of pronouns. For example, students often used the personal pronoun *they* to mean the possessive *their*, and they used *us* and *our* interchangeably. They also were confused about the singular and plural forms of nouns and verbs. *They eats* is, for example, a mixing of the plural morpheme *s* with a verb in the present tense.

The students needed much more instruction and help than the textbooks offered, and I provided this in different ways. I combined direct and formal teaching of grammar rules with contextual activities such as guided writing and paragraph ending. We also worked on simple sentence structures in the present and the past tenses. The students never hid their reluctance to have anything to do with writing. Their lack of vocabulary was another major obstacle. I prepared vocabulary lists to use during warm-up activities. One successful strategy was the use of bilingual dictionaries. I encouraged and even insisted on use of their dictionaries. This practice, I felt, helped them build some confidence and a sense of achievement. I also used the English-Arabic part of the dictionaries to foster their skimming and scanning skills.

Overall, I followed the common EFL techniques of group, pair, and individual work. What my students needed most was continuous encouragement and individual attention. I needed to work on their morale and self-confidence. Because many of them did not know how to tackle their language problems, they tended to be quiet and pretend that they were making sense of the tasks at hand. It was clear to me that my students needed a very supportive teaching style and a nonthreatening atmosphere. In addition, some were shy and preferred to ask their classmates for explanation rather than me. As I became aware that this shyness and lack of confidence were hindering their progress, I resorted to giving the very shy students extra help after class.

One activity that helped boost their sense of achievement was called "one word a day." The students were asked to learn a new word every day and write it in a special vocabulary notebook. The word needed to be found outside the classroom context and outside the textbook. This simple yet demanding task made many of my students proud of their work. This was not seen as homework but as an individual project to raise learners' awareness of English outside the classroom boundaries. Many of them shared their work with me and said that they enjoyed using their dictionaries to check the meaning and use of the words.

Extra Help

I provided students with extra help in the form of frequent individual and group tutorials. These sessions allowed me to check on their progress and ask them for their feedback and suggestions. Students talked very openly about coping with the course requirements and their fear of failing the final exam. On many occasions I had to hide my frustration, instead showing enthusiasm and continuing to provide extra exam revision by working on test-taking skills. What was encouraging about this approach was that students did not complain about doing homework or being bored. They said that they had a better understanding of the content but were still worried about the exam.

Reflection

Success depends on how you define it. At the end of the course, 70% of my students passed the final exam and moved on to Level 3. By multiple repeaters' standards this is a high rate of success. My personal sense of achievement is that I feel that I managed to restore some confidence in my students, which if nonexistent, can do much harm to the learning process. Furthermore, many of my students made some linguistic improvement and even seemed interested in learning English outside the classroom.

Above all, including students in decision making and giving them control over their own learning helped me revisit my pedagogic strategies and enabled learners to have an impact on their own learning. They were not passive and did not have to follow all my instructions. Some of them gave me immediate feedback about an activity or a point I made. Others showed their disinterest in some activities and suggested doing something else. Negotiation, therefore, brought life to the classroom and helped reshape the syllabus.

This process also helped me examine the prevailing assumptions of the educational institution. Multiple repeaters were not entirely unmotivated and undisciplined. Many of them were victims of a system that did not recognize their special needs. In fact, a good number of my students were doing well in other subjects, so English could not be used to form a judgment about their academic performance. In addition to helping students with their immediate language problems, which was the main aim of the project, the study gave me reason to critically challenge the construct of the multiple repeater. Teacher research, therefore, can help us challenge stereotypes and suggest alternative meaning-making systems (Kanpol, 1997) while empowering the students and ourselves.

From personal experience, I find action research a useful and nonthreatening method of self-evaluation. In a previous project, I looked at myself in videotapes and was, of course, horrified at what I saw. I was, however, pleased to be able to discover my shortcomings. Reflecting on this action research project, I think that I would have learned more if I had worked collaboratively with other colleagues who had similar multiple-repeater students. Collaborative action research can be much more empowering to teachers because changes in practice and even institutional policies are more likely to happen if data were collected by a group of teachers rather than an individual (Burns, 1999; Oja & Smulyan, 1989; Wallace, 1998). My work, however, was not totally individual because my students took part in the study by suggesting activities they preferred and giving me feedback. I am very thankful to them.

Salah Troudi teaches language education, applied linguistics, and research methodology at the University of Exeter in England.

CHAPTER 13

Moodling in the Middle East
(*United Arab Emirates*)

Jason M. Ward

Issue

The conditions in many 1st-year composition programmes are often less than ideal and leave little time to achieve the desired objectives. In our department at an American University in the Middle East, the second language (L2) students receive less than 3 hours' writing instruction per week. This limited contact time, combined with heavily loaded syllabi and class sizes often in excess of 20 students, tends to restrict the amount of time available for genuine two-way communication between students and teachers. This issue is compounded by poor student motivation; therefore, many teachers are constantly seeking out new ways to keep the students on task, enthused, and learning. In this context, I investigated the current role of computer-assisted language learning in L2 education to see how computer-mediated communication might help make a difference.

This chapter describes the use of the open-source course management system (CMS) Moodle in a 1st-year writing class at an American university in the United Arab Emirates (UAE). Using Moodle in the UAE is a complex issue because administrations which spend thousands of dirhams annually on proprietary CMSs are often distrustful of an open-source software which costs nothing to download and upgrade. Many decision makers buy into the argument that if it costs nothing, then it cannot be worth anything. Furthermore, the tendency toward top-down decision-making processes at some universities in the region can prevent those who actually use the technology from making any decisions about it. At a number of institutions, teachers using Moodle have been effectively banned from using the software or driven underground. The issues surrounding the perceived administrative attitudes toward Moodle will be explored in another publication, but this chapter explains why so many language teachers still choose Moodle's particular design and features.

In this chapter, Moodle is advocated as the system currently best equipped to build community, empower students, assess authentically, and motivate. In support, student opinions during this study revealed that 90% of the students enjoyed using Moodle and thought it was useful for the course. Further, 77% thought that they read or wrote more as a result of this CMS, and 68% of students who had used other CMSs preferred to Moodle.

Background Literature

Keobke (1998) suggested, "In the ideal world, Computer Assisted Language Learning (CALL) software programmes would intuitively adapt themselves to each learner and offer a number of possible interfaces and challenges to match individual learning styles" (p. 46). However, the preconception of traditional CALL is that it favours a field-independent learning style. This is a point supported by Freeman and Freeman, who in 1998 pointed out that "advances in technology have increased [the] tendency toward individual learning" (p. 150). In the typical traditional CALL scenario which Freeman and Freeman refer to, the student works alone with a PC and CALL software and completes on-screen activities and tests. The computer "structures the learning environment" and acts as a "tutor" (Levy, 1998, p. 86); therefore, the teacher's role and class interactions are reduced.

Chapelle (2003) explained the logic behind the CALL software used in this context: "to design materials that can direct learners' attention to particular linguistic forms within the input. The suggestions that come from the research on instructed [second language acquisition] are to mark the forms that learners should attend to in some way or provide for repetition" (p. 41). Using such CALL software, the students can work at their own pace, focus on their own troublesome language forms, practice, and be rewarded by instant feedback. Such software is popular with grammar-hungry students and teachers in our context in the Middle East and may be helpful in the memorisation of particular grammatical points. But does it help our students communicate?

Freeman and Freeman (1998) stress the importance of meaningful communication when they describe how the language in many traditional grammar-based language classes is *controlled* by the teacher. Similarly, the traditional CALL lab sessions can be just as controlling when they offer the students few chances "to invent or construct meaning" (p. 133). Keobke (1999) explained that "a central defining characteristic of many CALL materials is their reliance on a behaviourist model of instruction, using behaviour modification principles in their design" (p. 232). Many traditional CALL software packages are more concerned with modifying wrong behaviour than with communication and language use. Furthermore, Freeman and Freeman argued that "grammar exercises are taken from someone else's experience . . . but students only acquire the correct forms when they find themselves in situations where they need them" (p. 133). Skill and drill processes, whether in a textbook or a sophisticated software package, are not truly meaningful or communicative.

Since, and arguably partly because of, the explosion of the Internet, there have been many changes in pedagogy and networked technology which have helped to make CALL more communicative. The overall tendency, as Levy (1998) asserted, is that CALL is now best considered a tool rather than a self-contained language tutor, with the teacher back in the picture "actively and intrinsically involved in the learning process" (p. 92).

CALL AS COMPUTER-MEDIATED COMMUNICATION

Computer-mediated communication (CMC) is a branch of CALL that is concerned with how learners communicate using technology. CMC is defined in Wikipedia (2007a) broadly as "any form of data exchange across two or more networked computers" or more narrowly as "communications that occur via computer-mediated formats (i.e., instant messages, e-mails, chat rooms) between two or more individuals." Rather than just using computers to disconnect from reality in order to cram for grammar quizzes, students applying CMC use computers as a communication tool to make meaningful connections with a wider audience, including but not limited to peers and teachers. As Healey (1999) suggested, "The point is neither to use technology for its own sake nor to practice skills for their own sake, but to keep the focus on the communicative goal—and to achieve it in a variety of ways" (p. 116).

THE COURSE MANAGEMENT SYSTEM

The CMS is an effective example of how computers are currently being used to mediate communication in language learning. The CMS is a type of interactive online resource for students and teachers and has a number of bewildering alter egos. It might also be referred to as a learning management system, a learning support system, a managed learning environment, or a virtual learning environment. For convenience, the single term *CMS* will be used throughout this chapter. Such systems were initially developed to provide e-learning through distance learning, but the CMS is now just as often used to enhance the weekly class content of face-to-face courses. This combination of on-line and face-to-face teaching is known as a *hybrid*, or more often fuzzily referred to as *e-learning*.

MOODLE

Moodle is an open-source CMS, which means that the code and thus the software are free for the user to modify, improve, and share. A relatively small software program that runs on a server, Moodle is accessed over the Internet like a Web site. It can be hosted at no cost on a university server or by a private Internet service provider for whatever it costs to rent the Web space.

Besides Moodle, a range of other open-source CMSs are available on the Web, such as Sakai, Magnolia, OpenCMS, and ATutor, which contain some similar features. There are also several long-established proprietary CMSs, which include systems such as Blackboard, WebCT, and Desire2Learn. Subscribers to proprietary software wait for the developers to add new features and components and can usually expect to pay extra for these add-ons and upgrades.

MOODLE'S FEATURES AND THE CLASSROOM

Like most CMSs, Moodle basically emulates online the things that a teacher already does in the real world, such as providing a drop box for assignments, encouraging journal entries, giving announcements, distributing resources, chatting with students, conducting surveys, assigning and grading quizzes, facilitating peer-review workshops, displaying grades, and checking participation and progress. Most important, Moodle provides the students with their own space to collaborate with peers, discuss issues, communicate informally, and express themselves beyond the constraints of the classroom and their L2.

Moodle features such as the asynchronous Forums and synchronous Chat, in particular, encourage a sense of community and use of students' L2. In my own classes, students' L2 use has often gone well beyond the minimum number of words required in the assignments. The Events calendar, which provides automated updates of the latest deadlines and activities, and the e-mailed Announcements and News features also keep the channels of communication open as students receive regular updates about their peers' and their teacher's activities on Moodle.

The Moodle community is further enhanced by the Profiles feature, which allows participants to express themselves with photographs and biographies. The participant's photo appears as an icon whenever he or she is online, and as with chat software such as MSM Messenger, users can communicate with each other in real time by simply clicking on a face. This creates a genuine L2 community in which students can immerse themselves.

In her article "Group Dynamics and the Online Professor," King (1999) observed that unlike face-to-face communications which employ a range of nonverbal signals, "computer-mediated communication strips these important emotional cues from the conversation, leaving only the typed words on a computer screen" (p. 243). However, Moodle's emoticons help go some way toward addressing this deficiency in the text-based environment, as shown in the following examples:

The students communicating in Moodle are no longer restricted to communicating in their L2 but can draw from a lexicon of *smileys* to express themselves. Each smiley has a one-word description of its function such as "thoughtful," "shocked," "cool," "shy," or "angry."

Of course there is also the danger that smileys, like words and gestures, can sometimes be misconstrued, especially when used to indicate irony. Nevertheless, the smileys add a sense of play, which helps build a nonthreatening atmosphere more conducive to language learning. My own students make frequent use of emoticons in their online communications, and a few have informally commented that they like the smileys used to illustrate otherwise austere assignment instructions. Emoticons have proved especially useful in the forums when my students have made comments on each other's views and used smileys to help defuse potentially inflammatory statements.

In my experience, Moodle seems to build community in the class, and even between classes, as students get to know each other first from chatting online. As Dunkel predicted of computer use in 1991, "Rather than isolating students and promoting asocial behaviour, as many have feared, there is a growing body of evidence that computer use can promote new ways of working together, productive peer teaching, as well as high-quality social and academic task-based interaction, and that these kinds of interaction are related to higher levels of interest, motivation, and achievement" (p. 65).

Another way that Moodle supports student-centred learning is by its user friendly open and accessible design. Product information on the Educational Technology Information Center (2004) suggested that Moodle's layout is unusual and differs from most existing CMSs but supports current developments in software: "Most e-learning platforms are organized around tools: ALL the contents here, ALL the quizzes there, ALL the forums in another place, . . . [the] Moodle approach is much more related to the modern concept of Learning Objects" (Useful Features section, ¶ 6). In fact, Moodle's name is an acronym of its modular nature, Modular Object-Oriented Dynamic Learning Environment. The whole program fits together like Lego bricks, facilitating flexibility and accommodating limitless appendages as new modules become available.

As Campus Source (2005) observed, Moodle promotes collaboration activities and critical reflection within a group. Moodle's peer-review Workshop module, for example, facilitates the whole peer-review process online while concealing the identities of the writers and peer reviewers throughout. To take part, the student uploads his or her anonymous essay to Moodle and then downloads another anonymous assignment written by a peer and provides feedback using an online form. Once the feedback process is completed, the essays are returned to their rightful owners with anonymous peer input included.

Another typical example of a function which promotes collaboration is the Moodle Glossary, which allows students to enter their own definitions of words and phrases to help each other learn new vocabulary. For example, once a definition has been entered, whenever these words or phrases occur in any part of the class use of Moodle, they will be hot-linked directly to the definition contributed by the student or teacher. This feature can also be used to automatically tag common L2 spelling and grammar errors across the whole site. The Wiki feature is an additional illustration of how Moodle facilitates student-centred collaborative learning. A wiki is "a website that allows the visitors themselves to easily add, remove, and otherwise edit and change available content" (Wikipedia, 2007b). Wikis facilitate public collaborations and can allow the students to brainstorm ideas together, compose tag stories, draft group essays, share resources, edit each other's grammar errors, and so on.

Another feature which helps to empower the student is the Choice feature, which enables the students to cast anonymous ballots and then view the results of the vote. This can be used for many purposes, such as permitting the class to democratically decide on the date of the next quiz, engaging in a reading by nominating a favourite character, or even voting for the most appropriate score on an anonymous student assignment. The Moodle Web site (moodle. org) explains that the development of the program is guided by a philosophy of learning that can lead to a more student-centred educational environment:

> Your job as a "teacher" can change from being "the source of knowledge" to being an influencer and role model of class culture, connecting with students in a personal way that addresses their own learning needs, and moderating discussions and activities in a way that collectively leads students towards the learning goals of the class. (Moodle Documentation, 2007, Conclusion section, ¶ 1).

Used creatively, many of the features in Moodle can prove to be intrinsically motivating. The authentic audience of peers provided by activities such as Chat, Forums, and Wikis can be attention grabbing for many students. Some of my students have voluntarily posted their own creative endeavours on Moodle, such as poetry, short stories, and opinion pieces, because they *wanted* to share their writing with an audience. Such *dis-inhibition*, which allows the student to feel less intimidated in an online environment, is surprisingly common. In addition, Felix (1999) suggested, "Higher motivation and a better attitude towards learning have been reported in Web-based teaching (Atkinson, 1997), which seems to reflect general findings in CALL, where positive affective factors have been consistently reported" (p. 94). Moodle's weblog feature will help provide even more space for student expression.

Procedures

To begin to examine the results of using Moodle in my own classes over two semesters, fall 2004 to spring 2005, I conducted two identical online anonymous student surveys—one each semester. Because the students were already using the system and it was familiar to them, I used Moodle's Questionnaire feature to collect and collate the data. This feature regulated who could respond to the survey by automatically allocating one survey opportunity for each participant's login.

The first survey involved 33 respondents, and the second involved 37. All of the participants were voluntary and were male and female 1st-year university students from a variety of backgrounds enrolled in the same writing course. The questions included five multiple-choice and two open-ended responses. The multiple-choice questions were intended to find out whether the students enjoyed using Moodle, thought that it was useful for the course, and thought that it encouraged them to read or write more. The students were also asked to nominate a favorite and least favorite Moodle feature. The open-ended questions asked about students' overall impressions of Moodle and, if they had used another system other than Moodle, which CMS they preferred and why.

The main shortcoming of this research is that it was conducted at different stages in each semester. The fall 2004 survey was conducted at the end of the semester, whereas the spring 2005 survey had to be brought forward to midsemester to meet a research deadline. This meant that the two groups of respondents had spent differing amounts of time using Moodle and thus did not have identical levels of experience and familiarity with its many features. Another limitation with the methodology was the comparison with another CMS. Because the students were using Moodle only for their writing class, their experience with other systems such as Web CT or Blackboard came from outside of my class, which brought in a range of variables beyond my control.

Results

The student responses discussed in this chapter dealt with the aforementioned concerns of motivation and communicative language learning. I asked the question, "Overall, did you enjoy using Moodle?" (see Figure 1) to consider the issue of motivation. I used the loaded word *enjoy* because I was interested in whether or not the students thought that Moodling was like play. The results in Figure 1 are displayed as a percentage, so that the two semesters, with an unequal number of responses (33 versus 37), could also be compared. Not one student said that he or she did *not* enjoy Moodle in either semester, which is why these results are not displayed, and the majority (79%) selected "Liked it a lot."

It is interesting to note that more students selected "Liked it a lot" in spring 2005 than in fall 2004. This may have been because the site was a lot more active during the second semester and contained Web pages linked to non-school-related games, activities, and discussion Forums for chatty issues such as, "Where is the best pizza in Dubai?" These communicative activities were intended to attract students to the site and help them get to know each other. I also hoped that fun activities and pictures might help the students associate Moodle with playful communication rather than just work, resources, assignments, and deadlines.

However, it is worth noting that the discussion Forum, which was voted the favourite feature of 2004 by the students on the questionnaire, slumped to fourth place in the 2005 survey. This may have been because of the timing of the research. The fall 2004 survey took place in Week 15, after the students had spent many weeks getting to know each other using the Forum, whereas the spring 2005 survey took place in Week 8, before many of the best discussions had really got going.

The least popular feature in 2005 was the Glossary. I think that this was because it was not integrated very effectively into my course. Many students

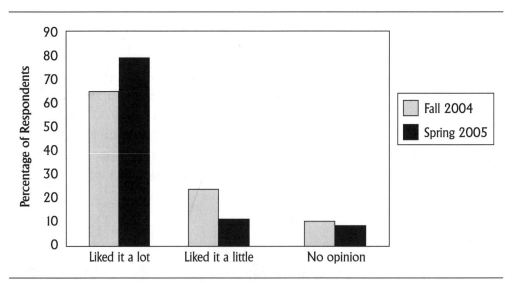

Figure 1. Student responses from both semesters (N = 70) to the question, "Overall, did you enjoy using Moodle?"

complained that their posts were never linked to anything and that they did not see the point. Both of these issues were a result of my own shortcomings, rather than any technical glitches, because I was still learning how to set up the Glossary and was not sure about how to fit it into an existing reading journal assignment. As Dunkel (1991) observed, computer-based activities need to be integrated into the content of the class: "The computer per se affects the social environment of the classroom. The critical factors that influence interaction centered around academic activities are the ways that tasks are defined and organized by the teacher and how they are construed by the students" (p. 66).

The least popular Moodle activity in the spring 2005 semester was the Workshop, and I think that this was for technical reasons. There were bugs in the earlier version of Workshop which we were using and so a couple of students did not get feedback on their essays or lost the comments that they tried to post. A bug-free version has since been made available in all current versions of Moodle.

Despite these minor flaws, the majority of students stated that Moodle was useful for the course in both semesters. The results in Figure 2 show combined answers from both semesters because they were virtually identical. Also, not one student in either semester said that he or she did not think that Moodle was useful, which is why "No" is not displayed.

However, not all students thought that they read or wrote more in English because of Moodle. According to the two pie charts in Figure 3, 27% of respondents thought that they did not read or write more. However, it should be noted that all of these "No" responses were from the spring 2005 research conducted

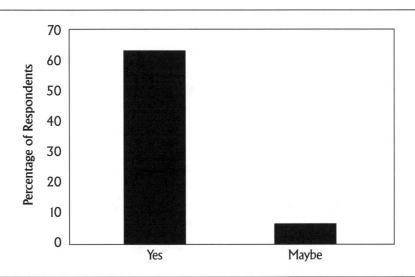

Figure 2. Student responses from both semesters to the question, "Do you think that the Moodle site has been useful for this course?"

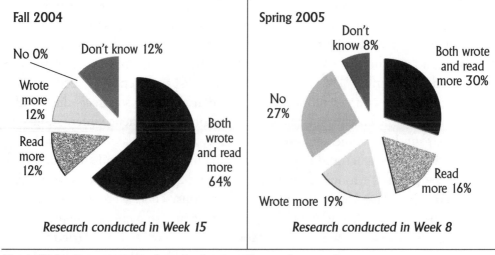

Fall 2004

No 0%
Don't know 12%
Wrote more 12%
Read more 12%
Both wrote and read more 64%

Research conducted in Week 15

Spring 2005

Don't know 8%
Both wrote and read more 30%
No 27%
Read more 16%
Wrote more 19%

Research conducted in Week 8

Figure 3. Student responses from both semesters to the question,
"Do you think that you read or wrote more in English because of Moodle?"

in Week 8. Nobody said "No" in the research conducted at the end of the course in fall 2004, when more Moodle-based assignments had been completed.

For the qualitative feedback, I asked two broad, open-ended questions:

1. What was your overall impression of Moodle, and could you make any recommendations on how I could improve this site?

2. If you claimed that you preferred Moodle to Blackboard or Web CT, why?

Out of 37 comments received in response to these questions, there was only one negative remark about Moodle. This was from Ahmed,[1] who stated, "I prefer Web CT because it had no hitches that need mentioning. I also prefer it because it is very user friendly." The hitches which Ahmed refers to were most likely problems with the peer-review Workshop mentioned earlier. This indicates the importance of consistently smooth functionality in a CMS. However, the other 36 comments either praised Moodle or denigrated the other most used CMS at the university.

Bashir provided a succinct introductory summary of most of the plaudits when he enthused, "Moodle is very impressive and usually makes work easier." Chaimaa illustrated the communicative nature of Moodle when she pointed out that "overall what moodle does best is help classmates interact with each other online." This is a point reiterated by Deena, who observed that "Moodle inhanced our ability to communicate with you and I think you should continue to use it."

Ebrahim demonstrated the motivational power of Moodle and its ability to facilitate student-centred learning when he confided, "Firstly you should definitely continue to use moodle, because it actully makes a students life a lot easier, secondly i loved moodle, its alot of fun, plus user friendly, and another thing(this is sort of a secret), moodle is the reason why i submitted all my essays on time, coz of the constant reminders." Faisal further illustrated this point when he opined, "i think that moodle is best way for submitting H.W and being away of forgetting it. more over it encourage us to use computer and practise the language alot." These students' uses of Moodle illustrate the following observation from Daniels and Brooks (1999): "On-line learning communities brought about by computer-mediated communication can enhance the individual's capacity to meet goals for motivated learners and may be helpful in encouraging unmotivated language learners through variety and teacher monitoring of effective feedback" (p. 86).

The enhancement of the teacher-student relationship was supported by Hadeel, who noted that "there is a greater relationship between the teacher and the student. . . . The student feels as if he is drawn more attention on rather than blackboard. . . . There is basically greater interaction between the two." Ismail had a similar complaint: "Blackboard is very dead . . . theres hardly any activity on it." The students' impression that Moodle is more active than Blackboard might be because Moodle displays a live feed of all the Moodle users currently online, which creates a lively buzz on the site. I can relate to this as a teacher because whenever I go to the site and see a long list of Moodle users online, some of whom I recognise as my own students and colleagues, it makes me feel as though I have been missing out on something and I am keen to reconnect and join the party.

In their appraisal of computer-mediated communication, Daniels and Brooks (1999) explained, "A traditional classroom can be enhanced by allowing student interaction to extend 24 hours a day via an on-line learning community" (p. 89). With Moodle running on the server, there is always a class in session. I was able to confirm this characterization by perusing Moodle's student Activity Reports, which revealed that students had been working on Moodle at all hours of the day and night.

Further evidence that the user friendly and accessible features of this CMS contributed to the students' motivation came from Leila, who explained that Moodle "was easier to access, more fun to view assignments, just more open, more useful and more organized." Mohammad concurred, suggesting that "moodle is better that blackboard, coz its way more user friendly . . . plus moodle is alot more fun, all those participant pictures, and discussion forums, and journals, and voting . . . i love MOODLE:)." Indeed, most of the students whom I spoke with informally also claimed that they "loved" Moodle because they thought that it was generally easier to use and more fun.

However, does this fun factor make Moodle better than the other systems or are there other variables here? Nawar sensibly pointed out that the software itself does not guarantee student satisfaction: "Moodle is good and yes u should keep using it. i think the problem is not with the site it is with the teacher. my friend in another class hates moodle cuz her teacher does not make it seem interesting." It should be noted that alternative CMSs such as Blackboard also have some facilities to allow students to chat informally with each other in discussion groups or to host fun material alongside the dry resources and threatening assignments. It depends on whether or not the teacher wants to use the CMS in this way.

Because my students appeared to have also been evaluating the online course rather than just the system, an impartial comparison between the Moodle and Blackboard systems needs to be conducted using exactly the same course and preferably the same instructor. Duzer and Munoz (2005) conducted just such a research project at Humboldt State University in California, titled *Blackboard vs. Moodle: A Comparison of Satisfaction With Online Teaching and Learning Tools*. In this study, the same course was taught using two different CMSs. The 35 students involved were randomly distributed into either Blackboard or Moodle. Duzer and Munoz's results (see Figure 4) revealed that Moodle users were more likely to suggest that this CMS enhanced instruction and preferred to use the same CMS again.

Did Blackboard/Moodle enhance instruction?		
	Blackboard	**Moodle**
Strongly agree	0%	7.1%
Somewhat agree	23.1%	21.4%
Neutral	23.1%	28.6%
Somewhat disagree	23.1%	28.6%
Strongly disagree	30.8%	14.3%
Would you like another course using this CMS?		
	Blackboard	**Moodle**
Strongly or somewhat agree	46.2%	57.2%
Neutral	30.8%	21.4%
Somewhat or strongly disagree	23.1%	21.4%

Source: Duzer & Munoz (2005)

Figure 4. Blackboard vs. Moodle: A comparison of satisfaction with online teaching and learning tools.

Reflection

More extensive and rigorous research needs to be done into the benefits of using particular course management systems and which features and approaches are most effective for meeting the needs of second language learners and writing students. Nevertheless, as we can see from this study, our own classroom-based research can begin to reveal what motivates and challenges our own students, what their needs may be, and how we can best meet them. Ninety percent of my students said that they enjoyed using Moodle and thought it was useful for the course. In addition, 72% of these students said they enjoyed it "a lot." According to the social constructivist model, learning is supposed to be enjoyable, and enjoyment was a factor supported by both the quantitative and qualitative data produced by these surveys.

Additionally, 77% of the students thought that they read or wrote more because of Moodle, which suggests that language learning through Moodle can be intrinsically motivating rather than just based on coercion and memorization. Finally, 68% of students who had used other CMSs said they preferred to use Moodle, which appeared to accommodate their requirements more effectively. From these two semesters of study and the students' feedback, it seems that using a CMS can certainly enhance the learning environment by providing the students and faculty with more communicative, student-centered, and motivating activities in a much bigger world than the classroom.

Many of our students come from educational backgrounds which rely on a predominantly behaviourist approach—based on memorization for quizzes. By using technology such as Moodle, it is now physically possible to make the course more student-centred, providing more opportunities for critical thinking and learning through interaction with peers. Furthermore, Moodle makes this learning environment freely available to any institution with a Web link and an open-minded policy toward open-source technology.

Since conducting this study, I have continued to survey my students each semester about their attitudes toward Moodle, and the results become more positive as Moodle improves. Through experience, I have continued to become better able to put its features to good use. The results from the most recent survey (Ward, 2006b), in spring 2006, showed that

- 61% of my students thought that they communicated more with other students because of Moodle.

- 81% of the students thought that they spent more time using their second language because of Moodle.

- 96% thought that they contributed more to class because of Moodle.

An additional survey of faculty (Ward, 2006a) revealed that despite such positive results, many administrators remain wary of Moodle, and many respondents felt that those who actually used a CMS did not make decisions about its use. My own classroom-based research has convinced me that the students' needs and preferences should play a role in the implementation of on-line technology. After 2 years of using this system and surveying my students every semester, I am confident that Moodle's features and functionality can effectively meet the needs of writing students and communicative language learning.

Jason M. Ward teaches at the American University of Sharjah, UAE.

Note

1. The students' original grammar and spelling is used throughout this chapter.

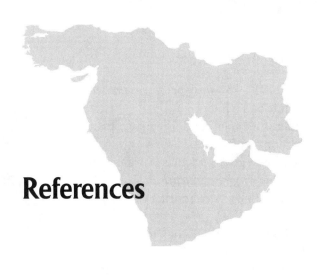

References

Abu-Rabia, S., & Siegel, L. S. (1995). Different orthographies, different context effects: The effect of Arabic sentence context in skilled and poor readers. *Reading Psychology: An International Quarterly, 16*, 1–19.

Ahmadi, M., Helms, M., & Raiszadeh, F. (2001). Business students' perceptions of faculty evaluations. *International Journal of Educational Management, 15*, 12–22.

Aida, Y. (1994). Examination of Horwitz, Horwitz, and Cope's construct of foreign language anxiety: The case of students of Japanese. *Modern Language Journal, 78*, 155–168.

Aleamoni, L. M. (1981). Student ratings of instruction. In J. Millman (Ed.), *Handbook of teacher evaluation* (pp. 110–145). Beverly Hills, CA: Sage.

Anderson, K. H., & Siegfried, J. J. (1997). Gender differences in rating the teaching of economics. *Eastern Economic Journal, 23*(3), 347–357.

Angoff, W. (1989). *Context bias in the test of English as a foreign language: Research Reports, Report 29* [Electronic version]. (Supplemental Report Number TOEFL-RR-29). Princeton, NJ: Educational Testing Service. Retrieved January 3, 2007, from http://www.ets.org/portal/site/ets/

Argaman, O., & Abu-Rabia, S. (2000). The influence of language anxiety on English reading and writing tasks among native Hebrew speakers. *Language, Culture, and Curriculum, 15*(2), 143–160.

Atkinson, D. (1997). A critical approach to critical thinking in TESOL. *TESOL Quarterly, 31*, 71–94.

Auerbach, E. (1993). Reexamining English-only in the classroom. *TESOL Quarterly, 27*, 9–32.

Bailey, K. M., Curtis, A., & Nunan, D. (2001). *Pursuing professional development: The self as source*. Boston, MA: Heinle & Heinle.

Bakhtin, M. (1984). *Problems of Dostoevsky's poetics* (C. Emerson, Trans.). Minneapolis, MN: University of Minnesota Press.

Bangert, A. W. (2004). The seven principles of good practice: A framework for evaluating on-line teaching. *Internet and Higher Education, 7*, 217–232.

Barell, J. (2003). *Developing more curious minds*. Alexandria, VA: Association for Supervision and Curriculum Development.

Bejarano, Y. (1987). A cooperative small-group methodology in the language classroom. *TESOL Quarterly, 21*(3), 483–504.

Berg, E. C. (1999). The effects of trained peer response on ESL students' revision types and writing quality. *Journal of Second Language Writing, 8*, 215–241.

Best, J. B., & Addison, W. E. (2000). A preliminary study of perceived warmth of professor and student evaluations. *Teaching of Psychology, 27*, 60–62.

Bitchener, J., Young, S., & Cameron, D. (2005). The effect of different types of corrective feedback on ESL student writing. *Journal of Second Language Writing, 14*(3), 191–205.

Blagg, N. (1991). *Can we teach intelligence? A comprehensive evaluation of Feuerstein's instrumental enrichment program*. Hillsdale, NJ: Lawrence Erlbaum.

Blagg, N., Ballinger, M., Gardner, R., Petty, M., & Williams, G. (1988). *Somerset thinking skills course*. Oxford, England: Basil Blackwell.

Boddy, C. R. (2004). From brand image research to teaching assessment: Using a projective technique borrowed from marketing research to aid an understanding of teaching effectiveness. *Quality Assurance in Education, 12*(2), 94–105.

Bonesrønning, H. (2004). Can effective teacher behavior be identified? *Economics of Education Review, 23*, 237–247.

Boudah, D. J., & Knight, S. L. (1996). *Participatory research and development* (Technical Report to the Office of Special Education Programs, U.S. Department of Education). College Station, TX: Texas A & M University.

Breen, M., & Littlejohn, A. (2000). *Classroom decision-making: Negotiation and process syllabus in practice*. Cambridge, England: Cambridge University Press.

Bress, P. (1995). It made me think . . . what teachers think, what students think. *Modern English Teacher, 4*(3), 47–48.

Bress, P. (2000). What makes a teacher special? *English Teaching Professional, 14*, 43–44.

Brown, N. (2004). What makes a good educator? The relevance of meta programmes. *Assessment & Evaluation in Higher Education, 29*(5), 515–533.

Brown, S., & McIntyre, D. (1992). *Making sense of teaching*. Buckingham, England: Open University Press.

Brundrett, M., & Silcock, P. (2002). *Achieving competence, success, and excellence in teaching*. London: Routledge/Falmer.

Bruner, J. (1985). Vygotsky: A historical and conceptual perspective. In J. V. Wertsch

(Ed.), *Culture, communication, and cognition: Vygotskian perspectives* (pp. 21–34). New York: Cambridge University Press.

Buckton, R. (2001). Classroom democracy—Letting the students choose. In C. Coombe, S. Riley, & S. Troudi (Eds.), *TESOL Arabia 2000: Bridging the gap between teacher and learner: Selected papers from the 2000 international conference: Vol. 5* (pp. 81–88). Dubai, UAE: TESOL Arabia.

Burge, E. J. (1993). *Students' perceptions of learning in computer conferencing: A qualitative analysis.* Doctoral thesis, Graduate Department of Education, University of Toronto.

Burns, A. (1999). *Collaborative action research for English language teachers.* Cambridge: Cambridge University Press.

Burr, V. (1995). *An introduction to social constructionism.* London: Routledge.

Campus Source. (2005). *Moodle.* Retrieved March 13, 2005, from http://www.campussource.de/org/software/moodle/

Canagarajah, S. A. (1999). *Resisting linguistic imperialism in English teaching.* Oxford, England: Oxford University Press.

Carroll, S. (1995). The irrelevance of feedback to language learning. In L. Eubank, L. Selinker, & M. Sharwood Smith (Eds.), *The current state of inter-language: Studies in honor of William E. Rutherford* (pp. 73–88). Amsterdam: John Benjamins.

Carroll, S. (2001). *Input and evidence: The raw material of second language acquisition* (Language Acquisition and Language Disorders, Vol. 25). Amsterdam: John Benjamins.

Cashin, W. E. (1988). Students' ratings of teaching: A summary of the research (IDEA Paper No. 20). Manhattan, KS: Kansas State University, Division of Continuing Education. (ERIC Document Reproduction Service No. ED 302 567)

Caulk, N. (1994). Comparing teacher and student responses to written work. *TESOL Quarterly, 28,* 181–188.

Chapelle, C. A. (2003). *English language learning and technology.* Amsterdam: John Benjamins.

Chen, Y., & Hoshower, L. B. (2003). Student evaluation of teaching effectiveness: An assessment of student perception and motivation. *Assessment and Evaluation in Higher Education, 28,* 71–88.

Cheng, Y. S., Horwitz, E., & Schallert, D. (1999). Language anxiety: Differentiating writing and speaking components. *Language Learning, 49*(3), 417–446.

Cimarolli, M. (1993). Observations of excellence in teaching. *Teaching English in the Two-Year College, 20*(3), 181–187.

Cochran-Smith, M., & Lytle, S. (1990). *Inside-outside: Teacher research and knowledge.* New York: Teachers College Press.

Codde, J. (1996). *Using learning contracts in the college classroom.* Retrieved January 3, 2007, from http://www.msu.edu/user/coddejos/contract.htm

Collinson, J. (1997). How to be a really rotten teacher. Keynote. *Modern English Teacher, 6*(1), 7–9.

Connor, U., & Asenavage, K. (1994). Peer response groups in ESL writing classes:

How much impact on revision? *Journal of Second Language Writing, 3*, 257–276.

Cook, V. (2000). The author responds. . . . *TESOL Quarterly, 34*, 329–332.

Cooksey, R., Freebody, P., & Bennett, A. (1990). The ecology of spelling: A lens model analysis of spelling errors and student judgments of spelling difficulty. *Reading Psychology, 11*(4), 293–322.

Corcoran, T. (1995). *Helping teachers develop well: Transforming professional development*. Madison, WI: Center for Policy Research in Education.

Crumbley, L., Henry, B., & Kratchman, S. (2001). Students' perception of the evaluation of college teaching. *Quality Assurance in Education, 9*, 197–207.

Daly, J. A., & Miller, M. D. (1975). The empirical development of an instrument of writing apprehension. *Research in the Teaching of English, 9*, 242–249.

Daly, J. A., Vangelisti, A., & Witte, S. P. (1988). Writing apprehension in the classroom context. In B. A. Rafoth & D. L. Rubin (Eds.), *The social construction of written communication* (pp. 147–171). Norwood, NJ: Ablex.

Daly, J. A., & Witte, S. P. (1982). Relationship of writing apprehension to teachers' classroom behaviours and emphasis on writing activities. Paper presented at the annual conference of the American Educational Research Association, New York.

Daniels, P., & Brooks, D. (1999). Building on-line communities for language learners. In K. Cameron (Ed.), *CALL and the learning community* (pp. 83–92). Exeter: Elm Bank.

de Bono, E. (1999). *Six thinking hats* (Rev. ed.). London: Penguin.

Dickinson, L. (1987). *Self instruction in language learning*. Cambridge, England: Cambridge University Press.

Drudy, S., & Chathain, M. U. (2002). Gender effects in classroom interaction: Data collection, self-analysis and reflection. *Evaluation and Research in Education, 16*(1), 34–50.

Dunkel, P. (1991). *Computer-assisted language learning and testing: Research issues and practice*. New York: Newbury House.

Duzer, J. V., & Munoz, K. D. (2005). Blackboard vs. Moodle: A comparison of satisfaction with online teaching and learning tools. Retrieved March 7, 2005, from http://www.humboldt.edu/~jdv1/moodle/all.htm

Educational Technology Information Center. (2004). Moodle. *Educational Technology Information Center: T.H.E. Journal*. Retrieved February 7, 2007, from http://www.edtechinfocenter.com/view/productdetail.cfm?fproductref=438

Educational Testing Service. (2003). *TOEFL test and score data summary, 2002–2003 edition*. Princeton, NJ: Author. Retrieved January 3, 2007, from http://www.ets.org/Media/Research/pdf/TOEFL-SUM-0203.pdf

Edwards, C., & Willis, J. (Eds.) (2005). *Teachers exploring tasks in English language teaching*. London: Palgrave Macmillan.

Ellis, G. (1991). Learning to learn. In C. Brumfit, J. Moon, & R. Tongue (Eds.), *Teaching English to children* (pp. 142–157). London: Collins.

Ellis, R. (2003). *Task-based language learning and teaching*. Oxford: Oxford University Press.

Elton, L. (2003). *Creativity and innovation in academic practice.* Paper presented at the Business Education Support Team Conference, Brighton, England.

Emery, C. R., Kramer, T. R., & Tian, R. G. (2003). Return to academic standards. *Quality Assurance in Education, 11*(1), 37–46.

Ennis, R. H. (1987). A taxonomy of critical thinking dispositions and abilities. In J. Baron & R. Sternberg (Eds.), *Teaching thinking skills: Theory and practice.* New York: W. H. Freeman.

Ericksen, S. (1984). *The essence of good teaching.* San Francisco: Jossey Bass.

European Ministries of Education. (1999, June 19). Déclaration de Bologne 1999. L'Espace Européen de l'Enseignement Supérieur [The Bologne Declaration 1999. European Higher Education Space]. Retrieved on October 15, 2005, from http://www.education.gouv.fr/realisations/education/superieur/bologne.htm

Felix, U. (1999). Web-based language learning: A window to the authentic world. In R. Debski & M. Levy (Eds.), *World CALL: Global perspectives on computer assisted language learning* (pp. 85–98). Lisse, Netherlands: Swets and Zeitlinger.

Feuerstein, R., Klein, P. S., & Tannenbaum, A. J. (1991). *Mediated learning experience: Theoretical, psychological and learning implications.* London: Freund.

Feuerstein, R., Rand, Y., Hoffman, M., & Miller, R. (1980). *Instrumental enrichment.* Glenview, IL: Scott Foresman.

Finch, J. H., Helms, M. M., & Ettkin, L. P. (1997). Development and assessment of effective teaching: An integrative model for implementation in schools of business administration. *Quality Assurance in Education, 5*(3), 159–164.

Fisher, A. T., Alder, J. G., & Avasulu, M. (1998). Lecturing performance appraisal criteria: Staff and students' differences. *Australian Journal of Educational and Child Psychology, 42*(2), 153–168.

Fobes, R. (1993). *The creative problem solver's toolbox.* Portland, OR: Solutions Through Innovation.

Francis, S., Hirsch, S., & Rowland, E. (1994). Improving school culture through study groups. *Journal of Staff Development, 13,* 12–15.

Freeman, Y. S., & Freeman, D. E. (1998). *ESL/EFL teaching: Principles for success.* Portsmouth, NH: Heinemann.

Frymier, A. B. (1993). *The impact of teacher immediacy on students' motivation over the course of the semester.* Paper presented at the Annual Meeting of the Speech Communication Association, Miami Beach, FL.

Frymier, J. R. (1965). *The nature of educational method.* Columbus, OH: Charles E. Merrill.

Ganschow, L., Sparks, R., Anderson, R., Javorsky, J., Skinner, S., & Patton, J. (1994). Differences in language performance among high, average, and low anxious foreign language learners. *Modern Language Journal, 78,* 41–55.

Gardner, R. C., & MacIntyre, P. D. (1993). A student's contributions to second language learning. Part II: Affective variables. *Language Teaching, 26,* 1–11.

Germain, M., & Scandura, T. (2005). Grade inflation and student individual differences as systematic bias in faculty evaluations. *Journal of Instructional Psychology, 32,* 58–67.

Goodgame, C., & McCoy, L. (1997). *High school students' perspectives on good and bad teachers*. Wake Forest University: Department of Education.

Gordon, R. L. (1997). How novice teachers can succeed with adolescents. *Educational Leadership, 54*(7), 56–58.

Goswami, D., & Stillman, P. (1987). *Reclaiming the classroom: Teacher research as an agency for change*. Upper Montclair, NJ: Boynton Cook.

Grassian, E. S., & Kaplowitz, J. R. (2001). *Information literacy instruction: Theory and practice*. New York: Neal-Schuman.

Greenwald, A. G. (1997). Validity concerns and usefulness of student ratings of instruction. *American Psychologist, 52,* 182–186.

Greenwald, A. G., & Gillmore, G. M. (1997). No pain, no gain? The importance of measuring course workload in student ratings of instruction. *Journal of Educational Psychology, 89,* 743–751.

Guefrachi, H., & Troudi, S. (2000). Enhancing English language teaching in the UAE. In K. Johnson (Ed.), *Teacher education*. Alexandria, VA: TESOL Publications.

Haggan, M. (1991). Spelling errors in native Arabic-speaking English majors: A comparison between remedial students and fourth year students. *System, 19*(1–2), 45–61.

Harley, K., Barasa, F., Bertram, C., Mattson, E., & Pillay, S. (2000). "The real and the ideal": Teacher roles and competences in South African policy and practice. *International Journal of Educational Development, 20,* 287–304.

Hassett, M. F. (2000, winter). What makes a good teacher? *Adventures in Assessment, 12,* 9–12. Retrieved on Sept. 15, 2004, from http://www.sabes .org/resources/adventures/vol12/12hassett.htm

Hativa, N., Barak, R., & Simhi, E. (2001). Exemplary university teachers: Knowledge and beliefs regarding effective teaching dimensions and strategies. *Journal of Higher Education, 72*(6), 699–729.

Healey, D. (1999). Classroom practice: Communicative skill-building tasks in CALL environments. In J. Egbert & E. Hanson-Smith (Eds.), *CALL environments: Research, practice, and critical issues* (pp. 116–136). Alexandria, VA: TESOL.

Hedgcock, J., & Lefkowitz, N. (1992). Collaborative oral/aural revision in foreign language writing instruction. *Journal of Second Language Writing, 1,* 255–276.

Hobson, S. M., & Talbot, D. M. (2001). Understanding student evaluations. *College Teaching, 49,* 26–31.

Hoekje, B. (1993/1994). Group work, the teacher's role, and the student-centered classroom. *TESOL Journal, 3*(2), 4–6.

Holliday, A. (2002). *Doing and writing qualitative research*. London: Sage.

Horwitz, E. K. (2000). Horwitz comments: It ain't over 'til it's over: On foreign language anxiety, first language deficits, and confounding of variables. *Modern Language Journal, 84,* 256–259.

Horwitz, E. K. (2001). Language anxiety and achievement. *Annual Review of Applied Linguistics, 21,* 112–126.

Horwitz, E. K., Horwitz, M. B., & Cope, J. (1986). Foreign language classroom anxiety. *Modern Language Journal, 70,* 125–132.

Horwitz, E. K., & Young, D. (1991). *Language anxiety: From theory and research to classroom implications*. Englewood Cliffs, NJ: Prentice Hall.

Hoyle, E. (1980). Professionalisation and deprofessionalisation in education. In E. Hoyle & J. Megarry (Eds.), *World yearbook of education 1980: Professional development of teachers* (pp. 42–54). London: Kogan Page.

Hudson, L. (1967). *Contrary imaginations: A psychological study of the English schoolboy*. Harmondsworth, England: Penguin.

Hyland, F. (2000). ESL writers and feedback: Giving more autonomy to students. *Language Teaching Research, 4,* 33–54.

Hyrkstedt, I., & Kalaja, P. (1998). Attitudes toward English and its functions in Finland: A discourse-analytic study. *World Englishes, 17*(3), 345–357.

Isaacs, G. (1994). Lecturing practices and note-taking purposes. *Studies in Higher Education, 19*(2), 203–216.

Jacobs, G. M., Curtis, A., Braine, G., & Huang, S. (1998). Feedback on student writing: Taking the middle path. *Journal of Second Language Writing, 7,* 307–317.

Jacobs, H., Zinkgraf, S., Wormuth, D., Hartfiel, V., & Hughey, J. (1981). *Testing ESL composition: A practical approach*. Rowley, MA: Newbury House.

Jay, J. K., & Johnson, K. L. (2002). Capturing complexity: A typology of reflective practice for teacher education. *Teaching and Teacher Education, 8,* 73–85.

Jimenez-Gonzalez, E. (1997). A reading-level match study of phonemic processes underlying reading disabilities in a transparent orthography. *Reading and Writing: An Interdisciplinary Journal, 9,* 23–40.

Kanpol, B. (1997). *Issues and trends in critical pedagogy*. Cresskill, NJ: Hampton Press.

Kemmis, S., & McTaggart, R. (Eds.). (1982). *The action research reader*. Geelong, Victoria, Australia: Deakin University Press.

Keobke, K. (1998). Computers and collaboration: Adapting CALL materials to different learning styles. In J. M. Reid (Ed.), *Understanding learning styles in the second language classroom* (pp. 46–52). Upper Saddle River, NJ: Prentice Hall Regents.

Keobke, K. (1999). The teacher in the machine: Making WWW technology serve pedagogy. In K. Cameron (Ed.), *CALL and the learning community* (pp. 231–241). Exeter, England: Elm Bank.

King, K. (1999). Group dynamics and the online professor. In K. Cameron (Ed.), *CALL and the learning community* (pp. 241–249). Exeter, England: Elm Bank.

King, P. E., & Behnke, R. R. (2005). Problems associated with evaluating student performance in groups. *College Teaching, 53*(2), 57–61.

Kinsella, K. (1996). Designing group work that supports and enhances diverse classroom work styles. *TESOL Journal, 6*(1), 24–30.

Kleinmann, H. H. (1977). Avoidance behaviour in adult second language acquisition. *Language Learning, 27,* 93–108.

Knowles, M. S. (1986). *Using learning contracts*. San Francisco, CA: Jossey-Bass.

Knowles, M. S. (1987). Enhancing HRD with contract learning. *Training and Development Journal, 41*(3), 62–63.

Kolitch, E., & Dean, A. V. (1999). Student ratings of instruction in the USA: Hidden assumptions and missing conceptions about 'good' teaching. *Studies in Higher Education, 24*, 27–42.

Kozulin, A. (1998). *Psychological tools: A sociocultural approach to education.* Cambridge, MA: Harvard University Press.

Kroll, B., & Reid, J. (1994). Guidelines for designing writing prompts: Clarifications, caveats, and cautions. *Journal of Second Language Writing, 3*(3), 231–255.

Lanteigne, B. F. (2004). *Task descriptions of non-Western English language use with cross-cultural evaluations and discussions of language choice.* Dissertation, Indiana University of Pennsylvania, Indiana, PA. Available: http://dspace.lib.iup .edu:8080/dspace/bitstream/1938/4/1/Test+WP+Dissertation.pdf

Leech, L. L. (2002). Asking questions: Techniques for semistructured interviews. *Political Science and Politics, 35*(4), 665–668.

Leki, I. (2001). "A narrow thinking system": Nonnative-English-speaking students in group projects across the curriculum. *TESOL Quarterly, 35*(1), 39–67.

Lesetar, P. (1997). *Say it right! English pronunciation dictionary.* Unpublished doctoral dissertation, University of Alberta, Canada.

Levy, M. (1998). Two concepts of learning and their implications for CALL at the tertiary level. *ReCALL Journal, 10*(1), 86–94.

Liang, K. Y. (2002). *English as a second language (ESL) students' attitudes towards nonnative English-speaking teachers' accentedness.* Unpublished master's thesis, California State University, Los Angeles, CA.

Lima, A. K. (1981). An economic model of teaching effectiveness. *American Economic Review, 71*(5), 1056–1059.

Little, J. W. (1993). Teacher professional development in a climate of educational reform. *Educational Evaluation and Policy Analysis, 15*(2), 129–151.

Lockhart, C., & Ng, P. (1995). Analyzing talk in peer response groups: Stances, functions, and content. *Language Learning, 45*, 605–655.

Long, M. (1996). The role of the linguistic environment in second language acquisition. In W. Ritchie & T. J. Bhatia (Eds.), *Handbook of second language acquisition* (pp. 413–468). Orlando, FL: Academic Press.

Long, M., & Porter, P. (1985). Group work, interlanguage talk and second language acquisition. *TESOL Quarterly, 29*(2), 207–228.

Lyster, R., & Ranta, L. (1997). Corrective feedback and learner uptake: Negotiation of form in communicative classrooms. *Studies in Second Language Acquisition, 19*, 37–66.

MacIntyre, P. D. (1999). Language anxiety: A review of the research for language teachers. In D. Young (Ed.), *Affect in foreign language and second language learning: A practical guide to creating a low-anxiety classroom atmosphere* (pp. 24–45). Boston: McGraw-Hill.

MacIntyre, P. D., & Gardner, R. C. (1989). Anxiety and second language learning: Toward a theoretical clarification. *Language Learning, 39*, 251–257.

Mahboob, A. (2004). Native or nonnative: What do students enrolled in an intensive English program think? In L. Kamhi-Stein (Ed.), *Learning and teaching from experience* (pp. 121–147). Ann Arbor, MI: University of Michigan Press.

Maloy, R., & Jones, B. (1987). Teachers, partnerships, and school improvement. *Journal of Research and Development, 20,* 19–24.

Mangelsdorf, K., & Schlumberger, A. (1992). ESL student response stances in a peer review task. *Journal of Second Language Writing, 1,* 235–254.

Mangubhai, F. (1993). *Anatomy of a good second language teacher: What it has to say about L2 teacher education.* Paper presented at the International Conference on Teacher Education in Second Language Teaching, Hong Kong.

Marsh, H. (1984). Students' evaluations of university teaching: Dimensionality, reliability, validity, potential biases, and utility. *Journal of Educational Psychology, 76,* 707–754.

Marsh, H. (1987). Students' evaluations of university teaching: Research findings, methodological issues, and directions for future research. *Journal of Educational Research, 11,* 253–288.

Marsh, H., & Dunkin, M. (1992). *Students' evaluations of university teaching: Handbook on theory and research* (Vol. 8). New York: Agathon Press.

Martin, J. R. (1998). Evaluating faculty based on student opinions: Problems, implications, and recommendations from Deming's theory of management perspective. *Issues in Accounting Education, 13,* 1079–1094.

Matsuda, P. (2003). Process and post-process: A discursive history. *Journal of Second Language Writing, 12,* 65–83.

McCroskey, J. C. (1977). Oral communication apprehension: A summary of recent theory and research. *Human Communication Research, 4,* 78–96.

McDonough, K. (2004). Learner-learner interaction during pair and small group activities in a Thai EFL context. *System, 32,* 207–224.

Mendonca, C., & Johnson, K. (1994). Peer review negotiations: Revision activities in ESL writing instruction. *TESOL Quarterly, 28,* 745–769.

Mingucci, M. (1999). Action research in ESL staff development. *TESOL Matters, 9*(2), 16.

Ministry of Higher Education, Tunisia. (2005, June 30). *Higher education in Tunisia and prospects for shifting to the bachelor, master, and Ph.D. system.* Tunis: Author.

Ministry of Higher Education, Tunisia. (2006, June 3). *Quality support project in higher education.* Tunis: Author.

Misson, R. (2006). Research in teacher education programs: Preparing for the future. In A. Warne, M. O'Brien, Z. Syed, & M. Zuriek (Eds.), *Action research in English language teaching in the UAE: Perspectives from teacher education at the higher colleges of technology.* Abu Dhabi, UAE: HCT Press.

Mitchell, R., & Myles, F. (2004). *Second language learning theories.* London: Arnold.

Moats, L. (1996). Phonological spelling errors in the writing of dyslexic adolescents. *Reading and Writing: An Interdisciplinary Journal, 8*(1), 105–119.

Moodle Documentation. (2007). Philosophy. *Moodle docs*. Retrieved January 9, 2007, from http://docs.moodle.org/en/Philosophy

Morris, L. (2001). Going through a bad spell: What the spelling errors of young ESL learners reveal about their grammatical knowledge. *Canadian Modern Language Review, 58*(2), 273–286.

Nelson, G., & Murphy, J. (1992). An L2 writing group: Task and social dimensions. *Journal of Second Language Writing, 1,* 171–193.

Nelson, G., & Murphy, J. (1993). Peer response groups: Do L2 writers use peer comments in revising their drafts? *TESOL Quarterly, 27,* 135–141.

Newcomb, L. H., & Warmbrod, J. R. (1974). *The effect of contract grading on student performance—Summary of research*. Columbus, OH: Ohio State University, Department of Agricultural Education. (ERIC Document Reproduction Service No. ED 093967)

Noffke, S. (1997). Professional, personal, and political dimensions of action research. *Review of Research in Education, 22,* 305–343.

Nunan, D. (1990). Action research in the language classroom. In J. Richards & D. Nunan (Eds.), *Second language teacher education* (pp. 62–81). Cambridge, England: Cambridge University Press.

Nunan, D. (1993). Action research in language education. In J. Richards & K. Richards (Eds.), *Teachers develop, teachers research: Papers on classroom research and teacher development* (pp. 39–50). Oxford, England: Heinemann.

Nunan, D. (1994). Action research in language education. In J. Edge & K. Richards (Eds.), *Teachers develop, teachers research: Papers on classroom research and teacher development* (pp. 39–50). Oxford, England: Heinemann.

Nyamasyo, E. (1994). An analysis of the spelling errors in the written English of Kenyan pre-university students. *Language, Culture, and Curriculum, 7*(1), 79–92.

Ogden, D. H., Chapman, A. D., & Doaks, L. (1994). *Characteristics of good/effective teachers: Gender differences in student descriptors*. Paper presented at the Mid-South Education Research Association Annual Meeting, Nashville, TN. (ED383657)

Oja, S., & Pine, G. (1987). Collaborative action research: Teachers' stages of development and school context. *Peabody Journal of Education, 64,* 96–116.

Oja, S. N., & Smulyan, L. (1989). *Collaborative action research: A developmental approach*. London: Falmer Press.

Oxford, R. L. (1999). Anxiety and the language learner: New insights. In J. Arnold (Ed.), *Affect in language learning* (pp. 58–67). Cambridge, England: Cambridge University Press.

Paulus, T. M. (1999). The effect of peer and teacher feedback on student writing. *Journal of Second Language Writing, 8,* 265–289.

Pennington, M. C., & Young, A. L. (1989). Approaches to faculty evaluation for ESL. *TESOL Quarterly, 23,* 619–646.

Philips, S. (1972). Participant structures and communicative competence: Warm Springs children in community and classroom. In C. Cazden, V. John, &

D. Hymes (Eds.), *Functions of language in the classroom* (pp. 370–394). New York: Teachers College Press.

Phillips, E. M. (1992). The effects of language anxiety on students' oral test performance and attitudes. *Modern Language Journal, 76*(1), 14–26.

Phillipson, R. (1992). *Linguistic imperialism.* Oxford, England: Oxford University Press.

Pitt, M. J. (2000). The application of games theory to group project assessment. *Teaching in Higher Education, 5,* 233–241.

Price, M. L. (1991). The subjective experience of foreign language anxiety: Interviews with highly anxious students. In E. K. Horwitz & D. J. Young (Eds.), *Language anxiety: From theory and research to classroom implications.* New York: Prentice Hall.

Radnor, H. (2001). *Researching your professional practice: Doing interpretive research.* Buckingham, England: Open University Press.

Raven, J. (2005). How not to integrate computers with group projects: An example from the field. *Technology, Pedagogy, and Education, 14*(2), 257–269.

Resnick, L. (1987). *Education and learning to think.* Washington, DC: National Academy Press.

Richards, J. C. (1990). The dilemma of teacher education in second language teaching. In J. C. Richards & D. Nunan (Eds.), *Second language teacher education* (pp. 3–15). New York: Cambridge University Press.

Richards, J. C., & Farrell, T. S. C. (2005). *Professional development for language teachers.* Cambridge, England: Cambridge University Press.

Richards, J. C., & Lockhart, C. (1994). *Reflective teaching in second language classrooms.* Cambridge, England: Cambridge University Press.

Richards, J. C., & Rogers, T. (1986). *Approaches and methods in language teaching.* Cambridge, England: Cambridge University Press.

Rollinson, P. (1998). *Peer response and revision in an ESL writing group: A case study.* Unpublished doctoral dissertation, Universidad Autonoma de Madrid.

Rollinson, P. (2005). Using peer feedback in the ESL writing class. *ELT Journal, 59,* 23–30.

Rosenshine, B., & Furst, N. (1973). The use of direct observation to study teaching. In R. Travers (Ed.), *Second handbook on research on teaching* (pp. 122–183). Chicago: Rand McNally.

Schmidt, R. (1990). The role of consciousness in second language learning. *Applied Linguistics, 11,* 129–158.

Schulz, R. (2001). Cultural differences in student and teacher perceptions concerning the role of grammar instruction and corrective feedback. *The Modern Language Journal, 85*(2), 244–258.

Scovel, T. (1978). The effect of affect: A review of the anxiety literature. *Language Learning, 28,* 129–142.

Seidman, I. E. (1991). *Interviewing as qualitative research: A guide for researchers in education and social sciences.* New York: Teachers College Press.

Sensenbaugh, R. (1995). *How effective communication can enhance teaching at the college level*. Washington, DC: U.S. Office of Educational Research and Improvement. (ED380847)

Shaw, E. L., Partridge, M. E., & Gorrell, J. (1990). Worlds apart, good teaching is the same. *Georgia Social Science Journal, 21*(2), 1–8.

Shehadeh, A. (2004). Modified output during task-based pair interaction and group interaction. *Journal of Applied Linguistics, 1*(3), 351–382.

Skehan, P. (1998). *A cognitive approach to language learning.* Oxford: Oxford University Press.

Skehan, P. (2003). Tasks in L2 learning and teaching. *Language Teaching, 36,* 1–14.

Slimani-Rolls, A. (2003). Exploring a world of paradoxes: An investigation of group work. *Language Teaching Research, 7*(2), 221–239.

Sojka, J., Gupta, A. K., & Deeter-Schmelz, D. (2002). Student and faculty perceptions of student evaluations of teaching: A study of similarities and differences. *College Teaching, 50,* 44–49.

Sorensen, S. M. (1981). *Group-hate: A negative reaction to group work.* Paper presented at the meeting of the International Communication Association, Minneapolis, MN.

Sparks, R., & Ganschow, L. (1991). Foreign language learning difficulties: Affective or native language aptitude differences? *Modern Language Journal, 75*(1), 3–16.

Sparks, R., & Ganschow, L. (1995). A strong inference approach to causal factors in foreign language learning: A response to MacIntyre. *Modern Language Journal, 79*(2), 235–244.

Stanley, J. (1992). Coaching student writers to be effective peer evaluators. *Journal of Second Language Writing, 1,* 217–233.

Stapleton, P. (2001). Assessing critical thinking in the writing of Japanese university students: Insights about assumptions and content familiarity. *Written Communication, 18*(4), 506–549.

Stenhouse, L. (1975). *An introduction to curriculum research and development.* London: Heinemann.

Storch, N. (2005). Collaborative writing: Product, process, and students' reflections. *Journal of Second Language Writing, 14*(3), 153–173.

Sullivan, P. N. (1996). Sociocultural influences on classroom interactional styles. *TESOL Journal, 6*(1), 32–34.

Susser, B. (1994). Process approaches in ESL/EFL writing instruction. *Journal of Second Language Writing, 3,* 31–47.

Syed, Z. (2003). The sociocultural context of English language teaching in the Gulf. *TESOL Quarterly, 37*(2), 337–340.

Tang, S. (1999). Student evaluation of teachers: Effects of grading at college level. *Journal of Research and Development in Education, 32,* 83–88.

Tatro, C. N. (1995). Gender effects on students' evaluations of faculty. *Journal of Research and Development in Education, 28*(3), 169–173.

Theall, M., & Franklin, J. (2001). Looking for bias in all the wrong places: A search for truth or a witch hunt in student ratings of instruction? *New Directions for Institutional Research, 109,* 45–56.

Treiman, R. (1991). Children's spelling errors on syllable-initial consonant clusters. *Journal of Educational Psychology, 8*(3), 346–360.

Triki, M., & Baklouti, A. S. (2003). *Pragmatic perspectives on persuasion*. Sfax, Tunisia: GRAD.

Tsui, A. B. M., & Ng, M. (2000). Do secondary L2 writers benefit from peer comments? *Journal of Second Language Writing, 9,* 147–170.

van Werkhoven, W. (1990). The attunement strategy and spelling problems. In A. Van der Ley & K. J. Kappers (Eds.), *Dyslexia '90*. Lisse, Netherlands: Swets & Zeitlinger.

Villamil, O., & de Guerrero, M. (1996). Peer revision in the L2 classroom: Social-cognitive activities, mediating strategies, and aspects of social behavior. *Journal of Second Language Writing, 5,* 51–75.

Vygotsky, L. S. (1978). *Mind in society: The development of higher psychological processes* (M. Cole, V. John-Steiner, S. Scribner, & E. Souberman, Eds. & Trans.). Cambridge, MA: Harvard University Press. (Original work published 1934)

Wachtel, H. K. (1998). Student evaluation of college teaching effectiveness: A brief overview. *Assessment & Evaluation in Higher Education, 23*(2), 191–211.

Wallace, M. J. (1998). *Action research for language teachers*. Cambridge, England: Cambridge University Press.

Ward, J. (2006a, March 3). *Faculty attitudes to Moodle survey*. Retrieved September 14, 2006, from http://www.surveymonkey.com/Report.asp?U=180051417617

Ward, J. (2006b, March 3). *Student attitudes to Moodle survey*. Retrieved September 14, 2006, from http://www.surveymonkey.com/Report.asp?U=158358987084

Warren, P. (1995). An investigation into the use of tasks that develop both second language learning and thinking skills with children. Unpublished MEd thesis, University of Exeter, England.

Weft QDA. (n.d.) *A free qualitative analysis software application*. Retrieved on April 24, 2006, from http://www.pressure.to/qda#intro

Weiss, R. S. (1994). *Learning from strangers: The art and method of qualitative interview studies*. New York: The Free Press.

Wennerstrom, A., & Heiser, P. (1992). ESL student bias in instructional evaluation. *TESOL Quarterly, 26,* 271–288.

Wikipedia. (2007a). *Computer-mediated communication*. Retrieved January 9, 2007, from http://en.wikipedia.org/wiki/Computer-mediated_communication

Wikipedia. (2007b). *Wiki*. Retrieved January 9, 2007, from http://en.wikipedia.org/wiki/Wiki

Williams, M., & Burden, R. L. (1997). *Psychology for language teachers: A social constructivist approach*. Cambridge, England: Cambridge University Press.

Williams, M., & Burden, R. L. (1999). On Reuven Feuerstein: Releasing unlimited learning potential. In D. Mendelson (Ed.), *Expanding our vision* (pp. 94–109). Toronto: Open University Press.

Willis, J. (1996). *A framework for task-based learning*. Harlow, England: Longman Addison-Wesley.

Wilson, W. R. (1999). Students rating teachers. *Journal of Higher Education, Special Anniversary Issue: A Look Back, 70*(5), 562–571.

Worthington, A. C. (2002). The impact of student perceptions and characteristics on teaching evaluations: A case study in finance education. *Assessment & Evaluation in Higher Education, 27*(1), 49–64.

Wrangham, C. (1992). Are you listening, teacher? Tape yourself and see. *Modern English Teacher, 1*(2), 25–27.

Young, D. J. (1986). The relationship between anxiety and foreign language oral proficiency ratings. *Foreign Language Annals, 12*, 239–448.

Young, D. J. (1991). Creating a low anxiety classroom environment: What does language anxiety research suggest? *Modern Language Journal, 75*(4), 426–437.

Zeichner, K. (1999). Teacher research as a professional development activity for P–12 educators. Washington, DC: U.S. Department of Education.

Zhu, W. (1995). Effects of training for peer response on students' comments and interaction. *Written Communication, 12*, 492–528.

Zhu, W. (2001). Interaction and feedback in mixed peer response groups. *Journal of Second Language Writing, 10*, 251–276.

Zohar, A., & Dori, Y. J. (2003). Higher order thinking skills and low-achieving students. *Journal of the Learning Sciences, 12*(2), 145–181.

Index

Contracts
background literature and, 101–103
interviews and, 106–107
introduction to, 4, 99–101
procedures and, 104–107
reflection and, 109–111
results and, 107–109
The Student Contract, 113–114
Student Questionnaire, 111–113
TOEFL Results From Level 4A, Spring Semester 2005, 109*t*
Total Class Hours Missed in Level 4 Section 1, 108*t*
Control, mediation and, 83, 84, 88*t*, 90
Convergent thinking, defined, 116
Course content, teacher management of, 140–144
Course management systems (CMSs), 175–176. *See also* Blackboard; Moodle
Critical thinking, defined, 116
Criticism, teacher skill and, 55
Cultural considerations
gender roles and, 68, 72*t*
introduction to, 3
secondary schools and, 104
thinking hats and, 120. *See also* Six Thinking Hats model
Curriculum, teacher/student autonomy and, 101

D

Data analysis, multiple repeaters and, 166
Decision-making, practitioner inquiry and, 2
Degree, Six Thinking Hats model and, 125
Delivery, best practices and, 135
Desire2Learn, 176
Development stages, language learning and, 43
Difficulty, course, student evaluation and, 24–25
Discussion, Six Thinking Hats model and. *See* Six Thinking Hats model
Dis-inhibition, technology and, 178

Distribution of Positive and Negative Comments for NESTs, NNESTs, and No Preference, 61*t*
Distribution of the Total Number of Correct Answers, 29*t*
Divergent thinking, defined, 116
Dubai Men's College, 54. *See also* Teacher skills
Dynamic assessment, 83

E

Editing, peer. *See* Feedback
Emoticons, 177
English as a foreign language (EFL)
language anxiety and. *See* Anxiety
mediation and. *See* Mediation
multiple repeaters and. *See* Multiple repeaters
peer feedback and. *See* Feedback
spelling errors and. *See* Spelling errors
teacher skill and. *See* Teacher skills
English as a second language (ESL). *See* Spelling errors
English for specific purposes (ESP). *See* Multiple repeaters
Enrollment statistics, 21
Environmental characteristics, student evaluation and, 24–25
Epenthesis, 45*t*, 49–50, 50*t*
Errors, spelling. *See* Spelling errors
ESL. *See* English as a second language (ESL)
Etiquette, classroom, 170
Evaluation. *See also* Feedback
AUS Teaching Evaluation Form, 36–38
best practices and. *See* Best practices
learning contracts and, 103
student. *See* Student evaluation
teacher skill and, 55
Evidence, Six Thinking Hats model and, 125
Exams
Arts Group's Average, Lowest, and Highest Scores, 12*t*
introduction to, 3–4
mediation and. *See* Mediation

M

Magnolia, 176

Management, best practices and, 135, 137, 140–142

Matching, phoneme/grapheme, 44t

Materials, instructional. *See* Instructional materials

Mean Total and Component Scores on the Posttest, 154t

Mean Total and Component Scores on the Pretest, 152t

Mechanics, scoring and, 152t, 154t, 155t

Mediation
background literature and, 82–86
best practices and, 135
Comparison of Teachers' and Students' Perceptions of Actual Practice of Mediation by Teachers, 88t
Interview Questions, 97–98
introduction to, 3–4, 81–82
procedures and, 86–88
reflection and, 91–92
results and, 88–91
Student Questionnaire, 93–94
Teacher Questionnaire, 95–96
technology and, 175

Memory, best practices and, 135

Messenger, MSM, 176

Metathesis, 45t

Methodology, teaching, 170–171

Missed classes, 108t

Modular Object-Oriented Dynamic Learning Environment. *See* Moodle

Monographicization, 44t

Moodle
Blackboard vs. Moodle, 184f
introduction to, 5, 173–174
procedures and, 179
reflection and, 185–186
results and, 179–184
student enjoyment of, 180f
student utilization of, 181f, 182f

Motivation, student evaluation and, 24–25

MSM Messenger, 176

Multiculturalism. *See* Cultural considerations

Multiple repeaters
background literature and, 163
introduction to, 4, 161–162
procedures and, 163–166
reflection and, 171–172
results and, 166–171

N

Nationality and Gender of Students Who Preferred to Work in Same-Gender Groups, 72t

Nativeness, teacher skill and, 58

Nativization, 49, 49t

O

Objectives
best practices and, 141
learning, 102

Observation, classroom, 164

OpenCMS, 176

Opinion, Six Thinking Hats model and, 125

Opportunities, Six Thinking Hats model and, 117

Oral proficiency
anxiety and, 9
peer feedback and, 158. *See also* Feedback
practice and, 16

Organization, best practices and, 141–142

Origin, student evaluation and, 30–31

Overview, Six Thinking Hats model and, 118

P

Pair work, language anxiety and, 16

Pakistan, mediation and. *See* Mediation

Paragraph Rating Scale for EFL Compositions, 159–160

PD. *See* Professional development (PD)

Peers
collaboration and. *See* Group work

Also Available From TESOL

CALL Essentials
Joy Egbert

Content-Based Instruction in Primary and Secondary School Settings
Dorit Kaufman and JoAnn Crandall, Editors

ESOL Tests and Testing
Stephen Stoynoff and Carol A. Chapelle

Gender and English Language Learners
Bonny Norton and Aneta Pavlenko, Editors

Learning Languages through Technology
Elizabeth Hanson-Smith and Sara Rilling, Editors

Language Teacher Research in Asia
Thomas S. C. Farrell, Editor

Language Teacher Research in Europe
Simon Borg, Editor

Language Teacher Research in the Americas
Hedy McGarrell, Editor

Literature in Language Teaching and Learning
Amos Paran, Editor

More Than a Native Speaker: An Introduction to Teaching English Abroad
revised edition
Don Snow

Perspectives on Community College ESL Series
Craig Machado, Series Editor
Volume 1: Pedagogy, Programs, Curricula, and Assessment
Marilynn Spaventa, Editor
Volume 2: Students, Mission, and Advocacy
Amy Blumenthal, Editor

PreK–12 English Language Proficiency Standards
Teachers of English to Speakers of Other Languages, Inc.

*Planning and Teaching Creatively within a
Required Curriculum for School-Age Learners*
Penny McKay, Editor

*Planning and Teaching Creatively within a
Required Curriculum for Adult Learners*
Anne Burn and Helen de Silva Joyce, Editors

Professional Development of International Teaching Assistants
Dorit Kaufman and Barbara Brownworth, Editors

Teaching English as a Foreign Language in Primary School
Mary Lou McCloskey, Janet Orr, and Marlene Dolitsky, Editors

For more information, contact
Teachers of English to Speakers of Other Languages, Inc.
700 South Washington Street, Suite 200
Alexandria, Virginia 22314 USA
Toll Free: 888-547-3369   Fax on Demand: 800-329-4469
Publications Order Line: 888-891-0041
or 301-638-4427 or 4428
9 am to 5 pm, EST

ORDER ONLINE at www.tesol.org/

TESOL